Made in Yorkshire

Made in Yorkshire

Tony Earnshaw & Jim Moran

For Danni and Abigail

First published 2008
guerilla books limited
www.guerilla-books.com

Made In Yorkshire.
Copyright © guerilla books limited 2008
Text © Tony Earnshaw 2008
Tony Earnshaw has asserted his right to
be identified as the author of this work in
accordance with Copyright, Designs and Patents
Act 1988 UK.
Foreword © Ronald Harwood 2008.
Photo copyright at the back of the book.

Cover Design and book layout by Nebulo Strata.
Printed by C & C Offset Printing.

A catalogue of this book is available
from the British Library.

ISBN 13   978-0-9554943-1-4

Contents

above: Director Peter Yates, star Tom Courtenay and Ronald Harwood outside the Alhambra Theatre Bradford.
below: York Station's starring role in The Dresser.

Foreword

When I was a lad growing up in South Africa, I first heard of Bradford as the city in which one of my heroes, J. B. Priestley, was born, and which he called Bruddersford in many of his books and plays. Years later, in 1982, my heart quickened a little on being told that Bradford was to be the place where we would shoot some of the scenes in *The Dresser*, the film based on my stage play, starring Tom Courtenay, Albert Finney, Eileen Atkins and Edward Fox.

On arrival my first impression was one of astonishment. I had always thought of Bradford as an 'industrial city', a phrase that conjures up images of dark Satanic mills. I was astonished because I quickly discovered that Bradford is a decidedly handsome city with notable architecture, especially its proud cathedral and trustworthy, down-to-earth Wool Exchange, typically Yorkshire, a place without pretensions.

No wonder a host of people have been attracted to film there and in the breathtaking countryside around. This book by Tony Earnshaw rightly casts Yorkshire as the star of numerous movies, among them some of my favourites, *Billy Liar,* directed by John Schlesinger, *The Railway Children*, directed by Lionel Jeffries and Jack Claytons' *Room at the Top* which, incidentally, contains one of the best performance given in a film by Sir Donald Wolfit, whose dresser I was and who was the inspiration for my play.

So it was apt in many ways that we chose to make our film in Bradford and its surrounds. Peter Yates, the director, had already paid a visit to decide on locations. Not surprisingly, he had fallen in love with the superb Alhambra theatre, built in 1914, and now lovingly restored. Here he filmed in the foyer, the auditorium and backstage. But he was keen to show us what he rightly believed was the ideal setting for our wartime market scene, the magnificent Piece Hall in Halifax. The enormous space framed by graceful arches and colonnades, forming a kind of piazza, would do justice to any Italian city of the Renaissance.

We journeyed, too, to York, for scenes at the railway station, built in 1877, then the largest in the world, with its ornate bridge spanning the platforms. From the steps of that bridge, Albert Finney as Sir, yelled, 'Stop that train!' to bring a departing train to a halt.

It is impossible to leave York without paying homage to the Minster, a glory of Gothic architecture, almost a thousand years old. And, for me, it is impossible to leave Bradford without wandering towards the National Media Museum and give an affectionate nod to Ian Judd's fine statue of the man who first introduced me to Bradford and Yorkshire, J. B. Priestley.

Ronald Harwood
Slindon, West Sussex
January 2008

Introduction

Like all filmmakers, I have that dream film sitting on my shelf - the project that has everything except finance, the one that I cannot let go. Mine is called *Robbery in Motion* and is based on a 1980 BBC short play. A few years ago I was given some money by an investment group to further develop the package because they saw its potential.

In 1969, at Benton Park School in Rawdon, Leeds, I told my English teacher and assembled classmates that one day I would make a feature film in the West Riding of Yorkshire. Although they laughed, within one year I was a professional actor. I have subsequently become a producer and film distributor and, although I have been involved with well over 100 feature films, I still have not managed this ambition. I have however filmed documentaries and other projects in Yorkshire, but never a feature.

Now I could change that. The original script, an Ealingesque comedy caper set in London works, I believe, far better artistically if set in Leeds, Bradford and Harrogate. My investors did not agree; they could only see the story working if set in a 'capital city'. I pointed out that *The Full Monty* and *Calendar Girls* were both highly successful films based in Yorkshire. "Yes, we know that", they said. "Everyone knows they were Yorkshire films. *They* could not have worked anywhere else."

I argued that this was the case with *Robbery in Motion* - that there is more to Yorkshire than these two films. They claimed "It's a heist film and heist films can not work in Yorkshire." "Why not?" I said. "Is there no crime in the county?" My strategy was unsuccessful. I was told that if I did not relocate and shoot the entire film in London they would withdraw their funding. I did not change my mind and, to date, I've been unable to finance the Yorkshire film elsewhere.

Therefore when Tony Earnshaw and Jim Moran approached me to publish their book of the movies shot, fully or partly, in Yorkshire I jumped at the opportunity. We would be able to show the world just what a great location Yorkshire is. What surprised even me was just how many motion pictures have been filmed in the county. Take away the counties of England where there are (or were) film studios - Middlesex (Shepperton, Twickenham, Isleworth and Teddington), Surrey (Merton Park and Bray) Buckinghamshire (Pinewood) and Hertfordshire (Elstree and Leavesden) - and Yorkshire can probably boast more films shot in its diverse acreage than any other county in England. Add to that the plethora of television productions and the county is brimming over with other filmmakers who agree with my assessment.

As a location, Yorkshire has more to offer the filmmaker that any other county in the country. There is the stunning and varied scenery of the dales and moors, the medieval cities and towns of York and Richmond, the atmospheric harbours of Whitby and Staithes, the cosmopolitan thrust of Leeds and

Sheffield, the lush rural valleys of the Swale, Ure, Nidd and Wharfe and the magnificent industrial valleys of the Aire and Calder. From coalfields to cornfields, from the almost otherworldly outcrop that is Brimham Rocks to the down-to-earth charm of Bradford, Huddersfield and Halifax. Yorkshire has it all. Throw in the seaside resorts of Scarborough, Filey, Bridlington and the port of Hull then there is everything any filmmaker could want, all nestling within one very large county.

Those of us from Yorkshire already know what is on offer. Through the work of a growing legion of filmmakers dating back to the dawn of cinema in 1888, the rest of the world is also becoming more and more acquainted with "God's own county". So, yes, there is much, much more to Yorkshire's cinema heritage than *The Full Monty* and *Calendar Girls*.

Tony, Jim and I are indebted to the rich and well-stocked picture libraries of many of Yorkshire's top newspapers, among them the *Huddersfield Examiner, Halifax Evening Courier, Keighley News, Hebden Bridge Times, The Press (York), Bradford Telegraph & Argus*, and, in particular, *Yorkshire Post Newspapers* in Leeds. Our gratitude goes to the various editors, picture editors and photographers for granting permission to reproduce them.

We would also like to place on record our thanks to the extras, technicians, location owners, freelance photographers, picture agencies and passers-by, all of whom have contributed a huge array of largely unseen and unpublished photographs. Without the talent, creativity and generosity of many of these people, this unique celebration of Yorkshire's films would not have been possible.

David Nicholas Wilkinson
London,
January 2008

Yorkshire –
The unlikely birthplace of the movies

Cinema was born in Yorkshire. On a sunny autumn day in October, 1888, four people larked about as an unseen relative used the most rudimentary of moving picture cameras to capture the moment for posterity. It was an epoch-making moment, and one that has survived for 21st century audiences to savour. More than 120 years later, progress has changed the movies beyond all comprehension. But when Louis Le Prince shot those few fleeting seconds of footage, and then followed up a short while later with a view of horses, people, trams and traffic on Leeds Bridge, Yorkshire's place in the history of film was well and truly cemented.

As his name suggests, Louis Aimé Augustin Le Prince was not a Yorkshireman but a Frenchman. Born in Metz in 1841, he had worked intermittently in Leeds in a workshop at 160, Woodhouse Lane. It was there, following his mysterious disappearance in 1890, that his equipment was found by the joiner and mechanic who had worked with him on his invention.

The son of a French army officer, Louis Le Prince was a maths and physics graduate who had enjoyed his first brush with photography via the atelier of Louis Daguerre, the father of commercial photography, who was a friend of his father. In Leipzig Le Prince met Englishman John R. Whitley, who invited him to Leeds. Le Prince was to spend two-fifths of his life in the city, meeting and marrying Elizabeth, the daughter

title page: Louis Le Prince's legendary images of traffic on Leeds Bridge, 1888.

above: Louis Le Prince

of Joseph and Sarah Whitley and living in Oakwood Grange, in Roundhay, Leeds. After working as a photographer and painter he joined the Whitleys' engineering firm, first as a designer and then as manager of the valve department. Following military service in the Franco-Prussian War of 1870-1871 he returned to Leeds and, with his wife, set up Leeds Technical School of Art in Park Square.

According to his daughter, Marie, Le Prince had been "thinking about moving pictures" as early as the 1870s. He was later inspired by the work of Eadweard Muybridge, who had developed sequential photography depicting a trotting horse using 24 separate cameras. But while Le Prince worked on his own projects, others were racing towards their own goals. In 1882 Étienne-Jules Marey perfected the revolving-gun camera which took up to 12 pictures a second. In 1885 George Eastman's American paper roll film became available, followed four years later by his commercial development of celluloid film.

Le Prince produced a complex 16-lens camera in 1886. He was granted an American patent on January 10, 1888. A British patent, containing an extra clause relating to a single-lens camera and projector, was issued on November 16 that same year. The work, which had begun during a five-year spell in New York where Le Prince and wife lived from 1882, was completed at the Woodhouse Lane workshop in Leeds after his return from the United States in May 1887. The single-lens camera that resulted was used to create the moving picture sequences at Roundhay, and later on Leeds Bridge, in October 1888.

above and right: Leeds Bridge: now and then

Speaking in 1930, Marie Le Prince recalled: "In 1882 we went to New York where my mother's brother was interested in the introduction of the Lincrusta Walton wallpaper process. He wanted my father to design the decorations. My mother became a teacher of art at the Institute for the Deaf at Washington Heights, New York, and through that connection my father had permission to use the workshop and a large studio. One evening in 1885 I went to the school building and, seeing a ray of light beneath the studio door, I peeped in and saw projected on the white-washed wall some moving pictures. That was my first sight of moving pictures."

There is evidence to suggest that what Marie witnessed was her father's experimental use of celluloid film, which he

had obtained from the Lumière Brothers in Lyon. He is also believed to have developed a 'deliverer' or projector with which he projected images in his workshop, though the apparatus has not survived.

On or around October 14, 1888, Le Prince gathered his parents-in-law, the Whitleys, his son Adolphe and young Harriet Hartley in the garden at Oakwood Grange. This quartet then performed for what would become accepted as the first-ever sequence of moving pictures, and simply wandered around the grounds of the house. It is an eerie, haunting record of a long-lost autumn day, made all the more so by the knowledge that Sarah Whitley was to die just ten days later. Thus the film can be accurately dated. Only a tantalising two-second fragment has

survived. It shows dark-suited Adolphe striding across the lawn, Harriet turning from the camera, Sarah appearing to move backwards and Joseph's coattails blowing in the breeze.

A little over 18 months later, Le Prince carefully packed his apparatus – a single lens moving picture camera and a projector – in preparation for a trip to New York. First, however, he had business in France. He also planned to take a trip around various gothic cathedrals with his friends from Leeds, the Wilsons. On September 16, 1890, Le Prince boarded a Paris-bound train in Dijon station. His brother bade him farewell. He was never seen again. In Paris the Wilsons were puzzled by his non-arrival but assumed he had been delayed. Across the Atlantic in New

York, his wife Lizzie endured a similar wait. After some weeks had passed she reported him missing. Detectives were hired to locate him but found nothing. On the brink of unveiling one of the greatest inventions in the history of mankind, the creator of the world's first single lens motion picture camera had disappeared from the face of the earth.

Darker forces were at work. There were those who recognised the embryonic film industry for what it was: not merely entertainment or artistry, but a licence to print money. There was much at stake. Whoever sprinted first across the finish line would not only enter the history books but also be feted as the inventor of a major new technical achievement: the movies. Shortly after Louis

Le Prince vanished Thomas Alva Edison stepped forward and claimed motion pictures as his invention. Lizzie, outraged and mad with grief, attacked her husband's US rivals. He had, she said, been "removed by agents of the American inventors who wished to get control of the moving picture situation". Was Louis Le Prince murdered on the orders of a rival inventor? His family certainly believed so. Neither his body nor any trace of his luggage was ever found but, in 2003, French police archives yielded an image of a drowned man, circa 1890. It looked uncannily like Le Prince.

By the mid 1890s inventors on both sides of the Atlantic had perfected their techniques. Auguste and Louis Lumière presented their first film, shot outside their factory, on March 22 1895. In America Grey and Otman Latham screened a boxing film to an audience of New Yorkers from May 20. The Lumières had the Cinématographe; the Otways used their Eidoloscope projector. In 1902 agents working for Edison bribed a London theatre owner and took away a copy of Georges Méliès' *A Trip to the Moon*, which was then duplicated and shown at dozens of venues across New York City. Méliès, who had plans to screen the film across the United States, was never compensated and was forced into bankruptcy by the move – an indication, should any be needed, of Edison's ruthlessness.

Four years earlier Adolphe Le Prince had appeared as a witness for the defence in a court case brought by Edison against the American Mutoscope Company, claiming that Edison was the first and sole inventor of cinematography. Adolphe was prevented from presenting his father's cameras

as evidence, thus establishing his father's prior claim as inventor and the court ruled in favour of Edison. A year later the ruling was overturned but, by then, and despite the efforts of his widow, the name of Louis Le Prince was fading into obscurity.

In December, 1930, Le Prince's daughter Marie returned to Leeds for the unveiling of a memorial to her father and his work. The brass plaque was erected on a garage standing on the site in Woodhouse Lane where Le Prince's workshop once stood. It read: "LOUIS LE PRINCE. The pioneer of cinematography had a workshop on this site where he invented a one-lens camera and projecting machine." E. Kilburn Scott, convenor to the memorial fund for Le Prince, argued strongly that he was the father, not merely a father, of motion pictures. Others spoke of their indignation that the honour and glory which should have gone to Le Prince had been given to others.

The years after Le Prince disappeared saw an explosion of interest in motion pictures. Incomplete records of titles, release dates and the identities of the filmmakers makes it impossible to present a full and accurate record of turn-of-the-century film production, but what is certain is that industrious little studios sprang up everywhere. In Bradford were based R.J. Appleton, William Phillips, Cecil Hepworth and William & Herbert Riley. R.J. Appleton – the initials stood for Richard James – hit upon an ambitious plan: he would travel to London, film the State procession as part of Queen Victoria's Diamond Jubilee Celebrations, develop the footage in a special dark room on a speeding train and present it to paying audiences the very same night using his Cieroscope machine. What's

more, he did it. It was Tuesday, June 22, 1897. The event was described as "a triumph in science". Four days later 10,000 people assembled in Bradford's Forster Square to watch the film projected on a giant white sheet. The evening concluded with the National Anthem.

Bradfordian William Riley visited Paris in 1895 and saw the Lumière Brothers present their famous first show at the Grand Café in the boulevard des Capucines on December 28. He rushed back to the family firm and promptly built his own camera and projector. Later two other local men, Henry Hibbert and C.J. Cutliffe Hyne, started the Captain Kettle Film Company in 1912 and made a wide range of movies, including westerns, around the area. Actresses like Kitty Vernon (real name Catherine Appleton; she was part of the Appleton family) earned £1 a day – a splendid wage in pre-WWI England – and was whispered about as "the film star" by reverent neighbours.

The Pyramid Film Company, based on Manchester Road, Bradford, made a series of early newsreels in the late teens and early '20s with titles like *Bradford Gazette* and *Roll of Honour*, which listed the names of soldiers killed at the Front. Another Pyramid effort was *My Yorkshire Lass*, starring actress Mabel Jaye from Headingley, Leeds. The film, written by Herbert Pemberton, was a five-reeler shot in Bradford and Leeds. One romantic sequence was filmed in Idle Churchyard. *My Yorkshire Lass* was premiered at Hunslet Pavilion in 1916, during which Mr. Pemberton conducted a live orchestra.

The Imperial Film Company fixed a camera to the fixed to the front balcony of tramcars as they followed routes through Bradford, Leeds, Halifax and Huddersfield. Sheffield was home to Frank Storm Mottershaw and the Sheffield Photo Company which, between 1903 and 1908, produced ambitious fiction films including *The Life of Charles Peace*, a documentary on the exploits of a master burglar who was later hanged at Armley Gaol in Leeds.

And, in Holmfirth from 1899, James Bamforth churned out scores of mini documentaries, dramas and comedies. Among the most popular were the 50-plus slapstick shorts featuring the ne'er do-well character of Winky. Bamforth's prolific output was halted by the outbreak of the Great War. By the time war ended in 1918, Bamforth's had ceased to

previous page and right:
The first ever adaptation of Wuthering Heights.
This book has been filmed more times than any other novel set in Yorkshire.

Milton Rosmer as Heathcliff:
"a monomaniac wracked by
lust for vengeance".
(The Bioscope, August 5, 1920)

be a major player in the embryonic British film industry. Ironically, as the war brought Holmfirth's film industry to a halt, Bamforth's received an order for 100 films from Russia. Said Bamforth's son, Frank: "We were streets ahead of America in production methods and technique."

Across the Pennines in Blackburn, Sagar Mitchell and James Kenyon saw ready profit in the filmmaking process. These two Edwardian entrepreneurs were not interested in art. Instead, they determined to bring working class folk face-to-face with themselves: "see yourself how others see you" was their sales pitch. They filmed everything: processions and parades, brass bands, workers leaving factories and football, rugby and cricket matches. Their efforts were not confined to Lancashire. They travelled to Manchester, Liverpool and Yorkshire to capture their subjects on film and processed the film the same day in order to maximise audiences and profit. More than 800 of their short films were discovered in 1994.

To all intents and purposes, Yorkshire's heritage of feature film making began in 1920 with a majestic adaptation of Emily Brontë's *Wuthering Heights*. For the time, the film was an epic: a five-reeler running around 90 minutes. The stars were Milton Rosmer, playing Heathcliff, Warwick Ward (Hindley Earnshaw), John Lawrence Anderson (Edgar Linton), Albert Brantford (Young Heathcliff), Louis B. Furniss (Young Edgar) and three actresses including Annie Trevor and child star Twinkles Hunter as Cathy.

Director A.V. Bramble, writer Elliot Stannard, the crew of Ideal Film Productions and the cast arrived in Haworth in May, 1920. The production caused much excitement in Haworth which still resembled the village that Emily Brontë had written about in the 1840s. Crowds turned out to see the cast, in full costume, as they prepared to shoot near the Parsonage. Bramble was determined to produce his picture on authentic locations. Ponden Hall, his first choice to double as Thrushcross Grange, was not in a fit state to receive the film forcing Bramble to repair to Kildwick Hall, a 17th century Jacobean mansion in extensive grounds. Kildwick, north of Keighley and just nine miles from Haworth, would surely have been known to Emily Brontë when she began work on *Wuthering Heights*. The owners at the time were the Currers, and Brontë took as her pseudonym the name Currer Bell so as to pass for a man without adopting a definitively male Christian name. Exteriors were shot at Cold Knowle, Stanbury, where Bramble and his actors used the Brontë Waterfall.

The film was previewed in August, 1920, two months before release, and earned rave reviews. *The Bioscope* called it "a real triumph of film art," adding "the silent picture becomes as eloquent as the silent print of the book". Much of the success of the film was associated with the authentic moorland settings.

"*Wuthering Heights* is a drama of character and atmosphere and of the interplay between the two. Heathcliff, sinister, cruel, strong, was a creation of the dark and desolate moors upon which he was bred. Emily Brontë, who conceived him, shaped the hero of her famous tale as an embodiment of the sad grey uplands where her short life was spent. In the cold hatred which obsesses the soul of this amazing character, you feel the fierce passion of the devastating storms which sweep the bleak and lonely wastes of the Haworth district in the dreary winter months – an environment that, we know, made an indelible impression upon the sensitive spirit of the girl-genius pent, far from the warmth and colour of normal life, in her cheerless home," wrote the Bioscope reviewer.

"You are made to realise the isolation of the wilderness-prison in which it was possible for human souls to be tortured and deformed by the malevolence of man and the harsh influence of unkindly Nature. Removed from the setting which inspired it, *Wuthering Heights* would have seemed an improbable story, and Heathcliff an inhuman character. Thanks to the production of Mr. Bramble and the extraordinary acting of Milton Rosmer, its poignant truthfulness is even intensified on the screen."

In November, 1920, the film played to packed houses at The Palace in Cavendish Street, Keighley. The town's newspaper, the *Keighley News*, announced "Never has the coming of a picture been so eagerly anticipated." *Wuthering Heights* ran for six days – double the length of the normal booking. Two years later Bramble returned to West Yorkshire to make another film. The Elizabethan manor house Oakwell Hall, in Birstall, was immortalised as Fieldhead, the home of the heroine in Charlotte Brontë's *Shirley*.

Sadly, *Wuthering Heights* is now considered a "lost" film. Despite being considered the first-ever adaptation of the novel – "Emily Brontë's tremendous story of hate" – and possibly the most accurate, covering the entire length of the book, it appears not to have survived. Nonetheless it adds lustre to Yorkshire's reputation as a hot spot of pioneering silent era filmmakers.

left: Cameraman, director and two assistants going to next set-up.

left: Onlookers throng the manicured lawns of Kildwick Hall. Producer A.V. Bramble and cameraman Horace Wheddon watch their actors as the camera turns unassisted. The sheer numbers of observers watching the performances is not surprising, for as long as the cast could concentrate and not be distracted by onlookers, no sound would be recorded.

1935

Turn of the Tide

Director: Norman Walker

Producer: John Corfield

Writers: J.O.C. Orton, L. du Garde Peach

Production Company: British National Films Ltd

Year of Production: 1935 (Released October 1935)

Where filmed: Robin Hood's Bay, Whitby, Ramsdale and Staithes, North Yorkshire between March/April and June, 1935.

Synopsis: Old Isaac Fosdyck resents the presence of rival fishing family, the Lunns, and vows to stop the burgeoning romance between his granddaughter Ruth and young John Lunn. But he is forced to accept both the reality of true love and the inexorable march of progress.

Credited cast: John Garrick (Marney Lunn), J. Fisher White (Isaac Fosdyck), Geraldine Fitzgerald (Ruth Fosdyck), Wilfrid Lawson (Luke Fosdyck), Moore Marriott (Tindal Fosdyck), Sam Livesey (Henry Lunn), Niall MacGinnis (John Lunn), Joan Maude (Amy Lunn), Derek Blomfield (Steve Lunn), Hilda Davies (Mrs. Lunn).

Uncredited cast: "Stowaway" Dryden, Tom Dryden, Elliot Duke, George Duke, Henry Duke, Robert Storm (fishermen), Henrietta Walmsley (infant), Thomas Welham (Lifeboat Coxswain).

Movie lore points to *Turn of the Tide* as J. Arthur Rank's entry into British cinema, and indeed it was. However while the film is rightly acclaimed as a classic, Rank's motives for selecting it had more to do with evangelical zeal than a wish to deliver quality cinema. Born in Hull in 1888, Joseph Arthur Rank was a millionaire industrialist whose fortune had been made in the flour mills. His business acumen was matched by his religious fervour – he was an ardent Methodist – which was to manifest itself in a proselytising mission.

During the early 1930s Rank funded a series of short films, all featuring religious overtones, to be screened in church halls, prisons, pits and youth clubs across the country. Rank's intention was to convert the masses – or at least

some of them – via the subtle messages and imagery in his films. Cinema was the great new form of communication – a powerful suggestive medium – so what better way to spread the gospel? The 'movie with a message' was about to be born, and J. Arthur Rank, the self-styled celluloid missionary, was both its author and publisher.

Mastership, made for £2,700 in 1934, featured a Methodist evangelist. *Inasmuch*, which starred Donald Wolfit as St. Francis of Assisi and featured the screen debut of Greer Garson, appeared the following year. In July 1934 Rank had formed a triumvirate with Lady Yule, widow of the banker and Calcutta Jute magnate, Sir David Yule, and John Corfield to raise the standard of British cinema and put home-grown films on the American map. Their intention was to make a series

of high quality family-friendly feature films that presented British life, tradition and culture in a positive light. Together they set up British National Films. Rank's ambition to produce a larger, more commercial and accessible picture than his religious shorts led him, via a curious route, to *Turn of the Tide*.

Turn of the Tide was chosen following a spat between the *Methodist Times*, which Rank owned, and the *Evening News*. Railing at what it considered to be low morality in the British films on the circuit, the *Methodist Times* argued for quality productions that oozed moral fibre. A journalist with the *Evening News* threw down the gauntlet and suggested that Yorkshire writer Leo Walmsley's novel *Three Fevers* might be appropriate for family audiences. Rank, on behalf of the

title page: Writer Leo Walmsley, cameraman Eric Cross, cinematographer Franz Planer and director Norman Walker on location in Robin Hood's Bay, 1935.

previous page: Franz Planer, Eric Cross (behind camera), unknown crew member and a very young Gil Taylor (with cigarette), who later went on to shoot Star Wars, *on the beach at Robin Hood's Bay.*

opposite: Tindal Fosdyck (Moore Marriott) at sea.

above: An aerial shot of Robin Hood's Bay from 1940 – just five years after the making of Turn of the Tide.

Methodist Times, accepted. Thus it was that J. Arthur Rank, the accidental movie mogul, helped bring to the screen one of the quintessential Yorkshire movies.

Born in Shipley, West Yorkshire, in 1892, Leo Walmsley moved with his family to Robin Hood's Bay on the coast of North Yorkshire when he was barely two years old. Though initially considered a 'foreigner', Walmsley became a firm advocate of the North Yorkshire coastline and its people, immersing himself in village life and the lives of his fishermen neighbours. Eventually he immortalised their ways and traditions in his books. Published in 1932 his novel *Three Fevers* was a semi-biographical story that chronicled the feud between two rival fishing families, the Fosdycks and the Lunns, in the tiny fishing village of Bramblewick. In truth the book,

a best-seller, had been based on two real-life families, the Dukes and the Storms, both of whom lived in Robin Hood's Bay, just a few short miles from the seaport of Whitby.

The book focused on three fevers, those periods in the year when fishermen would take their cobles – short, single-masted fishing boats – to sea and brave the elements in search of cod, lobster and salmon. It was an atmospheric tale of hardy seafaring people and their battles with the cruel sea. Moreover, it offered a sympathetic and unpatronising portrait of a unique way of life that city folk could never imagine. And yet it stirred the imagination of J. Arthur Rank, who saw in *Three Fevers* all the requirements for a feature film that represented quality entertainment and a commercial undertaking.

Out of the blue Walmsley received a letter from John Corfield, Rank's managing director at British National. It made an ambiguous invitation: "We have read this book and believe that it contains distinct filmic possibilities - provided that it is treated something on the lines of *Man of Aran* - but we should like to know from you whether conditions today in any part of Northumberland or Durham are approximately as they are described in your book. We should also like to know if you are ever in town, or if you are likely to be in town in the near future, in order that we might have a chat on the subject generally."

Walmsley travelled to London and was swept away by the idea that his book might be transformed into a motion picture. He accepted £300 for the rights to *Three Fevers* as an advance on a promise of five per cent of the film's projected net profits. In addition he was offered a salary of £6 per week to act as technical advisor to director Norman Walker.

Turn of the Tide broke new ground by eschewing the restrictions of the studio and instead filming largely on location. Leo Walmsley had based his story in and amongst the people of the East Coast, so Walker took his cast and crew to the very heart of the novel. Lovers of the superb countryside will recognise several key scenes from their locations. Ramsdale Mill and its beck is the setting for the scene where Marney and Steve Lunn attempt to catch a salmon while in their Sunday best. In 1935 the mill's redundant waterwheel was made to work for the movie. Another moment sees Ruth Fosdyck (Geraldine Fitzgerald) watching the arrival in Bramblewick of the Lunns' new boat engine yet she is standing near the Cod and Lobster in Staithes. A sequence shot in Whitby shows the hustle and bustle of a fish auction. Real people drift in and out of shot, lending *Turn of the Tide* a documentary style that Walker may not even have realised when he made it. As for Robin Hood's Bay itself, the tiny village remains much the same as it did when the film was made in 1935. Time seems to have stood still.

Rank poured £30,000 into his maiden production, but the budget was insufficient to attract 'name' actors. Indeed, initial reports of the filming suggested that the film would be populated by non-actors; given the ability required on screen there were rumours – all reported in the local Press – that local men would be hired. A story that reads suspiciously like a publicist's release appeared in the

opposite: A posed portrait of the Lunns: John Garrick, Sam Livesey and Niall MacGinnis.

above: Joan Maude and Geraldine Fitzgerald on the promontory in Whitby.

Whitby Gazette in February, 1935. It said: "The picture is designed to be an epic of the fishing industry, full of the life, love, laughter and fierce drama of unending struggle with the elements which is typical of the coastal race. A preliminary survey of the locality is being made with a view to selecting places for actual film shots. As far as possible, local fisher-folk will be used in casting the film and it is likely that many of them will be given leading roles. While the picture will have a strong love interest, as well as highly dramatic and humorous parts, it is probable that it may go down in history as one of the greatest of all British films made without the aid of a recognised star."

Among those considered perfect for one of the rough-hewn seafarers was Douglas Fairbanks Jr. When he proved to be unavailable (not to mention too expensive) Rank and his team went with an array of tried and trusted theatre performers, reliable veterans and newcomers like Niall MacGinnis and Geraldine Fitzgerald. Both would later make an impact and enjoy success in much bigger productions.

The line-up included Bradford-born Wilfrid Lawson, radio star John Garrick and, as Tindal Fosdyck, 50-year-old Moore Marriott, a prolific jobbing actor who, since 1908, had made his living (and his reputation) in more than 100 films as a scene-stealing Everyman. He is best remembered for playing Harbottle in four films with Will Hay. Before the likes of Marlon Brando made it fashionable, the versatile Marriott adopted his own personal form of method acting

when playing his parts, be they butcher, baker or candlestick maker. For *Turn of the Tide* (filmed under its original title *Three Fevers*) he spent six weeks amongst Whitby's fishermen in an attempt to pick up their mannerisms while learning something of the complexities of the job.

"Put me in a boiled shirt and I just can't act!" he told *Film Weekly*. "But ask me to play a navvy, or a butcher, or a postman, or a liftman and I'm happy. I'm the world's best 'worst sailor' but I used to go out in their trawlers enduring untold agonies. It was worth it. I got to know intimately some of the finest men in the world. I based my characterisation on an old character called Tom Dryden, from whom I was inseparable. We used to talk together for hours, and I even borrowed some of his clothes for the picture. When the film was over Old Tom gave me 14 lobsters and a couple of crabs as a present!"

"Nine out of ten times, I find that if I base my screen characterisations on actual people they are credible; the tenth time some particular idiosyncrasy may have to be toned down to avoid a suggestion of burlesque. Of course, I am sometimes unable to spend any time with the type

opposite: Feuding families: Luke and Tindal Fosdyck (Wilfrid Lawson and Moore Marriott) with John and Marney Lunn (Niall MacGinnis and John Garrick).

above: Wilfrid Lawson, J. Fisher White and Moore Marriott close to the slipway in Robin Hood's Bay.

of character I am playing in a film. I have to delve in my memory for some curious persons I have met, and try and work out a suitable composite study."

For six weeks in March and April, 1935, Walker and his crew filmed on location in Robin Hood's Bay, doubling as Walmsley's fictitious Bramblewick, and occasionally went further afield to Whitby (renamed Burnharbour for the film), Staithes and Ramsdale Mill, Fylingdales, for extra scenes. Walmsley was continually on set; having been hired as technical advisor he took his new role extremely seriously.

Walmsley had a great deal invested in the making of the film. He had lived with and grown up amongst the fisher

folk of the Bay. He wanted their lives and experiences to be honestly and truthfully represented on screen. What he witnessed made him cringe. A fastidious – some might say obsessive – overseer of Walker's film treatment of his novel, he sought absolute authenticity and volunteered advice which, at first, was welcomed. Later, however, Walmsley's obsession with the meticulous replication of the minutiae of fishing life began to wear down even Walker's patience. Walmsley's painstaking approach to detail was well-meant – he wanted his friends and neighbours to be proud of what appeared on screen. His conscience would not allow him to accept falseness, even though the vast majority of those seeing the film would not be able to tell anything was amiss. It was a purely provincial perspective – his loyalty was to the people of Robin Hood's Bay, and he was embarrassed

and frustrated that the filmmakers would employ studio trickery to circumvent a problem.

Yet Walker was also keen to present the Bay's sturdy fisher folk as experts of their craft. Local men were hired to undertake skilled work that Walker's cast could not manage. Consequently it is the practiced and weather-beaten hands of genuine fishermen seen baiting lines and netting crab pots. Still, accuracy only went so far: there was amusement when lobsters were shown being caught in pots that had no bait.

Among the little ruses employed were simple tactics such as throwing water over the actors' hands as they worked in their boat. Doing so ensured the close-up could be shot in the safety of the dock rather than the open water. To replicate a rising gale, smoke from a chimney was made to billow by blowing it from vertical to horizontal with the aid of a vacuum cleaner. Another sequence involved the 'jumping' of a salmon from a pool upstream from Ramsdale Mill with the aid of catapult elastic. This fiddly task was achieved by teenager Arnold Storm, then a pupil at Whitby School.

Writing in the school magazine, *The Viking*, young Storm recalled the daily business of the shoot: "It is a difficult matter to make a film at sea even in calm weather, especially when in a small boat, and it was fine weather when the shot of the Lunns hauling their lobster pots was taken. It was most interesting to see how things were made to appear so real; for example, the scene of the ship ashore was taken on an extraordinarily fine afternoon, and the convincing fog was produced by the use of a smoked glass lens on the camera. There was a scene taken of some washing blowing about, to give the effect of a gale. However, there was very little wind, so, in order to get the effect, a man jerked the line to and fro from one end. One housewife earned an easy five shillings by shaking the window curtains of her cottage to simulate the effect of a gale. A real salmon refused to leap to order, so a rubber one, more capable of gymnastics when manipulated by a string, was substituted."

Perhaps the film's most impressive sequence comes courtesy of a tremendous collaboration between filmmakers and lifeboat men. It is a brilliantly executed recreation of a real-life event from five years before when a steamship had run aground at night in a dense sea fog and had to be helped off again by the crew of the Bay's lifeboat. Walmsley, a member of the lifeboat crew that put to sea to salvage the vessel, had incorporated the incident into his book.

Speaking prior to filming the scene, Norman Walker revealed his commitment to realism. "We want this film to be absolutely true to the life of the coast," he said. "It is all very well reproducing a shipwreck from models in a studio, but often it is more costly, and perhaps less satisfactory in the long run than photographing the real thing. When our ship has been run ashore the lifeboat will turn out, not to rescue the crew but to take part in salvage operations."

Perhaps the film's most impressive sequence comes courtesy of a tremendous collaboration between filmmakers and lifeboat men. It is a brilliantly executed recreation of a real-life event from five years before when a steamship had run

opposite: John Garrick, Sam Livesey and Niall MacGinnis.

above: An atmospheric shot of Niall MacGinnis on the beach at Robin Hood's Bay. Over time the cliffs have been badly eroded by the sea. This scene could not be pictured today; huge boulders block the view.

aground at night in a dense sea fog and had to be helped off again by the crew of the Bay's lifeboat. Walmsley had incorporated the incident into his book.

The location was a sandy stretch of shore between two treacherous shelves of rock to the south of Robin Hood's Bay. To achieve maximum effect, Walker did it for real. No models or studio water tanks here. The steamer Plawsworth, a 1,500 ton collier, was stranded and run aground to form the dramatic centrepiece of a scene that showed lifeboat men and a rival tug crew in a race for salvage. Crowds gathered to watch the action, and there were gasps as the tide left the boat with only a few feet of water around its hull. However, only local people would have noticed the difference between reality and what appeared on screen.

And since the Bay's lifeboat station had been closed for four years, its crew could only watch from the beach. The glory went to their Whitby counterparts, who became film stars for a day.

The unpredictability of Yorkshire weather prompted Walker to shoot whenever the sun shined. But the industriousness of the filmmakers provoked criticism from the vicar of Robin Hood's Bay, the Revd. Gordon Sayle, when Walker and his crew worked on a Sunday. While technicians laboured in the Bay, Revd. Sayle made his feelings known from the pulpit. "The making of a film is a purely commercial proposition. I informed my congregation that we, as Christians, could not encourage or countenance a desecration of God's Day in this manner," he said.

Walker was courteous but firm in his pragmatism. "It was very much against our wishes that we had to work last Sunday," he replied. "Our work is extremely difficult because of the vagaries of the weather. We have, therefore, to seize every opportunity when the weather is suitable. I should like the vicar to know that we are quite content to work six days a week; but supposing we are standing idle for several days and then perfect weather conditions prevail on a Sunday, we have to make the most of them."

When Walker and his crew moved to London to shoot interiors, Walmsley went with them. He was staggered to discover that art director Andrew Mazzei, for added realism and with painstaking attention to detail, had made plaster casts of the Bay's paving stones, cottage walls and cobbles and had reproduced them on sets at British and Dominions Studios, at Elstree. But the recognition and acceptance of such meticulous research could not salve Walmsley's concerns. After a series of increasingly confrontational clashes with the filmmakers, Walmsley announced his resignation, washed his hands of the picture and returned to Yorkshire. He had long suspected that his vision was not shared by Norman Walker and his crew. Inevitably, his desire for perfection on screen led to him meddling in the making of the movie. Once he had left, Walker was able to continue, unencumbered by Walmsley's suggestions.

On October 20 Leo Walmsley was astonished to read glowing reviews of the film in the Sunday papers. By then the film's title had been changed from *Three Fevers* to *Turn of the Tide* - the result of a competition run by *Picturegoer* magazine. A few days later Walmsley's astonishment grew as the manager of Whitby's Empire Cinema revealed he had taken a week-long booking of *Turn of the Tide* after being inundated by requests from local people eager to see it. Walmsley and his wife, Margaret, were invited to attend the first performance. She was delighted, he less so. In fact, it was a decidedly nervous Leo Walmsley who took the bus into Whitby that night. He was greeted with a lengthy queue that snaked its way from the cinema to the harbour quay and beyond. He was recognised and people began to stare. The Empire's manager, in full evening dress, hustled the Walmsleys into the theatre and into their reserved front row seats. The screening, packed with members of the fishing community, was a sell-out. As the opening credits appeared on screen all Walmsley's fears evaporated.

Writing in his 1944 memoir *So Many Loves*, Walmsley recalled: "From that moment I surrendered my possessive literary pride in the authorship of *Three Fevers*. I forgot my feud with British National Films, my quarrels with Norman Walker, my disillusionment, my fears of what Henry Lunn and the other fishermen were feeling and what afterwards they were going to say to me. I had the immeasurable thrill of feeling that all round us and below us in the 'shillings' and 'ninepennies' and 'fourpennies' the folk, the grown-ups and youths and children of my own town and village had, to quote the *Graphic* review, their eyes riveted to the screen, that the film had got them from the first title!"

It was a remarkable premiere for a remarkable little film, yet while *Turn of the Tide* was widely seen and well received it was not a financial success, mainly due to the accounting methods operated by distributors Gaumont-British. Released on the bottom half of various 'B' picture double-bills, it never yielded a profit, much to Walmsley's chagrin. He had been promised five per cent of the net profits but the film never recouped its costs.

Yet the appeal of *Turn of the Tide* is timeless. In 1992, the centenary of Walmsley's birth, the film was revived for a special Whitby screening in the presence of camera operator Eric Cross, then in his 91st year. It was Cross, a former stills photographer, who had had the inspired idea to use up off-cuts of nitrate film in his camera, thus capturing some wonderful candid shots of cast and crew at work.

In recent years the film's flame has been kept burning bright thanks to the efforts of both The Walmsley Society and the British Film Institute. In 1996, during the Cinema 100 celebrations marking the centenary of British Film, a commemorative plaque was erected to permanently mark the making of *Turn of the Tide*. It clings to the wall of the harbour's Bay Hotel – the crew's headquarters while making the film – and faces out towards the grey waters of the North Sea. Another, affixed in 1968 by the Whitby Literary & Philosophical Society, adorns a cottage in King Street, Robin Hood's Bay – Leo Walmsley's home between 1894 and 1913. All who love the film praise Norman Walker's impressive use of locations, cinematographer Franz Planer's exquisite black-and-white photography, the soaring score by Arthur Benjamin, the lean and authentic dialogue and the forthright simplicity of the story. In reviewing the finished film in 1935 the *Sunday Chronicle*'s critic raved "If I had a big drum I'd bang on it until the entire twenty million of you went along to see this one."

And, always, the star of the film remains the sea.

opposite: Art director Andrew Mazzei and director Norman Walker making plaster casts of real Yorkshire cobbles that were then reproduced in the studio.

We of the West Riding

Director: Ken Annakin

Producer: Ken Annakin

Writer: Phyllis Bentley

Production Company: Greenpark Productions

Year of Production: 1945 (Released February 7, 1946)

Where filmed: Halifax, Huddersfield, Haworth, West Yorkshire; Blubberhouses, Burnsall, Bolton Abbey, Skipton Castle and Upper Wharfedale, North Yorkshire between March 19 and April 15, 1945.

Synopsis: A charming portrait of a typical West Riding textile family at work and play featuring magnificent black-and-white cinematography that contrasts the soot and grit of industrial towns with the open spaces of the Yorkshire Dales.

Credited cast: Albert Coldwell, Ethel Coldwell, Kenneth Coldwell, Ivy Coldwell, Eva Coldwell, Edna Sutcliffe, Jack Standeven, A. C. Bamforth, Revd. W. Cornelius Williams, Louie Hirst, Margaret Weavill, Ernest Armitage, Leonard Sykes, Huddersfield Choral Society, Holme Valley Male Voice Choir, the Black Dyke Mills Band and members of the Clarion Cycling Club.

Commentary spoken by Philip Robinson and Philip Wade.

March, 1945. The war in Europe was winding, inexorably and inevitably, to its close. Across the continent exhaustion at six-and-a-half years of war was slowly metamorphosing into a genuine belief that the end was near. At home in England, ordinary people were beginning to recognise that some sort of normality was about to return to lives blighted by conflict. For the British Council, such a feeling was to be encapsulated by a new documentary featurette showing how the stoic folk of Yorkshire's West Riding spent their leisure time. The resultant film, *We of the West Riding*, would be translated into 23 languages and screened in more than 100 countries around the world as a slice of pro-British propaganda, showing the importance of the West Riding textile industry.

We of the West Riding was written by the distinguished Halifax novelist Phyllis Bentley (1894 - 1977). She chose a simple and dignified theme, contrasting the bleak moors of the Brontë country and sheep pastures on millstone grit hills with the giant water wheels that powered the county's great textile industry. Bentley largely eschewed dialogue, relying primarily on a commentary spoken by BBC broadcasters Philip Robinson and Philip Wade to communicate the ways of the West Riding to foreign audiences.

Production began in the third week of March, 1945, in Halifax, where the Coldwell family was selected to portray a typical Yorkshire working class household at work and play. The Coldwells – Albert and Ethel, with daughters Ivy and Eva and son Kenneth – became the "Sykes family" and were filmed at their home in Woodside Place, Boothtown, near Halifax. The Sykes family was enlarged by the inclusion of Edna Sutcliffe, a young amateur actress with Halifax Thespians, who played the Sykes's third daughter.

The Sykes family's pastimes did not parallel the Coldwells', and some dramatic license was required to deliver what the film required. Albert, in reality a motor driver, was cast as a textile worker and pigeon fancier. Since he had always wanted to keep pigeons he was delighted when his character was filmed releasing his birds at Longwood and Milnsbridge L.M.S. railway station. Another member of the family was revealed to play a cornet, thus allowing for the introduction of the Black Dyke Mills Band, seen during a rehearsal. Edna Sutcliffe was seen participating in a rehearsal for Halifax Thespians' production of Jane Eyre. Other scenes featured the cup-tie on March 24 between Halifax Town and Chesterfield, filmed at The Shay.

Forty members of the Clarion Cycling Club gathered to assist with another scene, shot outside the 18th century Pole Moor Baptist Chapel in Scammonden, on the moors above Huddersfield, on Sunday 15 April, 1945. An atmospheric site so isolated that worshippers often brought packed lunches with them, Pole Moor was chosen as it represented a typical West Riding moorland chapel. In the morning cameras recorded the cyclists delivering a lusty version of On Ilkla Moor baht 'at. Later that evening the chapel was packed with more than 700 extras as a combination choir made up of Huddersfield Choral Society and Holme Valley Male Voice Choir sang the Hallelujah Chorus during the annual Messiah. Among the singers was Phyllis Bentley, who had earlier featured Pole Moor Chapel in her 1932 novel Inheritance. The scene made for a rousing finale to *We of the West Riding*.

A comfortable six-week filming schedule allowed Beverley-born filmmaker Ken Annakin to jump from the mills and chapels of Halifax and Huddersfield to the pastoral beauty of Upper Wharfedale. Annakin, only 30 when the film was shot, landed the job after delivering another British Council documentary, the 31 minute short *London 1942*. He would return to the county of his birth in 1947 to make his first feature, *Holiday Camp*, followed by *Value for Money* in 1955. His later feature films included *Swiss Family Robinson, The Longest Day, Battle of the Bulge* and *Those Magnificent Men in Their Flying Machines*.

In his 90's and living in Beverly Hills, California, Annakin remembers his first Yorkshire film with great warmth. "It showed the wonderful strength of Yorkshire people despite World War II," he wrote in 2006 – more than six decades after making the film. "All the performances were by mostly Halifax people (not actors) and they were marvellously co-operative. My film showed how these West Yorkshire people came together in soccer, amateur dramatics and chapel life. There is a magnificent singing of Handel's Messiah which I am very proud of, I suppose because my father competed in many parts of Yorkshire with the Beverley Methodist Choir. How many people saw this movie I don't know, but it gives the best coverage of life and outdoor joys of the West Riding that I know of – the sources of the five main rivers, the building of stone walls and the home of the Brontës."

We of the West Riding premiered on February 11, 1946 at Bradford's New Victoria Cinema.

1948

A Boy, a Girl and a Bike

The whirr of wheels on the open road!

Director: Ralph Smart
Producers: Ralph Keene, Alfred Roome

Writers: Ralph Keene, John Sommerfield, Ted Willis

Production Company: Gainsborough Pictures Ltd

Year of Production: 1948 (Released 23 May 1949)

Where filmed: Elland, Hebden Bridge, Halifax, Mytholmroyd and Ilkley, West Yorkshire, and Grassington, Skipton, Kilnsey, Rylstone, Buckden, Arncliffe and Malham, North Yorkshire between May 19 and mid-August, 1948.

Synopsis: A love triangle set against the backdrop of a Yorkshire cycling club as a pretty young lass finds herself pursued, in life, in love and on two wheels, by rival suitors: a plain-speaking working class lad and his smooth, upper class competitor.

Credited cast: John McCallum (David Howarth), Honor Blackman (Susie Bates), Patrick Holt (Sam Walters), Diana Dors (Ada Foster), Maurice Denham (Bill Martin), Leslie Dwyer (Steve Hall), Anthony Newley (Charlie Ritchie), Megs Jenkins (Nan Ritchie), John Blythe (Frank Martin), Hal Osmond (Mr. Bates), Thora Hird (Mrs. Bates), Amy Veness (Grandma Bates), Margaret Avery (Ginger), Cyril Chamberlain (Bert Gardner), Barry Letts (Syd), Vera Cook (Helen Gardner), Julien Mitchell (Mr. Howarth), Alison Leggatt (Mrs. Howarth), Lyn Evans (Policeman in café), Margot Bourke (Mary Bates), Geoffrey Best (Harry), John Howlett (Alf Pearson), Patrick Halstead (Willie), Joan Seton (Beryl Howarth).

Uncredited: Cyclists: Roland Bancroft, S. Cooper, Joe Farrand, Granville Fox, Jim Gibson, Ronnie Pickles, Allan Ruddock, Jimmy Savile, Bill Sugden (doubled for John McCallum), James Wilde.

A joyous, free-wheeling (pun intended) celebration of innocence, devotion and fresh air, *A Boy, a Girl and a Bike* is a slight fable that dedicates itself to simple folk and simple pastimes. Filmed just three years after the end of the Second World War it is a hugely evocative story that harks back to an era when courtesy and politeness went hand-in-hand with the pursuit of true love.

A quintessential Yorkshire film, *A Boy, a Girl and a Bike* (originally called *Wheels within Wheels*) truly captured the essence of post-war Yorkshire and, for many, exemplifies the spirit of the broad acres. Shot between May and August 1948 the film leaps nimbly between the steep cobbled streets and towering mill chimneys of the West Riding and the dry stone walls and winding lanes of the Dales. Thanks

to the superb editing of James Needs, the movie's patchwork nature is only evident when it shifts to Gainsborough Pictures' studios, where the artificial painted backdrops can be clearly distinguished against the genuine locations that have gone before. All are seamlessly interconnected to provide a glimpse of parallel worlds: the muck and grime of the industrial Pennines versus the freshness and freedom of open roads of the Dales.

Sydney-born Smart arrived in Grassington in mid-May, several days before the majority of his 60-strong cast and crew, to scout locations. At the same time 50 new drop-handled racing bicycles were delivered to Skipton railway station in readiness for the shoot. Smart planned on a three-week schedule in Upper Wharfedale but reckoned without

previous page: You can just spot Sir Jimmy Saville in his cycling shirt reacting to star John McCallum. Also in the photograph is Googie Withers, one of the UK's biggest stars of the time, who is not actually in the film. In real life she was Mrs McCallum

television and a tireless charity fundraiser (he would be knighted for his charity work in 1990), Savile had spent the war years working as a Bevin Boy. He and a friend, both racing cyclists, heard about the filming, volunteered their assistance and were promptly hired. For more than a month they cycled every day and were paid for their pleasure. Savile and a friend moved into digs in Grassington, close to the unit base at Malham. Every morning they would head off to the day's location. They couldn't believe their luck.

"Riding a bike was the most marvellous thing for me. I'd just come out of the pit and was getting used to being able to stand upright without banging my head," says Savile. "I wasn't really doing anything other than trying to get a few quid to live. When this film came along it was like heaven on earth. It was the most amazing time in the world."

Other locals were persuaded to add depth to crowd sequences while members of Bradford Civic Players and Halifax Thespians were hired as extras. Teenager Margaret Avery, just 16, was plucked from obscurity in the Thespians' ranks to play Ginger, a young girl who becomes involved with troubled Charlie, played by future star Anthony Newley. A junior clerk in a Halifax bank, Avery was one of five aspiring actresses granted screen tests for the role after Smart had been made aware of her untapped talents. She was chosen by Gainsborough Pictures' executive Sydney Box.

the area's early morning mist. To add to his woes, the sun was found to be on the 'wrong side' of the valley during the brightest part of the day. While Smart and his actors – including lead triumvirate John McCallum, Patrick Holt and 21-year-old Honor Blackman in one of her earliest films – prayed for sunshine, Upper Wharfedale treated its visitors to day after day of rain.

Smart shot his first sequences on roads outside Grassington on May 20, mixing his actors with 14 real cyclists from Halifax, Leeds, Bradford and Keighley who had volunteered to swell the ranks of the fictional Wakeford Cycling Club. Among the various cyclists hired as extras was a 21-year-old former coalminer from Leeds. His name: Jimmy Savile. Later to become one of the best-known faces on British

"It was arranged that I should meet her without it becoming known who I was," Smart told the *Yorkshire Post* during one of the many unscheduled breaks in filming "A few days later she wrote to say she had found out I was a director and her parents were willing for her to give up her job if there was any future in films. I wrote and told Margaret that it might be unwise to do that. Straight away she wrote back and said she was giving up clerking anyway." She joined the rest of the cast on June 6.

A Boy, a Girl and a Bike allowed Avery to turn professional. She was active on the repertory circuit in the 1950s, working in Nottingham and Huddersfield where she met (and later married) the affable and popular actor Jimmy Hanley. Ralph Smart's encounters with wannabe performers were not always so positive. One aspirant launched into an impromptu (and uninvited) audition, delivering an energetic rendition of Shakespearian prose while driving the director in a hire car along a particularly treacherous stretch of highway. Smart was amused by the man's novel approach – until he took his hands off the wheel to demonstrate his flair for drama. Smart demurred and gently rejected his enthusiastic companion's exhortations, including his firmly stated opinion that he was prime film material since taking third prize for elocution at a recent musical festival!

With inclement weather regularly halting filming Blackman, McCallum, Holt and Co frequently found themselves with little to do. Holt and Barry Letts, playing a supporting role, explored the countryside on the racing bikes that had been supplied for the film. Others in the cast and crew, marooned in their hotels or 'digs', busied themselves with reading, writing letters, knitting, playing darts or going for long walks – often in the rain. Temporary relief from boredom was provided when, on Tuesday, June 1, a small fire broke out at the Wilson Arms, Grassington, where many actors and technicians were staying. They stood by to man the pumps and help fight what may have been a major blaze but the drama was quickly dealt with by Skipton Fire Brigade, after which cast and crew returned to the tedium of involuntary indolence. With even the most junior stars like Anthony Newley and Diana Dors receiving upwards of £30 a week, the production office estimated the ongoing cost of such enforced inactivity at several hundred pounds per day.

Three weeks would be insufficient to get the picture 'in the can', and that unless the weather improved dramatically the production would have to reassemble in Grassington following further location work in Halifax and district. The unit moved across country in early July, setting up a new production base on Skip Hill, in Midgley. By that point Gainsborough Pictures had announced a title change: *Wheels within Wheels* had become *A Boy, a Girl and a Bike* and a small part of Yorkshire movie history was born.

Bad weather followed Smart and his crew from Grassington to the Calder Valley. The stop-start shoot meant the actors had to remain in costume for hours on end, ready to climb into the saddle the moment the sun broke through the clouds. One sequence, shot at the scissors junction at Long Wall, in Elland, involved the majority of the central cast including Diana Dors, Anthony Newley, Cyril Chamberlain, Thora Hird and Leslie Dwyer. When they weren't filming they cupped warm mugs of coffee in their hands or ate roast chicken provided by the catering wagon. Six decades later Jimmy Savile remembered it well. "At the locations was this marvellous food van. We all had a dinner at lunchtime – we'd never had that in our lives! It was wonderful, a dream time. I've done a million things since but that was the first film, which is what makes it important. I loved it then, and I love it now. It was special, different and, for me, totally amazing bearing in mind that I had just come out of the pit."

It was reported that the absence of hot, shimmering days allowed the camera to pick up clear distances. The general quality of outdoor scenes was said to be extremely high, and the crispness of the cinematography (by Ray Elton and Phil Grindrod, the latter an experienced exterior cameraman responsible for the location photography) remains one of the film's strong points. Other Pennine locations, all seamlessly stitched together to portray the town of Wakeford, included Elland Bridge (glimpsed in the background of the race scenes at the Long Wall), Birchcliffe in Hebden Bridge and the main Burnley Road, also in Hebden Bridge, heading towards Mytholmroyd. Another key sequence involved filming the start and finish of the Charles Fox Memorial Race, which provided the film with its climax. Technical assistance was provided by 24-year-old Geoffrey Binns, team leader of Halifax Cycling Racing Club, who, like his fellow riders, received 30 shillings a day for his efforts.

Jimmy Savile can be glimpsed in the road race that forms the film's closing sequence. Smart took his cameras all over the Dales, with four separate teams of riders jostling for space on narrow lanes as they fly through 60 miles of countryside. The start and finish of the race, which John McCallum and Patrick Holt eventually win for Wakeford, were shot in Skipton High Street. The majority of the actors' scenes in the saddle were filmed in the studio against the convenience of back projection. Thus they were seldom seen.

"We rarely saw the actors because they were doing the acting bit and we were doing the cycling bit. It was two entirely separate worlds," recalls Savile. "We saw Patrick Holt as there were times when he had to ride a bike

because he actually pretended to win the race. The bits we did as racing cyclists were obviously only during the bike race. It was like the Tour de France: 'x' number of bike riders set off and after a few miles they all drop into different parties of fitness. There were about 20 riders and they would just film us by coming up alongside in cars, by driving in front [of us] or standing by the side of the road as we came speeding past over bridges. It looks like a real race, but obviously it wasn't. It was linked together via many separate locations and at the behest of the director. For the finish the riders hid round the corner from Skipton Castle [near The Castle pub on Mill Bridge]. Then, when they were ready, we all belted round the corner past Holy Trinity Church and into a sprint finish in High Street. We did that about four times."

A Boy, a Girl and a Bike presented Yorkshire in a favourable light. On its release in May 1949 critics were sympathetic to the actors' attempts at northern accents. Looking back at a film that has become a beloved nostalgia piece it is refreshing to consider that the clipped tones of actors like 36-year-old Patrick Holt (who, during the war, had been a Lieutenant Colonel in the Punjab Regiment with a voice to match his rank) were substituted, at least temporarily, by something amounting to the broad vowels of homely Yorkshire folk. English with a faint trace of Yorkshire accent had been replaced by Yorkshire accent - with a faint trace of English.

Like all films shot on location it left its mark among the Dalesmen and women who, albeit fleetingly, became wrapped up in its production. Mused one: "We don't mind film studios coming to Yorkshire, so long as they show the rest of the country what Yorkshire is really like." His words were echoed by another tyke, who summed up the land known as God's Own Country with surprising eloquence. "This is the finest part of the country to provide background to a film," he mused aloud. "The studios will capture the real atmosphere by bringing the cameras into Yorkshire. There is romance in every inch of the soil."

above, from left to right: publicity shots from Anthony Newley, John McCallum, Leslie Dwyer and Patrick Holt personally signed for Barbara Brown.

1951

Another Man's Poison

She had everything you could give a woman to torment a man!

Director: Irving Rapper

Producer: Daniel M. Angel

Writer: Val Guest

Production Company: Angel Productions

Year of Production: 1951
(Released November 20 1951)

Where filmed: Malhamdale, North Yorkshire
during April 1951.

Synopsis: A mystery writer living in an isolated house
on the Yorkshire moors kills her bank robber husband
and thinks she has committed the perfect murder.
But she reckons without the appearance of a convict
who claims to be her late husband's partner in crime.
Suddenly, she is faced with a dangerous man who
inveigles himself into her life. The only way to be rid of
him is to kill again.

Credited cast: Bette Davis (Janet Frobisher),
Gary Merrill (George Bates), Emlyn Williams (Dr.
Henderson). Anthony Steel (Larry Stevens), Barbara
Murray (Chris Dale), Reginald Beckwith (Mr. Bigley),
Edna Morris (Mrs. Bunting).

Uncredited cast: Peter Colton (Station Master),
Brian Percy (Shop Boy).

When Bette Davis arrived in England in early 1951 to make *Another Man's Poison* she was riding high on the success of *All about Eve* – the 'comeback' movie that had temporarily restored her credibility as a leading lady. But *All about Eve* proved to be only a momentary blip on Hollywood's radar. Davis did not win the Oscar she craved and, soon, she was looking around for work again.

She arrived in the UK after accepting an offer from producers Douglas Fairbanks Jr. and Daniel M. Angel to star in *Another Man's Poison*, a murky murder/mystery melodrama based on a play by Leslie Sands called *Deadlock* and set on the dark and foggy Yorkshire moors. Davis would play Janet Frobisher, a rich mystery writer who has murdered her husband.

Her leading man was fourth husband Gary Merrill. The two had met during the making of *All about Eve* in 1950 and were married shortly after filming ended. They treated the trip as an all expenses paid family honeymoon. To Press and public they put on a show of loved-up marital bliss but in reality they frequently rowed, particularly when Davis found the script wanting and demanded changes to her lines. In this she enlisted the assistance of playwright Emlyn Williams, who was in the cast as a nosey country doctor.

Davis, Merrill and their four-year-old daughter, Barbara, arrived in Settle late on the evening of Sunday, April 8 and moved into the Ashfield Hotel with other members of the seven-strong cast and 50-plus crew. Conscientious

title page: A shoeless Bette Davis between takes at the door of her caravan in Malham. Of local folk she remarked: "They have the good sense to know when to leave."

opposite title page: Lovers on horseback: Bette Davis and screen boyfriend Anthony Steele prepare for a hard ride across country.

previous page: Setting up a shot in Malham village.

below: Gary Merrill and Bette Davis fill in their census forms shortly after arriving in Yorkshire assisted by Edward Bradley, manager of the Ashfield Hotel, Settle.

reporters and photographers who had lain in wait since the morning were caught on the hop and frantically gathered to get what news they could of the stars' arrival. They needn't have worried. diva and husband held court in the Ashfield's small cocktail bar, bought drinks for all and, with director Irving Rapper and co-star Anthony Steel, surrendered to what amounted to an informal Press conference.

Among the Press corps were Derrick Boothroyd, later to see his own book *Value for Money* turned into a comedy/drama by Yorkshire-born filmmaker Ken Annakin, and 17-year-old Barbara Taylor later to add her husband's surname Bradford to her own, and to enjoy her success as a best-selling authoress.

Davis and Merrill made a perfect double-act. He rhapsodised over dry stone walls and the dramatic limestone scenery. She offered her thoughts on the "awful weather". "We're New England stock, and it's just as bad there. The rain is just exactly like we have at home. Gary and I were brought up to this weather. Why, we even have snow in April in New England," she chirruped obligingly. Merrill joined in the fun. "In London they told me and Miss Davis that Yorkshire was the end of the world – all except one doctor, who told us it was the greatest place in England. I guess he had the right idea. If it's the end of the world it's a mighty nice end to come to. Anyway, I like the country better than London. You can't use night life when you are working."

It was left to director Irving Rapper, who had worked with Davis on four previous pictures including 1942's *Now, Voyager,* to talk movies. "If I can average three minutes a day of what you seen on the screen, I'm a quick, dependable and economic director," he said. He too professed to adore the "arresting" limestone landscape that was so vital to the melancholy mood of his film. Malham and Settle, he announced, possessed a cold, earthy quality.

Filming began late on Monday, April 9 with a lengthy night shoot at Malham's Bell Busk railway station – renamed Tarnmoor for the picture. The cold, wet and blustery conditions did not deter hundreds – some claim thousands – of hardy locals from turning up to watch the filming. It was a perfect case study in how movies are made in piecemeal fashion. Two hours of rehearsals were followed by take after take of Davis walking along a station platform to make a clandestine 'phone call. The scene was lit by huge arc lights placed on nearby banking.

"The scene did not amount to much," reported Derrick Boothroyd in the *Yorkshire Post.* "Bette Davis, as a novelist who has killed her husband, is seen walking down the platform of an isolated Yorkshire station called Tarnmoor. She enters a 'phone box and makes a secret call. On her way out she meets Emlyn Williams, the local veterinary surgeon, and has a short conversation with him. That is all."

Several takes were required. First a steam engine (Number 46440 for enthusiasts) missed its cue and thundered forward, spoiling the shot. Then a camera on a dolly shattered a station lamp, showered splinters of glass on cigar-smoking producer Daniel M. Angel. Finally the

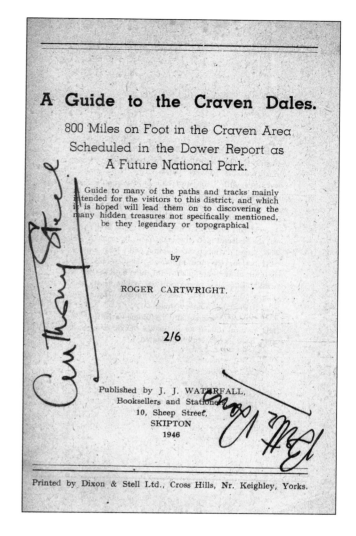

camera failed to function. It was 5am before the scene was 'in the can'. Continued Boothroyd: "For the crowd of eager onlookers, freezing slowly to death in a bitter north-east wind, it could hardly have been ideal entertainment. For me it was perfect misery. When I left Miss Davis had still not got to the 'phone box. What time Emlyn Williams came into the picture I do not know. I suspect he will still be waiting about that platform as you read this. These film stars earn their money."

Alongside New Englanders Davis and Merrill, Welshman Williams and Londoners Anthony Steel and Barbara Murray were two northern talents: Reginald Beckwith (born in York) and Edna Morris (born in Bolton). Both were allowed to use a Yorkshire accent provided, said one newspaper report,

"they do it moderately and without risk of confusing the mentality of the Middle West".

Other key sequences were later shot at the 19th century mansion Tarn House (sandwiched between the limestone crag of Highfolds Scar and the north shore of Malham Tarn), the waterfall at Janet's Foss, on the banks of the Tarn, at the local post office and at majestic Malham Cove. At Tarn House the men of Settle Fire Brigade were enlisted to "water down" the set to add to the damp look of the film. New gates were fitted to the entrance of the grounds to provide a suitably gothic feel. And on Langcliffe Brow a speeding car was driven off the road to crash into a stone quarry. The vehicle, left there by the filmmakers when shooting was complete, was later recovered and repaired by a local farmer who used it for years afterwards.

Arnold Kellett and his fiancée Pat Horsfall were enjoying a walk through Malhamdale when they stumbled across the *Poison* crew filming on an outcrop of rock facing the picturesque waterfall of Janet's Foss. It was Saturday, April 21, and the young couple were on a day trip. Surprised to witness a genuine Hollywood legend at work, Pat requested an autograph. Davis and co-star Steel duly signed their names - on the title page of a guide book to the Craven Dales! The moment – Davis signs while Steel looks on – was captured by Kellett with his 120 camera. "When they resumed filming we felt bold enough to move in a bit closer. The director, however, asked us if we would move well back because they were going to film 'an intimate love scene' for which the stars needed privacy! So we went on to Gordale Scar and got on with our own courting," recalls Kellett.

above: Arnold Kellett and his wife Pat stumbled on the filming of Another Man's Poison *at Janet's Foss. Mr. Kellett sneaked one photograph of the filming – the man with his back to camera is Anthony Steel – before snapping another of his then-fiancée as she asked for, and received, autographs from Steel and Bette Davis.*

right: Local lad Bryan Percy with Bette Davis. Only a teenager when he met the legendarily tempestuous star, he recalls her only with affection. And no wonder. When he posed for a photograph, the camera that took it belonged to Davis. Back in Hollywood she had the film developed and made sure it was posted on with a very touching letter, much to the surprise and delight of her teenage fan, which belies her "monster" image.

Davis and Merrill had little free time whilst on location. They did manage a trip to White Scar Caves (although Davis left after seeing the first waterfall as she did not feel safe) and hoped to catch a screening of *All about Eve* – which they had not seen outside a studio projection room – at The Plaza, Skipton. *Another Man's Poison* was completed at Nettlefold Studios, Walton-on-Thames, Surrey. It was not a hit and failed to add lustre to what Davis hoped would be a continued comeback. Dubbed 'box office poison' by critics, it was a pale shadow of the work she had done for Warner Bros at the height of her success in the 1940s, when she had picked up five successive Oscar nominations as best actress between 1939 and 1943.

above: A rehearsal at the edge of Malham Tarn. Gary Merrill (on horseback) and Emlyn Williams (wearing trilby) run through a scene between an escaped convict and a nosy village doctor. Director Irving Rapper, in black coat, stands near the giant 'brute' lamp. To the left of the picture two crew members take the opportunity to grab a bit to eat.

1958

Room at the Top

A savage story of lust and ambition

Director: Jack Clayton

Producers: James Woolf, John Woolf

Writer: Neil Paterson, from the novel by John Braine

Production Company: Remus Films

Year of Production: 1958 (Released January 1959)

Where filmed: Bradford, Bingley, Halifax, Keighley, West Yorkshire, between June 2 and 19, 1958.

Synopsis: An ambitious working-class civil servant sets his sights on money and success via the gauche daughter of a wealthy industrialist but finds himself drawn into an all-consuming love affair with a sensual married woman.

Credited cast: Simone Signoret (Alice Aisgill), Laurence Harvey (Joe Lampton), Heather Sears (Susan Brown), Donald Wolfit (Mr. Brown), Donald Houston (Charles Soames), Hermione Baddeley (Elspeth), Allan Cuthbertson (George Aisgill), Raymond Huntley (Mr. Hoylake), John Westbrook (Jack Wales), Ambrosine Phillpotts (Mrs. Brown), Richard Pasco (Teddy), Beatrice Varley (Aunt), Delena Kidd (Eva), Ian Hendry (Cyril), April Olrich (Mavis), Mary Peach (June Sansom), Avril Elgar (Miss Gilchrist), Thelma Ruby (Miss Breith), Paul Whitsun-Jones (Laughing Man in Pub), Derren Nesbitt (Tow Path Thug).

Uncredited cast:
Derek Benfield (Man in Bar), Wendy Craig (Joan), Basil Dignam (Priest), Jack Hedley (Architect), Miriam Karlin (Gertrude), Wilfrid Lawson (Uncle Nat), John Moulder-Brown (Boy), Prunella Scales (Girl in Council Office).

Extras: Tony Allsopp, Edith Bailey, Jim Birch, Garth Boyd, Sheila Bradley, Audrey Brown, Jane Brown, Beryl Carter, Barbara Chaffer, Nicholas Chaffer, Harry Chapman, Margaret Chapman, Sydney Cross, Tony Cross, Angela Culbert, Michael Doak, Peter Doak, Anthony Elgar, Ronald Elms, Roy Emerson, Kathleen Fox, David Gore, W.W. Gregg, Anne Gunning, David Hardy, Olive Hunter, Fred Kynnersley, Bernard Lambert, Denis Linford, Helen Linford, Sandra McKnight, Lorna Mawson, Arthur Midgley, Pam Milnes, Sally Milnes, Mary Newton, Kenneth Paine, Walt Parkinson, Peter Reeve, Bert Scaife, Jesse Scarfe, Francis Smith, Clifford Stansfield, Laurence Swaine, Harold Swift, Lacy Swift, Nona Swift, Sandra Thompson, Maureen Wilkinson, Newton Wood.

It was 10 o'clock on the morning of Monday, June 2, 1958. Under a bright blue sky partly obscured by the drifting smoke of mill chimneys, a taxi drew up outside Halifax Town Hall. Out of it leapt tall, dark and handsome Laurence Harvey, who quickly hurried inside. The scene was repeated several times until director Jack Clayton was satisfied. Thus the first moments of *Room at the Top* were safely 'in the can'. It was the beginning of shooting on a film that was to become a critical and commercial hot potato, equally lauded and condemned as filmic art and celluloid pornography.

John Braine's scorching book had been published in 1957. It was a sensation - a brutal and sensual tale of love and malevolent ambition. At its heart was Joe Lampton, a self-seeking snake of a human being who pursues wealth and

title page: Simone Signoret and Laurence Harvey.

above: Filming in Crossley Street, Halifax, for the very first scenes of Room at the Top, *June 2, 1958. The watching crowds were praised for their good behaviour.*

above: The writer and the movie star during the making of Life at the Top. *John Braine was never entirely happy with the casting of Laurence Harvey as cold-hearted Joe Lampton. Harvey had problems with his northern accent and asked Braine for advice. His cigarette holder was an affectation that Braine later remembered and remarked upon, describing the actor as "an exotic butterfly".*

opposite: Arc lights bite through the gloom of a dull day at Halifax Station.

social standing with frightening vigour. An archetypal man-on-the-make, Lampton latches onto the daughter of a textile magnate in the sleepy northern town of Warnley where he works as a council employee. Soon, however, he is embroiled in an affair with an older woman. His callous approach to life and love eventually brings about his downfall, but not before he is confronted by tragedy the like of which he had never imagined.

Clayton and a 60-strong crew arrived in Bradford on June 1, 1958, and set up a production base in the Victoria Hotel, overlooking the noisy Exchange railway station. It prompted Laurence Harvey to ask, each morning as he arrived for breakfast: "Tell me, what time does the hotel pull into London?" For three weeks an ensemble that included Harvey, Heather Sears, Sir Donald Wolfit, Donald Houston, Allan Cuthbertson, Raymond Huntley and the French star Simone Signoret filmed extensively in the city as well as in Halifax, Keighley and Bingley. It was arguably the biggest motion picture ever to come to Yorkshire at that time – a contemporary, ground-breaking slice of small-town sexual politics that would pick up nominations for six Oscars, seven BAFTAs and a slew of other awards. With its 'New Wave' stable mate *Look Back in Anger* it ushered in a stark new dawn of permissive cinema. Yorkshire had never seen anything like it.

Anxious to give his film a degree of authenticity, Clayton set about creating the fictional town of Warnley and its people. He had sketches made of the inside of Bradford Town Hall to aid in the design of studio sets. He selected locations that supported the look, feel and atmosphere of a provincial town far from the metropolitan delights of London. "Local colour", as it was known. And he recruited extras from the ranks of the players at Bingley Little Theatre – the amateur group that included within its members a certain John Braine, former librarian turned overnight success with his debut novel. Charged with finding 60 extras a day was the late Lorna Mawson, the BLT's publicity manager, who was appointed liaison officer between the unit and the theatre. And the job didn't end there. Mrs. Mawson also had to provide costumes. Extras were paid a daily rate of £2 with an extra £1 for any overtime. Given that some days lasted from 8am until 3am they earned every penny. Some earned the equivalent of a week's wage for a day's labours.

Throughout June, 1958, the *Room at the Top* unit hot-footed from one outdoor location to another, attracting attention

wherever it went. Condemned houses in Park Place, Keighley, were given a brief respite from the bulldozer and 'cast' as the street where Joe Lampton lived before the war. The abandoned properties were fitted with new window frames and curtains to pass muster as lived-in quasi-slums – and mightily effective they were, too. At the other end of the scale, Bingley's Bankfield Hotel and Bradford's Cartwright Hall were used to host a dance sequence and a civic ball scene where the awkward Lampton commits a cringe-worthy faux pas in front of his would-be fiancé and her brusque industrialist father. In Bradford city centre the Manor Ice Creamery, close to the Boy and Barrel pub, on Jamesgate, was used as the stage door for scenes involving the film's amateur theatre and its players. A downstairs room of the creamery was decorated with billposters and floodlit from the inside. A worker who gave the crew a key was rewarded with a fiver and a free cup of tea. When filming was over the key was posted through the letterbox.

Inevitably there were problems. The on-off closure of the public library in Undercliffe Street led to complaints that borrowers were unable to select their books before closing time. They can't have been happy with the multitude that thronged the doors, either. More than 200 people, many of them children, waited outside for a glimpse of Harvey and Sears. The crowd was so vast that the two stars had to be smuggled out through the cellars. "We don't know where all the children came from," said PR manager Freddie Oughton. "But come they did. The Pied Piper must have been in the cast." Another example of disharmony occurred when more onlookers packed the narrow thoroughfare of Ivegate, watching avidly as Harvey jumped off a bus to go window-shopping. Furious traders claimed they had collectively lost more than £1,000 in takings.

Problems of a different kind arose during a night shoot on a canal tow path in which Lampton is attacked and beaten by a gang of youths led by 23-year-old Derren Nesbitt. Harvey, bored of waiting around with little to do, consumed several glasses of white wine. When it came to shoot the scene he was more than a little unsteady on his feet. Nesbitt, who had been told to swing a punch and miss the star, was terrified his knuckles might actually connect with Harvey's square jaw. "Harvey was swaying all over the place," he remembered. "Jack Clayton said to me 'You're missing him by a mile' and I said 'Unless you are not aware, he is pissed.' He said 'Well, we've got no time. Just go for it.' It was an absolute miracle that I didn't hit him."

The film's depiction of free-spirited adults who drank, smoked and had sex before (and outside of) marriage caused uproar when it opened in 1959. There were accusations that Room at the Top – both book and movie – had assisted in corrupting the youth of the nation. Among those most incensed by the film was the Archdeacon of Halifax, the Ven. Eric Treacy, who denounced it from the pulpit. "This film, adjudged the best British film of the year, presents a story of sordid sexual filth which may have made a lot of money for the producers, the author and the exhibitors but which must have done incalculable harm to the enormous number of young people who saw it." And see it they did, in their thousands, no doubt drawn by the hypnotic effect of the 'X' certificate that burned from posters advertising "a savage story of lust and ambition".

Joe Lampton continued his single-minded journey to the upper classes in Life at the Top, Braine's sequel, filmed in 1965. Harvey and Wolfit returned as Lampton and Abe Brown, but Heather Sears had been replaced by Jean Simmons. Scenes were shot in Bradford's Wool Exchange and council chamber where Harvey, as a new councillor, makes his maiden speech. The film explored some of the same ground as its predecessor but by then the world, like so many of the original cast, had moved on.

previous page, left: Courtroom scene from Life at the Top.

previous page, right: The legendary Sir Donald Wolfit who was the inspiration for another Yorkshire based film, The Dresser.

right: A grim-faced Laurence Harvey and a smiling Heather Sears exit All Souls' Church, Halifax, as Jack Clayton's crew films the closing scenes of Room at the Top. *Also pictured are co-stars Donald Houston and Sir Donald Wolfit.*

1959

Hell is a City

From dark till dawn... From dives to dames... From cops to killers...

Director: Val Guest

Producer: Michael Carreras

Writer: Val Guest, from the novel by Maurice Procter

Production Company: Associated British Picture Corporation Limited/Hammer Film Productions

Year of Production: 1959 (Released May 9 1960)

Where filmed: Marsden Moor, West Yorkshire, from September 21–23, 1959.

Synopsis: Detective Inspector Martineau of the Manchester City Police vows to catch fugitive career criminal Don Starling who, after escaping from prison, leads a robbery in which a young woman is killed.

Credited cast: Stanley Baker (Inspector Harry Martineau), John Crawford (Don Starling), Donald Pleasence (Gus Hawkins), Maxine Audley (Julia Martineau), Billie Whitelaw (Chloe Hawkins), Joseph Tomelty (Furnisher Steele), George A. Cooper (Doug Savage), Geoffrey Frederick (Devery), Vanda Godsell (Lucky Lusk), Charles Houston (Clogger Roach), Joby Blanshard (Tawny Jakes), Charles Morgan (Laurie Lovett), Peter Madden (Bert Darwin), Dickie Owen (Bragg), Lois Daine (Cecily), Warren Mitchell (John Hartley, Commercial Traveller), Sarah Branch (Silver Steele), Alastair Williamson (Sam), Russell Napier (Superintendent).

"Police! Quick! I think there's been a murder!"

Filmmakers are renowned for making the best of any situation. So it was on a dismal morning on the isolated road that winds through the bleak, windswept moorland above Marsden. Warren Mitchell was the commercial traveller who got more than he bargained for when he disturbed a gang of crooks as they dumped the body of a girl, accidentally killed during a bungled cash snatch. Horrified by his discovery – the lovely corpse was played by newcomer Lois Daine, whom writer/director Val Guest was grooming for stardom – the shocked man tried to flag down a passing car, but to no avail.

Inside the car were a reporter and photographer from the local newspaper, the *Huddersfield Daily Examiner*, who had been sent along to investigate reports of a film unit shooting in the remote spot a few miles from the town centre. Having been given their story, they were invited to join in the film as occupants of an anonymous vehicle who ignore the pleas of the man who stumbled across the girl's body. Minutes later, anxious and rattled, he calls the police from a telephone box.

The sequence began filming on Monday, September 21, 1959 and marked the beginning of eight weeks shooting on *Hell is a City*, a gritty crime thriller in which a flawed, driven and all-too-human detective, Harry Martineau (played with tenacity and more than a touch of world-weary realism by 32-year-old Stanley Baker, an actor who always looked older than his years), plunges headlong into

title page and above: Sir Stanley Baker.

previous page: Shooting a scene on bleak, windswept Marsden Moor, above Huddersfield.

opposite: Actor Warren Mitchell, seated in the white car, waits for his cue.

the hunt for escaped convict-turned-killer, Don Starling (John Crawford). On that first day Baker was on location for a sequence in which he and a detective constable begin the process of laying out a crime scene.

Guest adapted a semi-autobiographical novel (by former Manchester copper Maurice Procter) for the screen and shot the majority of the movie in Manchester. The finale – a gun fight between Baker and Crawford – was filmed 200 feet above the pavements of Manchester on the roof of the Refuge Assurance Building and assisted greatly in winning over the critics. Most agreed that *Hell is a City* was a magnificent modern crime thriller and compared it favourably to American films of the same genre.

Seen today the picture benefits greatly from Guest's hectic semi-documentary style and the realistic nature of Arthur Grant's engrossing black-and-white cinematography. In fact, realism was Guest's watchword throughout the shoot. He peppered his script with authentic, rat-a-tat dialogue, had Martineau tempted by an attractive vixen as his marriage to his nagging wife disintegrated and showed how violence came easy to desperate men. Naturally it became a controversial subject. The film received a gala premiere on April 10, 1960, at Manchester's vast Apollo Theatre and was, not surprisingly, a hit with the people of the city in which it was based. However the Chief Constable of Manchester City Police insisted on each screening being preceded by a filmed statement in which locals were earnestly reassured that the film was fiction and not a true picture of crime in Manchester.

Hell is a City was sufficiently successful for Hammer producer Michael Carreras to consider turning Martineau into the focus of a spin-off TV show. The idea lasted as long as the late 1960s until it was dropped. The series never materialised.

1962

This Sporting Life

Never before has the screen exploded with such raw emotions!

Director: Lindsay Anderson

Producer: Karel Reisz

Writer: David Storey, from his novel

Production Company: Independent Artists

Year of Production: 1962 (Released January 1963)

Where filmed: Wakefield, Leeds and Thrum Hall, Halifax, West Yorkshire; Bolton Abbey, North Yorkshire between March and June, 1962.

Synopsis: Frank Machin is a young miner whose strength and aggression bring him big rewards in the rough world of professional rugby but only conflict and suffering in love. Trapped by his brutal way of life, he is unable to communicate with the strange, complex woman with whom he lives.

Credited cast: Richard Harris (Frank Machin), Rachel Roberts (Mrs. Margaret Hammond), Alan Badel (Gerald Weaver), William Hartnell ('Dad' Johnson), Colin Blakely (Maurice Braithwaite), Vanda Godsell (Mrs. Anne Weaver), Anne Cunningham (Judith), Jack Watson (Len Miller), Arthur Lowe (Charles Slomer), Harry Markham (Wade), George Sewell (Jeff), Leonard Rossiter (Phillips), Katherine Parr (Mrs. Farrer), Bernadette Benson (Lynda Hammond), Andrew Nolan (Ian Hammond), Peter Duguid (Doctor), Wallas Eaton (Waiter), Anthony Woodruff (Head Waiter), Michael Logan (Riley), Murray Evans (Hooker), Tom Clegg (Gower), Ken Traill (Trainer), Frank Windsor (Dentist), John Gill (Cameron).

Uncredited cast: Edward Fox (Barman), Glenda Jackson (Girl singing at party), Bryan Mosley (Man in bar), Albert Rayner (Referee), Tommy Fisher (Pub compère), Paddy Armour (physiotherapist).

Wakefield Trinity RLFC: Brian Briggs, Albert Firth, Neil Fox, Colin Greenwood, Ken Hirst, Keith Holliday, Johnny Malpass, Geoff Oakes, Gerry Round, Alan Skene, Fred Smith, Derek Turner, Don Vines, Jack Williamson.

Wooden faces stared lifelessly from beneath cloth caps and scarves. Scattered amidst them was the occasional human being. Together they formed a phoney crowd for a *faux* rugby match starring a fake player. And as a rangy, long-legged loose-forward powered past to catch a ball before scoring a conversion, they cheered their hearts out. They would repeat their joy and emotion again and again and again. It was March, 1962. In a corner of Wakefield Trinity's Belle Vue ground, mothers, wives, schoolboys and the unemployed shivered together alongside crude people-shaped cut-outs. On the pitch a scene was played out repeatedly for the cameras as Frank Machin ploughed through the mud to take his fleeting moment of glory.

title page: A rare colour shot of a behind-the-scenes moment involving Richard Harris and Rachel Roberts. Playing Machin's doomed landlady offered Welsh-born Roberts, an actress of great sensitivity and emotional power, her biggest film challenge to date. "I was frightened of her," said Roberts. "She's such a strange, knotted Northern English character. I was scared stiff of her. But Karel resolved all my doubts and Lindsay was a tower of strength all through the shooting of the film."

above: A group shot of cast and crew. Pictured with real-life Wakefield Trinity players are Richard Harris, Jack Watson, Colin Blakely and director Lindsay Anderson. The first man on the back row is Keith Holliday. Referee Albert Rayner is on the far left of the front row.

top: The director's life is never an easy one.

above: Lindsay Anderson in better spirits.

opposite: Lindsay Anderson directs children at a concert party in Fitzwilliam during the making of Wakefield Express. *Walter Lassally is behind the camera.*

Machin was in fact Richard Harris – actor, poet and hellraiser. The ground had been conveniently watered with hundreds of gallons of water by the local fire brigade to make it sufficiently sodden for the requirements of director Lindsay Anderson. There may even have been a touch of cruelty to his fastidiousness. To add to the realism and energy, Anderson ordered a trench, four feet deep, dug along the edge of the pitch in which a camera, on a dolly, would capture the action from ground level. The action was consistent throughout: play, block and tackle, always heading towards the camera.

From the Agbrigg End of Trinity's ground a gang of lads from Richard Sutcliffe's Universal Works in Horbury watched and cheered on cue as Harris scored his try. It was in fact a replica of a terrific try scored in an earlier league match when Alan Skene passed to Neil Fox who then tore down the wing to make the score. The place erupted – 8,000 people made quite a din. Some months later Anderson sought to replicate the moment with Harris. Repeatedly Harris took the ball from the final overhead pass and dived over the line to the cheers and jeers of the crowd. On the final take Harris dived over, stood up, grinned and made a theatrical bow to the crowd, who roared with laughter, mock boos and applause.

The people of Wakefield had flocked to Belle Vue on a cold Monday morning following an appeal in the *Wakefield Express*. It had been advertised as a big outdoor bingo session for free. The queues started at eight o'clock. By nine o'clock there was a queue of Wakefield women in their finery waiting to play bingo. Thus the cardboard figures dotted around the ground had to be disguised as males; otherwise the crowd would have been 95 per cent women. More than 200 extras were needed for a sequence that complemented real-life crowd scenes shot a few weeks earlier at a match between Wakefield and Wigan. The scene both opened the film and introduced the lead character.

As interpreted by Harris, Machin was a scarily focused player with ambition. Determined to be noticed by scouts, and prepared to remove anyone who stands in his way, he ruthlessly disables a rival and allows a team mate to take the blame. Moments later Machin himself is being carried off the pitch, his teeth in pieces after a particularly vicious tackle. All was artifice, but Harris learned precisely how rough rugby could be during those early days on the pitch.

Lindsay Anderson's Wakefield

*In six films over 14 years, Lindsay Anderson put Wakefield on
the movie map. His earliest connections with the town came
via a series of industrial documentaries for Desmond Sutcliffe,
husband of his friend Lois Sutcliffe. It was Lois who, on a snowy
night in January 1948, offered Anderson the chance to become
a filmmaker. The project was a promotional featurette for her
husband's company, Richard Sutcliffe Limited, to be made almost
immediately. Anderson, having never directed a film before,
happily accepted.*

The resulting film was entitled Meet the Pioneers *and focused on
belt conveyors for coal mines. More importantly, it illuminated
the personality of the company that constructed them. Anderson
would later remember it as primitive and amateurish. Over
the next five years Anderson would return to Wakefield to make
four more shorts:* Idlers That Work, Three Installations, Wakefield
Express *and* Trunk Conveyor.

The best (and best-known) was Wakefield Express, *a celebration
of the town's newspaper. A 33-minute quasi-travelogue, it was
filmed without dialogue and completed with a commentary
spoken by George Potts, an Express reporter. Shot in Horbury
and Fitzwilliam, Pontefract, Sharlston and Selby, it followed
the daily life of a journalist as he gathers news for his paper. It
was a paean to the semi industrial heart of the West Riding and
completed on a budget of just £600.*

*Those early attempts at creating a film style are still
remembered today. In the early 1950s Bob Sykes was a junior
in the drawing office of Richard Sutcliffe Limited, based in
Horbury. He never thought for a moment that the man with the
scarf to whom he was handing a cup of coffee would one day be
a world-famous film director. The man with the scarf was, of
course, Lindsay Anderson. The film was* Three Installations.

*"Anderson filmed all over the works and in the drawing office
where I worked," recalled Sykes more than half a century later.
"A memorable shot was of the lads in their overalls swinging
over a beck on a rope as they did habitually at dinner time.
'Happy' Hainsworth is on the rope and, of course, many a lad
finished up in the beck over the years."*

above: *Lindsay Anderson and Richard Harris on*
the pitch at Belle Vue.

He had not endeared himself to his fellow players, most of them real-life Trinity regulars. A cocky, strutting figure fond of shocking people with his casual (and perhaps deliberate) profanity, Harris found that life on and off the pitch was very different. Off the pitch he was the movie star who had just held his own opposite Marlon Brando in MGM's mammoth *Mutiny on the Bounty*. On it he was merely a man labouring at convincing the watching crowds that he was a coal miner with a talent for rugby and violence.

Among those watching Harris slide into character was Keith Holliday. Like the other part-time professionals in the 1962 squad 28-year-old Holliday had jumped at the chance to earn £20 a week. He joined the likes of Neil Fox, Ken Hurst and Jack Williamson on the pitch while Brian Briggs, Geoff Oakes and Derek Turner helped form the opposition. Harris continued to play to the crowd, peppering his speech with profanities, secure in his status as the number one man on the pitch. No-one said a word.

"There were a lot of lads at Belle Vue that had never met an actor, and Richard Harris wasn't liked at first," recalls Holliday. "No-one liked him. His language was atrocious. Derek Turner [then Trinity team captain] was going to tackle him because he was the other forward [on the opposing team in the film]. Harris had been effing and blinding on the field. Derek came round the blind side and copped him a real 'un. He gave him a right bloody handful – bust his nose. Richard went down on his back. He wasn't knocked out but he was stunned. They stopped the game because they had to look at him. He went to the director and said 'Tell Derek he's coming too hard'. Anderson said 'You tell him' and Richard replied 'YOU ****** tell him! It's your job!' He was trying to prove he was a hard man, but when you are playing nobodies you don't push it as hard. They would have killed him in a real match." Thus the opening scenes of *This Sporting Life* are played out on the screen.

Published in 1960, *This Sporting Life* was a runaway success. It came from the personal experiences, both social and sporting, of David Storey, a 27-year-old wannabe writer who, in the early 1950s, had played for Leeds A-team for four seasons as second-row and loose-forward. A miner's son from Lupset, Storey broke away from the pits and studied at London's Slade School of Art. He was working as a supply teacher in the capital, travelling back to games in Leeds at weekends, when *This Sporting Life* was picked up. It was his seventh novel; six unpublished companions preceded it.

The seed of what would become *This Sporting Life* came via an actual match when Storey was still a teenager. Unlike Machin, Storey was an aesthetic player who preferred to avoid hard tackles and the risk of serious injury. "I was in the second row, with a player who was playing out his last days. At one moment the ball was at my feet, and I realised that if I picked it up I'd get my face kicked. And I hesitated just that amount, and he didn't, and he got his face kicked. He came up with a very bloody mouth, not knowing what had happened to his teeth. He just turned to me and said 'You ****.' The guilt induced by that was enormous, which was what prompted me to start writing about it."

The book emerged as an intense and visceral portrait of 1950s Rugby Union – a hard game for hard men. Tied to it was the locale: a grim, unforgiving northern town in which anti-hero Arthur Machin (the character was renamed for the film), coiled like a watchspring, rages against the world while yearning for a sign of love from his buttoned-up landlady, the widowed Mrs. Hammond. Storey always imagined Machin as an unsophisticated man thrust into a world where he is out of his depth. In truth he only exists on the rugby pitch, where he is able to balance his aggression with his latent tenderness. Said Storey: "I felt that a man's inner life is in endless conflict with his outer life – I could see no solution, and intuitively I was looking for some kind of synthesis between the two. So *This Sporting Life* is the physical side. Machin has a great appetite for society and people, and a capacity to fulfil himself through them."

The passion required for Machin flowed through Richard Harris. Only 31 when he landed the role, he arrived in Yorkshire as a bonafide movie star. His stand-in on the pitch was John Teasdale, who seemed to have been hired to lie in the mud so Harris didn't have to. Teasdale didn't complain. Out of work, he was on the film for more than a month and received £3 10s a day. "It was a pretty bloody miserable experience. My job meant lying in the mud and, when the lighting was all perfect, Harris lay down for two minutes. Harris was very much the man of the moment. He had just worked with Marlon Brando so was "god". He said 'thank you' when I got in the mud but there was no close conversation. I don't think he had much to do with anybody."

Running with the players was real-life referee Albert Rayner. He had been persuaded to take part by Trinity players Derek

Turner and Brian Briggs, who turned up on his doorstep one morning and uttered the immortal line "Do you want to be a film star?" It is Rayner who sends off the wrong player at the beginning of the film – a combination of nervousness, being made to laugh by Richard Harris and forgetting his lines. Anxious and desperate to do the right thing, Rayner collared the wrong man, took his name and number and dismissed him from the pitch. Anderson, who enjoyed the heightened realism of such errors, kept the scene in the picture.

Rayner, a non-actor like trainer Ken Traill and masseur Paddy Armour, was not used to the ways of movie-makers. Good-natured and pleasant, he failed to see the hidden threat in a seemingly innocuous question from Lindsay Anderson. "Albert, if you were refereeing a match in these conditions, would you still be as clean as you are now? Wouldn't you be as dirty as the players?" said the director with a wicked gleam in his eye. "No," said Rayner. "Only my boots would be dirty and there would be a few odd splashes on my stockings." It was a quick answer that tripped off the tongue, but it failed to save him. Rayner took off like a jack rabbit but was duly caught and rolled in the mud. On *This Sporting Life*, democracy was all. Everybody got filthy.

There are those who believe that *This Sporting Life* was a guaranteed success even before a foot of film had been shot. The disciplined Harris put in an incredible amount of preparation for the role and allowed himself to be consumed by the character he was playing. To bulk up for the role – he hadn't played rugby for more than a decade – he hit the gym. He also signed on anonymously to a London rugby club whose members were, in his words, "lawyers and bank clerks". Their awareness of his roots and Irishness had the desired effect: they totally ignored him, allowing Harris to concentrate on the rugby itself. Later, when he arrived in Wakefield, he was ready. "Physically I thought I was big enough, but I wasn't as big as most rugby players really are," recalled Harris. "I hung about the dressings rooms making mental notes on how they behaved. I worked at preparing my body but I was worried in the end that I wouldn't look the real thing in the movie." Later, on meeting David Storey for the first time, Harris decided to dye his naturally red hair jet black – just like Storey's. Thus Richard Harris became Frank Machin by way of David Storey.

The film was made on a variety of locations across Wakefield, in Leeds, at Bolton Abbey and in Halifax, where the Thrum Hall ground of Halifax RLFC was used for the off-pitch moments when Harris and his fellow actors – Alan Badel, Arthur Lowe, William Hartnell – discuss the game. A dance sequence was filmed on consecutive mornings in the Mecca Locarno Ballroom, in Southgate. A rowdy night out, with Machin and his pals cheering a local singer, was shot in The Dolphin, a notorious town centre pub run by Tommy Fisher, who landed a small role as a compere. The pub, on Warrengate and Kirkgate, is now the Zeus Bar. Another Wakefield pub put to good use was The Beehive.

Harris enjoyed his time on *This Sporting Life* and vowed to work again with Anderson and Storey. His pet project was a film of *Wuthering Heights*, co-starring with his idol Merle Oberon, by then ageing and semi-retired. A script was written and Storey scouted locations. There was a glimmer of interest in the picture when Harris was nominated for an Oscar and his box office cachet increased, but the film never got further than a dream.

opposite: Writer David Storey, producer Karel Reisz and star Richard Harris on location at Belle Vue, Wakefield. Harris was reluctant to let journalists on the set when he was working. "It is unbelievably distracting. Acting is such a personal, intimate business that it's impossible to do it in front of sightseers. You expose yourself too much," he said.

1962

Billy Liar

The truly hilarious adventures of a boy whose imagination runs away with him!

Director: John Schlesinger
Producer: Joseph Janni
Writers: Keith Waterhouse, Willis Hall, from their play
Production Company: VIC Films Limited
Year of Production: 1962 (Released 1963)
Where filmed: Bradford, Baildon, Leeds, West Yorkshire between October and December, 1962.

Synopsis: Lowly undertaker's clerk Billy Fisher longs to escape the drudgery of his monotonous existence for the bright lights of London and a new life as a scriptwriter. But his life is one long round of tightly-knotted but steadily fraying lies: to his family, to his boss, and to his three girlfriends. Ever the dreamer, Billy weaves an ever-growing web of deceit as his outrageous fantasies spiral out of control.

Credited cast: Tom Courtenay (Billy Fisher), Wilfred Pickles (Geoffrey Fisher), Mona Washbourne (Alice Fisher), Ethel Griffies (Florence, Billy's Grandmother), Finlay Currie (Duxbury), Gwendolyn Watts (Rita), Helen Fraser (Barbara), Julie Christie (Liz), Leonard Rossiter (Emanuel Shadrack), Rodney Bewes (Arthur Crabtree), George Innes (Stamp), Leslie Randall (Danny Boon), Patrick Barr (Inspector MacDonald), Ernest Clark (Prison Governor), Godfrey Winn (Disc Jockey).

Uncredited cast: Alexander Browne, Jack Cunningham, Sheila Fearn, George Ghent, Reginald Green, Natalie Kent, Margaret Lacey, Leslie Lawton, Ted Morris, Bryan Mosley, Elizabeth Murray, Robin Parkinson, Graham Rigby, Jessie Robins, David Scase, Neville Smith, Elaine Stevens, John Tordoff, Anna Wing, William Wymar.

Extras: Adrian Goodwin, Carl Gresham, Davril Foster Jones, Kate Lee, John Lensky, Jean Noon, Rita O'Neil, Mary Saville, Veronica Ward, Steve White.

The hero drew imperturbably at his cigarette as the soldiers cheered. Women threw flowers or clambered aboard his armoured car to embrace him. Smoke curled out of the wreckage of houses and flames flickered in the distance. Soldiers struggled over the battlefield, brandishing their rifles, while others trundled across in jeeps or armoured cars – and the people of Leeds looked on rather amused, perhaps a little excited. 'Billy Liar' was experiencing the fruits of war – the moment of triumph. Goggled, jack-booted and carrying binoculars and revolver, he looked every inch the revolutionary hero.

Then reality intervened, and the fantasy was over for a while. 'Billy Liar', funeral director's assistant, and a hero only in his fantasies, became once again Tom Courtenay, star of the film

of Keith Waterhouse's novel. It was October, 1962, and a demolition site off Wellington Road, Leeds, had temporarily been transformed into a battle zone as part of one of several dreamlike scenarios that brighten up the monotonous life of Billy Fisher. Courtenay, playing Billy, was in command of an imaginary army but, in truth, it was director John Schlesinger who was giving the orders. A veritable battalion had arrived to do their bit for William Fisher, President of the Democratic Republic of Ambrosia. All had been recruited after responding to newspaper advertisements appealing for 20 6ft-tall Amazons to join Billy's make-believe militia. When only three six-footers turned up the height specification was lowered to 5ft 7ins. Nine girls varying in age from early 20s to mid-30s were chosen. They included shopgirls, housewives, clerks and a stenographer.

title page. A never-before-published photograph of director John Schlesinger and actress Topsy Jane, who was originally cast as Liz, on location in Bradford.

previous page: John Schlesinger, Tom Courtenay and Rodney Bewes filming in Southgate, Bradford, autumn 1962.
Almost 50 years later the scene is remarkably unchanged by time and progress.

below: In order to see Bradford in the background of the scene the bench had to be raised almost three feet.

They were joined by women from Leeds Old People's Central Club, Territorial Army soldiers and students from Leeds University. Hundreds were hired for the sequence; more still were needed for an impressive parade past Leeds Town Hall. Among them were 20 girls, acting as nurses, "because Billy Liar thinks all nurses look like Pan-Am Airline hostesses," said a wag.

Billy Liar burst onto the screen as part of the British 'New Wave' that had begun in the late 1950s with the kitchen sink revolution that had produced Look Back in Anger (directed by Bradford-born Tony Richardson), A Kind of Loving and Saturday Night and Sunday Morning. Billy Liar proved to be a remarkable catalyst in the careers of many of those involved in its transition from novel to stage play to movie screen. It launched Courtenay and co-star Julie Christie on the road to international success, and did the same for Schlesinger, later to make Darling, Midnight Cowboy and Sunday, Bloody Sunday.

Schlesinger had first happened across the book when he was working on the TV series The Four Just Men in 1959. The project only got off the ground three years later when producer Joseph Janni, with whom Schlesinger had just made A Kind of Loving, offered him the film having bought the rights. Schlesinger jumped at it. It seemed he had been fated to make the film. Earlier, when Janni wanted to test his mettle as a filmmaker, he suggested he shoot a ten-minute test. The subject turned out to be Billy Liar, and the actor was Tom Courtenay.

Hull-born Courtenay had originally played Billy on stage. Albert Finney had initiated the part in 1960 at the Cambridge Theatre and when he left the production – directed by Lindsay (*This Sporting Life*) Anderson – Courtenay took over. Finney is said to have been offered the film but, fearing typecasting, turned it down. Anthony Newley is also rumoured to have been considered. In Schlesinger's eyes, there was no-one but Courtenay. Casting the character of the free-spirited Liz, who offers Billy a passport to freedom and an escape from his humdrum existence, proved trickier.

Filming began in late autumn 1962 with Courtenay and Topsy Jane, an actress who had appeared in *The Loneliness of the Long Distance Runner*. When, during filming, she fell ill, a replacement had to be found, and quickly. Speaking

in 1997, John Schlesinger recalled what happened. "When we started casting *Billy Liar* I saw a magazine. We kept saying to each other 'What sort of girl are we looking for?' 'Well, *this* sort of girl' and pointing to the photograph on the cover. And it was Julie. We did not one but two tests of her. I decided against casting her because she wasn't the image of the girl that I had in mind for Liz. I wanted a more bosomy, earth mother figure. So we cast Topsy Jane. She started work but got ill and was unable to continue. We had to very quickly decide who we would employ instead. So we went back to the tests that we had shot and Julie Christie was there. Joe and I both said 'Why on earth didn't we cast her in the first place? She's so gorgeous'. There are other qualities that she has other than big breasts and an earth mother image. So we quickly cast her and re-shot what we

top: Billy's amazons. When too few six-footers turned up, the height requirement was reduced.

above: A candid snapshot of star Tom Courtenay and extras Jean Noon and Davril Foster Jones during filming in Leeds. October, 1962.

opposite: Filming one of Billy's grand fantasies in Bradford. Director John Schlesinger (in sheepskin jacket) watches from behind the camera. Tom Courtenay is directly in front, leading the parade and saluting with his left hand.

had done, although the weather didn't match. If you look very carefully you can see snow in the background."

Julie Christie remembers delivering "an appalling test because I was in a state of terror". It was a feeling that prevailed throughout the filming. "I was so terrified. My life was dominated by absolute terror and thinking I didn't know what the hell I was doing. I can't look at the experience rationally. I just did what I was told to do, basically. I was a great admirer of Tom's, who was quite a lot more experienced than me and certainly knew much better what the hell *he* was doing. He was already a very developed actor. It takes my breath away, his performance – I think it's a great, great performance."

Schlesinger and Janni were deliberate in their choice of northern locations for the movie. When Janni secured the rights – he paid £12,000 after negotiations with Tony Richardson's Woodfall Films fell through – he vowed to make the film where it was set: an imaginary industrial town in Yorkshire. They settled on Bradford and selected locations across the city and in its suburbs. Scenes were shot in Southgate, Petergate, Forster Square, Bank Street, Midland Road, Broadway, Cheapside, Church Bank, Undercliffe Cemetery, the war memorial on Prince's Way and the Mecca Locarno nightclub on Manningham Lane. Billy's house was a real residence: 'Hillcrest', 37 Hinchliffe Avenue, Baildon. It was considered perfect for the job and barely altered, unless one ignores the gnomes surreptitiously added to the garden.

Extras were recruited at the Midland Hotel and at Bradford Civic Playhouse, which was scouted by Schlesinger's assistant. Many women were hired for a supermarket sequence involving Leslie Randall as comic Danny Boon. At the heart of the scene was Topsy Jane. Her illness threw the production into chaos. Extras who had queued in the cold had to be re-located and brought back to film their scenes again. Audrey Raistrick was given a walk-on part as the Lady Mayor of Bradford and shot a scene in the Great Northern Hotel (now The Victoria). When Topsy Jane left the film and Christie took over, it was impossible to match the scenes and Audrey's fleeting moment of glory was cut.

"It was a natural choice, really, to use Bradford, which I knew slightly from my schooldays as one of my best friends came from Shipley," said Schlesinger. "I used to go there during the school holidays and stay up there. I knew the moors

a bit and enjoyed them very much. I liked the hilliness of Bradford because I like levels to shoot in – streets that go up or down always make a better visual than flat streets. We didn't necessarily want to go back to Manchester where I'd made *A Kind of Loving* again – although I think the big dance scene at the end, the Twisterella, was shot [at Ashton-under-Lyme], near Manchester."

Writer Willis Hall, who co-wrote the play with Keith Waterhouse and then collaborated on the film's script, was always slightly peeved that so much of the film was made in Bradford. Born in Leeds, he always considered *Billy Liar* to be a Leeds movie. Still, he paid tribute to Schlesinger's involvement in transforming the project into a cinema piece via several brainstorming sessions with himself and

Waterhouse. "John brought a great deal to the screenplay. Many of the fantasy ideas were his. We did about three drafts of the screenplay and he contributed to each one."

"It was my second film, I loved the subject and I understood it," added Schlesinger. "The first film I made was a totally realist film. This had the element of fantasy about it which I've always enjoyed as well. Many of my movies have dealt with an insider in some way or other who has to either break out of his own environment or compromise and stay in it. The character of Billy Liar is something that so many people can identify with: underneath the rebel but on the surface quite conventional and unable to break his chains to the roots of his existence. I loved the ending. I thought the idea that he wants to go to London to be a screenwriter and finally

can't really pluck up enough courage to go with this more adventurous girl was lovely. Instead he's content to resort back to the fantasy of his imaginary army and marching in triumph home. It's an ironic end to the film which I'm rather fond of. I never, ever re-thought that. *Billy Liar* wasn't as popular commercially as *A Kind of Loving* but it's a film I look back on with a great deal of pleasure and pride."

left: Julie Christie

below left: John Schlesinger with selected members of the cast and crew unveiling a plaque in Southgate, Bradford in 1996.

below right: John Schlesinger in 1996.

"Billy Liar *makes comedy of the deepest terrors and fears. It's such a ghastly cliché, but it's truthful. It was exquisitely written; it never went off into sentiment or banalities. The sharp humour saved it from that, along with Tom's virtuoso performance. It was very nice to have a balanced group of women. All sorts of women were represented and I was very lucky to have the part of the 'free' person. All those people who were trapped and chained into awful social behaviour by fear. I was the only person who was free of fear. That's what was so remarkable: the character was so important. The chaps who fancied me were more likely to have had pictures from* Billy Liar *than almost anything else I'd done. There was something about that woman that really excited them, and people confused that with me. Even now, people talk about that. Somehow that liberated woman's personality got confused with my own. It was a great bonus to me."*

– Julie Christie, 1997

1965

Lady L

Director: Peter Ustinov

Producer: Carlo Ponti

Writer: Peter Ustinov

Production Company: Metro-Goldwyn-Mayer

Year of production: 1965
(World Premiere November 25, 1965)

Where filmed: Castle Howard, near Malton, North Yorkshire (doubling as Lendale Castle) between March 9 and April 4, 1965.

Synopsis: Elegant octogenarian Lady L reminisces about her colourful life as a laundress in a Parisian bordello and her romantic entanglements with a French revolutionary and an English aristocrat.

Credited cast: Sophia Loren (Lady Louise Lendale, aka Lady L), Paul Newman (Armand Denis), David Niven (Dicky, Lord Lendale), Claude Dauphin (Inspector Mercier), Philippe Noiret (Ambroise Gerome), Michel Piccoli (Lecoeur), Marcel Dalio (Sapper), Cecil Parker (Sir Percy), Jean Wiener (Krajewski), Daniel Emilfork (Kobeleff), Eugene Deckers (Koenigstein), Jacques Duphilo (Beala), Tanya Lopert (Agneau), Catherine Allegret (Pantoufle), Peter Ustinov (Prince Otto).

Uncredited cast: France Arnel, Dorothee Blank, Jean-Paul Cauvin, Lo Ann Chan, Sylvain Levignac, Laurence Lignieres, Moustache, Jenny Orleans, Hella Petri, Roger Trapp, Jean Ruppert, Joe Dassin, Jacques Legras, Mario Feliciani, Sacha Pitoeff, Arthur Howard, Dorothy Reynolds, Jacques Ciron, Hazel Hughes.

Extras: A. Blackstod, Bobbie Croskin, Clare Dunn, Gregory Dunn, Kenneth Dunn, Lee Dunn, Susie Dunn, Andrew Gillis, Alwyna Hale, Michael Howard, Karen Lewis, Bill Little, David Moore, Keith Nicholson, Joan Parkes, John Pickering, D. Pickles, Nigel Reay, Diana Schofield, Joan Topham, Sally Topham, Andrew Whalley, Christopher Whalley, Felicity Whalley, Joan Whalley, Joe Whalley, Guy Willoughby, J.H. Wresdell.

Try as he might, the little boy in the natty sailor suit could barely keep up with the leggy brunette in the glamorous evening gown. Both were dashing madly around the majestic Atlas fountain in the grounds of Castle Howard, near Malton in North Yorkshire. He was four-year-old Guy Willoughby, grandson of Lord Middleton and a junior member of the local gentry. She was Sophia Loren, statuesque Italian beauty and the star of *Lady L,* a multi-million dollar Metro-Goldwyn-Mayer blockbuster, based on the novel by Romain Gary, that had temporarily taken over Castle Howard as its production base.

It was March 9, 1965 and the first day of shooting had got underway with smooth efficiency, much to the delight of actor-turned-writer/director Peter Ustinov. Just 24 hours before Ustinov, Loren and a 150-strong crew had arrived in North Yorkshire to find Castle Howard and its magnificent grounds covered in snow.

After the heat of the South of France and the sunshine of Switzerland it was a disappointment to find their key English location hidden beneath a blanket of snow. Plans were hurriedly made to shoot a series of interiors within the 250-year-old country mansion. A day later and everything was back on track. The snow had vanished. Brilliant sunshine lit the scene. And to ensure the believability of an English spring, ice in the fountain was broken by members of the film unit wielding garden rakes as they bobbed along in a dinghy.

title page: Effortless elegance: Sophia Loren off-set as Lady L.

previous page: Day one, scene one. On her very first day on set at Castle Howard, 30-year-old Sophia Loren demonstrates, not entirely successfully, how to bowl a hoop to four-year-old Guy Willoughby.

above: Writer / director Peter Ustinov.

"It is warmer here than it was last week in the South of France where we have been filming for two months," said a relieved Ustinov as he prepared to call "action".

Loren spent an hour patiently coaching her juvenile co-star in the old sport of bowling a hoop. Guy, playing her son in the film, followed breathlessly in her wake as the 30-year-old superstar skipped along behind the yellow hoop. Ustinov shouted encouragement from the sidelines. "Guy is my son in the film," said Loren during a break. "It was a little difficult to get him moving and the camera could not focus on both of us at the same time."

Lady L had started its journey to the screen in 1961 with an entirely different cast. Studio chiefs at MGM had originally begun the film with director George Cukor. The stars were Gina Lollobrigida, Tony Curtis and Ralph Richardson. Production problems caused filming to cease and it remained uncompleted. Flash forward four years and the project had been picked up by Italian producer Carlo Ponti as a vehicle for his wife, Sophia Loren. Paul Newman, playing an unlikely French revolutionary, replaced Curtis and David Niven took the role originally intended for Richardson. On paper it seemed like a winner: three major international stars, a witty and sparkling screenplay written by one of the best film comedians in the business and globe-trotting drama that moved from Paris to Switzerland and on to England. It was sophisticated, chic and sexy.

The announcement of *Lady L* caused a sensation amongst the good people of Malton, York and Scarborough. The area was agog with excitement. The market town of Malton geared itself up to cater for the needs of a feature film crew – a major feat when the town's pubs could only muster 55 bedrooms together. And what of Miss Loren? Could Malton accommodate the needs of a major star and her retinue? Staff at The Talbot, Malton's grandest hotel, thought not. "She would want a whole suit of rooms and we don't run to that," said the manager. In the event Loren stayed at North Grimston House, home of the Hon. Michael Willoughby – father of young Guy Willoughby. Her reaction: "It is a lovely place". David Niven and Paul Newman, along with several of the Anglo-French crew, went to hotels in Scarborough.

More than 1,500 people, including members of some of the district's well-heeled families, applied to be extras and most were auditioned in the Milton Rooms, Malton. For most it meant tiring 12-hour stints, often starting at seven o'clock in the morning, for just £3 10s a day. (Six-year-old Michael Howard, youngest son of Castle Howard owners George and Lady Cecilia Howard, worked for three days on the film and asked for payment in sixpences. He got it: 420 coins which he stored in a dimpled whisky bottle.) Many extras were required for a gay masked ball that formed the backdrop to the start of the picture, when the aged Lady Lendale returns to her stately Georgian home and reminisces about her colourful past.

There were mothers, fathers and families, models, farmers and trawlermen's wives, town clerks, newspapermen and holiday camp managers. All of them queued for the chance of a brief moment on the movie screen. Some were lucky. Others were not. In a stinging letter to the *Yorkshire Post* a sports outfitter named Geoffrey Otley claimed the casting sessions amounted to nothing more than a publicity stunt because so many volunteers had been turned away. His comments were rejected by MGM which said all those granted an appointment were sent a form making it quite clear that there was no obligation to employ or interview them. "Disappointment was bound to be caused on a large scale but we had no alternative," explained a spokesman.

As well as human extras the *Lady L* production hired a trio of classic vehicles. Vintage car buffs will be able to spot a 1930 Bentley 8-litre Sportsman's Coupe, a super-charged 1934 Alfa Romeo straight 8 and a 1929 30hp Lanchester. All were provided by Monty Thackray and at least one of them was driven by Paul Newman – himself an avowed "petrol head" and something of an expert on the race track.

Prior to Ustinov and Co arriving in North Yorkshire MGM had built a *faux* summer house in the grounds of Castle Howard. Nestling close to the bullrushes near the lakes, the ornate domed building with its green painted lattice work was most realistic. Yet it was just another example of the artifice of the movies: costing £6,000 to create, it was doomed to destruction as part of the film's explosive finale. "It is always sad to see a set broken down at the end of a picture," said French art director Jean D'Eaubonne as he considered the fate of his creation – a prefabricated shell made of hardboard, three-ply wood and cork bricks. "The last thing of mine to be blown up was a three-masted ship I made for a German film before the war." The fate of the summer house was a major talking point among visitors, staff and owners at Castle Howard. Commented Lady Cecilia Howard: "It would have been quite an attraction this year

top: Behind-the-scenes in the ballroom.

above: Loren larks around.

above: *Different actors, different style:*
Method man Paul Newman and old-school
David Niven between takes with
Mr George Howard.

opposite: *The end of the fake summer house.*

"Lady L *wasn't the first time Castle Howard had been used for a movie because the south front façade had been used as the setting for the Kremlin in* The Spy with a Cold Nose. *Nonetheless the filming of* Lady L *caused quite an upheaval. The house was open to the public but they shut it during the filming. The long gallery was used for a ball scene and there were scenes in the great hall.*

It was just great fun at the time. The whole thing was a bit of a romp. I remember meeting quite a lot of the cast at dinner parties. They were interesting people. I was only about seven then but I fell in love with Sophia Loren. She's been my pin-up ever since.

My overriding memory is of the summer house, which they were going to blow up. It was built on the north front, about 500 yards from the house, down near the lakes. It was my first term at school and I was allowed out early to watch this thing being blown up, much to the horror of the headmaster.

Metro-Goldwyn-Mayer had hired a German explosives expert who they knew was over-keen on the use of combustibles. He set the whole thing up but they had to control it. The night before the big explosion they put in the relevant number of drums of fuel. Then they posted security guards on it in order to prevent the German coming in at night and adding extra!

All the filming around the summer house up to that point was in a foggy environment. The next day it was bright sunshine. There were Land Rovers driving over the lawns with what looked like big chestnut burners with smoke coming out of them in order to create a foggy atmosphere. Watching it all, quite a way back, was a big crowd with fire engines and God knows what else. They then blew it up.

The explosion was much larger than anyone had anticipated. It was quite spectacular and killed a tree, which meant that the German had managed to add his extra fuel! He had his knuckles suitably rapped afterwards.

After the event my father, George Howard, wrote a tongue-in-cheek letter to MGM saying "You've managed to kill off the tree next door to the summer house. Judging by when it was planted and the cost of maintenance this tree is worth 'x' amount." He got back a rather serious letter from MGM's lawyers saying they would take him to the courts. It was eventually all resolved amicably but he said it proved that the Americans didn't have a sense of humour."

– The Hon. Simon Howard, 2007

for the visitors, but, unfortunately, it is going to be blown up in the film. We are assured by the filmmakers that the explosion will not cause any other damage."

More artifice was provided by a York bakery which supplied a fake three-tier cake for Lady L's sumptuous 80th birthday celebrations. The four-foot high wooden cake was decorated with 30lbs of icing and took a fortnight to make. The trick was in creating a false slice on the bottom tier for Loren to cut.

Perhaps the film's defining moment was the transformation of an actress considered the most beautiful woman in the world into a tired, grey-haired old lady. For sequences that book-ended the beginning and end of the film Sophia Loren endured four hours in the make-up chair each day. It had to be dramatic, memorable and perfect – an elegant entry for Lady L into Castle Howard's Great Hall on the arm of her friend Sir Percy, played by Cecil Parker.

To achieve such a remarkable makeover veteran make-up man William Tuttle took a death mask of the 30-year-old's flawless face and used it as a template to which he added small pieces of moulded sponge rubber to manufacture a double chin, puffiness and latex crow's feet. "One becomes a little detached with this sort of work but it is always thrilling if you can produce something really convincing," he revealed. "I discussed with Peter Ustinov, the director, what kind of old lady we should try and create and it was decided on something regal. I think she has come close to something of the regal posture of a person like Queen Mary."

The sheer skill and artistry that went into the making of *Lady L* should have guaranteed its success, but it was a troubled picture and not a particularly happy one for those involved. When hired to write and direct the film Peter Ustinov crafted a script that combined farce with period comedy. He also poured detail into character and plot, so much so that the end result ran for almost three hours. But in the 1960s epics were the norm, and most were split by an intermission. Ustinov's film was geared for the same market but, when viewed by executives at MGM, it was considered to be too kaleidoscopic in its approach to be a hit.

The film was re-edited and released in a shorter version. Much of Ustinov's style and humour was lost. Audiences stayed away. Crucially, both punters and critics noticed

opposite top:David Niven smiles as nine-month-old Andrew Gillis, playing his baby son, refuses to be gentle. "He keeps on pulling my moustache and it makes my nose tickle," said the 55-year-old star, "but he is absolutely sweet and is as good as gold."

opposite bottom: Sophia Loren makes an interesting exit from Castle Howard.

above: Sophia Loren as an aged, regal beauty – the creation of veteran make-up man William Tuttle who envisaged "the regal posture of a person like Queen Mary".

the distinct lack of chemistry between Loren and Newman, playing her beau. Newman's forte was considered to be American heroes, and contemporary ones at that. In *Lady L* his good looks were hidden beneath a moustache, wigs and false beards. Playing a Robin Hood-style anarchist named Armand, circa 1905, he was fatally miscast. Loren, however, was in her element and thoroughly enjoyed camouflaging her looks beneath layers of rubber and latex.

Newman was awkward and ill-at-ease. An intense, nit-picking Method actor who masticated a part until it was in pieces, he riled his graceful co-star with an offhand manner she considered to be blue collar, vulgar and uncouth. Incompatible on set, they barely spoke off it. Ustinov, ever the diplomat, sought the on-screen magnetism he required and urged Loren to befriend her leading man. She agreed and, the next day, attempted to build bridges via harmless small talk. "Paul, how do you stick your moustache on every morning?" she asked. It was an innocuous question designed to break the ice. Newman turned the full glare of his blue eyes on Loren, smiled thinly and floored her with his response: "Sperm."

When it was finally released, *Lady L* bombed at the box office. It was a major disappointment to MGM, to Loren and to Ustinov. In a 58-year film career Ustinov directed just five movies; only one, *Billy Budd*, was a success. More than just a failure, *Lady L* was a debacle, so much so that, in his 1977 autobiography *Dear Me*, Ustinov omitted it entirely.

top: Paul Newman in disguise.

below: Script conference.

opposite: Sophia Loren: the epitome of screen beauty.

1968

Kes

A lad with a mind of his own –
and a life he shared only with Kes

Director: Ken Loach

Producer: Tony Garnett

Writers: Barry Hines, Ken Loach, Tony Garnett

Production Company: Woodfall Films/Kestrel Films

Year of production: 1968 (Premiere March 25 1970. Released March 29 1970)

Where filmed: Barnsley, Hoyland Common and Tankersley, South Yorkshire during July and August, 1968.

Synopsis: Sullen teenager Billy Casper lives in a northern mining village and has zero prospects. While out bird nesting he steals a kestrel chick and begins to rear and train it. Soon boy and bird are inseparable and, for the first time in his short life, Billy has something to break the monotony of his miserable existence.

Credited cast: David Bradley (Billy), Freddie Fletcher (Jud), Lynne Perrie (Mrs. Casper), Colin Welland (Mr. Farthing), Brian Glover (Mr. Sugden), Bob Bowes (Mr. Gryce).

Uncredited cast: Bernard Atha, Geoffrey Banks, Eric Bolderson, Laurence Bould, Duggie Brown, Beryl Carroll, Ted Carroll, Peter Clegg, Stephen Crossland, Billy Dean, Agnes Drumgoon, David Glover, Julie Goodyear, John Grayson, Desmond Guthrie, Trevor Hesketh, Michael Joyce, Joey Kaye, Martin Harley, Rose MacLean, Harry Markham, Joe Miller, Robert Naylor, Frank Norton, Michael Padgett, Jean Palmer, Julie Shakespeare, Mary Southall, George Speed, Leslie Stringer, Zoë Sunderland, Roy Turner, and The 4D Jones – David Hargreaves, Geoff Hollin, Alan Lodge, John Stenton, Les Stokes.

"In 1968 I was working at the BBC with Tony Garnett, the producer. He had met Barry Hines after his first book, *The Blinder,* and had asked him to do a TV script for *Play for Today.* Barry said "No, I want to finish the book I'm working on." So Barry finished the book, *A Kestrel for a Knave,* showed it to Tony in manuscript form, and Tony showed it to me. And we went on from there. I did a breakdown of the book and wrote down the scenes in the order that I thought we needed them in. I slimmed it down quite a lot and then knocked it backwards and forwards between Tony and Barry.

"We were going to do it in a school in Barnsley and so the dialogue had to be spoken in a Barnsley accent. It was completely implicit in the book. Language is central to everything. If you have to pick one element that is important in any culture, it's the language. It's the use of language, the humour in the language, the way you speak and the way it affects how your body works. Everything is connected to language so there was no way we could change it. After we finished the film United Artists did a bit of post-sync. They changed one or two lines and got the actors down to London to do bits. The version you see now has some bad post-sync: the opening lines are badly done. I didn't know about it and was really pissed off, but it doesn't change it hugely.

"Tony Richardson got *Kes* made. He had done *Tom Jones* for United Artists and it had been very successful. On his say-so United Artists put up about £170,000, which was more then than it would be now, obviously. That's why

title image: Kes star David 'Dai' Bradley at the premiere of the film. March, 1970.

previous page: A boy and his hawk. Three birds were used in the film. The crew christened them Freeman, Hardy and Willis.

below: Ken Loach (left), DoP Chris Menges (with beard) and David Bradley on location in Hoyland Common.

opposite: Together again: the men behind Kes reunite for a unique screening at the 12th Bradford Film Festival in 2006. Present on stage are, from left to right: author Anthony Hayward, director Ken Loach, writer Barry Hines, producer Tony Garnett, actor Colin Welland and author Simon Golding.

final spread, top left: Ken Loach directs David Bradley in St. Helen's County Secondary School.

final spread, top right: Teacher-turned-wrestler Brian Glover as games master Mr. Sugden.

final spread, bottom right: David Bradley, Kes and Colin Welland as the kind-hearted teacher, Mr. Farthing

Kes was done as a co-production with Woodfall Films – it was Tony Richardson's production company. Without him it wouldn't have been made because we couldn't raise the money. We didn't spend money on the things that a lot of films spend money on. There were no big actors' fees and nobody made a huge amount of money out of it, but it was a proper film on union rates and everything was done on a professional level.

"I think we saw *Kes* as a response to the 'kitchen sink' movement. Those films – *The Loneliness of the Long Distance Runner, Billy Liar, This Sporting Life, A Taste of Honey* - had been made within two or three years of each other and all the directors had abandoned the north, which made us very suspicious. We thought "It's just a location to them". John Schlesinger had gone to America, Karel Reisz somewhere else; Lindsay Anderson was doing things at the Royal Court.

"I've done about six or seven films in Yorkshire. I did quite a lot of films in Yorkshire between *Kes* and *The Navigators*. I did *Black Jack* in North Yorkshire. In South Yorkshire we did *The Price of Coal*, which was two films with Barry Hines. There was *The Gamekeeper*, which was based on another book of Barry's. *Looks and Smiles* was set in Sheffield and again was Barry. It's never felt that far away so I have to go back. I don't know if I have an affinity with that part of the country but I have an enjoyment of places that have got a very strong working class culture. South Yorkshire has it with the mines and steel. Liverpool has. Manchester has. Glasgow has. They are all places of very defined culture, very strong defined dialect and a strong tradition of working-class entertainers.

"In *Kes*, the comic who comes to the act in the pub was a Liverpudlian, Joey Kaye. All the Yorkshire folk were outraged that I'd asked a Liverpool comic and I did it because I'd worked with him on some films in Liverpool. Fortunately he's very funny, so they laughed, but there was a hostility that I hadn't reckoned with on inviting a Liverpool comic to play in a Yorkshire pub. I should have got a South Yorkshire comic, really.

"I don't think Barnsley was a particularly insular place. Any strong culture can seem insular in that it's so well defined. Those communities are usually outward looking because they are strong politically. They're about making links and connections with other communities and other people. It can often seem insular but if I have a real conversation then I don't find them insular at all.

"We decided to make it in St. Helen's County Secondary School, where Barry Hines had taught at, because the slag heap from the pit overlooked the school. Visually it was just right. Plus Barry had written it about that school so we just thought, why not? The headmaster was very helpful and we just auditioned the boys of that year. It was only a two form entry school so we only saw about 30 boys. David Bradley was one of them. Initially there were three or four boys that we had on our shortlist. Desmond Guthrie was one, and David Glover another. There were two others on the shortlist but David had a quality that was very special. The actual filming was very straightforward. We did it in the August holidays so for the kids it was just like still being at school. They just turned up and we did the filming instead of lessons. It was quite normal, in a way.

"David Bradley lived through it for the six or seven weeks that we shot *Kes*. He was brilliant to work with. Almost

whatever he did was okay because he was always true. So long as it was true – and it was really true how he would be in that situation – then that was good. He's in just about every shot and he was always spot-on. He carried the film. We had three kestrels called Freeman, Hardy and Willis. They were mainly trained by Barry's brother, Richard, and he took David along with him. They did it together. We didn't have any special bird handlers or any of that. It was just done within the family.

"Brian Glover was a teacher at a nearby school and a mate of Barry's, so we went and met him. He was a teacher by day and a wrestler by night. He used to travel the country, come back and be there for 'All Things Bright and Beautiful' the next morning in assembly. He said he wrestled under the name of Leon Arras, the Man from Paris, because Leon Arras had been on the same bill as him one night and hadn't turned up. He had to go on twice – the second time in a mask! He kept the name. But he'd done a funny thing. If you notice in the football game he wears strapping around his knee. He'd been on holiday in France before we did the

film. He said he'd been on a French toilet, where you put your feet in the two marks and his knee had gone while he'd been in this posture. So he'd had to be carried out of the toilet with his trousers round his ankles to be bandaged up! This was the story he told me, anyway. There was some fear that he wouldn't be able to play, but he played through the pain barrier and did it. If he hadn't have been a teacher then he couldn't have done it. The whole technique he uses is what a teacher would use to deal with the boys. Everything in the game I did through him. I got him to organise them so that they related to him the whole time – as a schoolmaster. They knew him as a schoolmaster from the other school. He wasn't Brian Glover to them; he was just the English teacher from the school down the road. He was very funny.

The stars were a bird and a boy. But, just as crucially, Barnsley played its part in a modest little film that was destined to become a classic of British cinema.

Forty years on from the shooting of Kes, *Ken Loach continues to prefer the freedom of location work to the restrictions of the film studio. And in* Kes *it is all there on the screen: the school, the council estate that Billy calls his home and the ruined farm from where he steals a kestrel chick.*

Billy's school was David "Dai" Bradley's seat of learning: St Helen's County Secondary School in Athersley South. Loach found the majority of his young cast within its walls. For the house Billy shared with his mother and older brother, Jud, a property was used on a big estate in Hoyland. The house was leased from a retired miner.

Old Hall Farm, on Black Lane in Tankersley (renamed Monastery Farm in the film), served as the quasi-gothic site for Billy's first glimpse of the bird that is to become his constant companion. Four decades later the remnants of the 18th century hall remain remarkably unaltered by time and weather.

Other locations familiar to locals and fans of the film include Barnsley Civic Library; the Cudworth Hotel (now The Dards) on Pontefract Road, Cudworth; Fitzwilliam Street, Hoyland Common; Barnsley Market; Skiers Spring and Rockingham collieries, in the village of Birdwell and James Miles Bookshop, Leeds, from where Billy steals a book on falconry.
"Got any books on hawks, missus...?"

"There were one or two guys that I saw for the part of Jud who could have done it differently. Freddie Fletcher was a dangerous choice. I don't think he'd done anything before and we needed somebody who had a sense of danger about him. There always was with Freddie, at that age anyway. You felt he could get quite angry. I can't remember where I met him. He came to one of the auditions. Lynne Perrie was a club act who was a singer. I always cast from club acts and I had met her through her agent. I'd cast newcomers before. In *Poor Cow*, the film before *Kes*, one of the parts was taken by a guy called John Bindon who was a villain from Fulham. He'd never acted before. I'd been veering that way for some time.

"I've always done everything on location, and the film became a little institution for a time. What we did then - which you wouldn't do now - is build a little construction to the interior of the house because we thought it would be too small to shoot in. So it was just slightly bigger. But we did it on the same location – right near where the real house was. Everything was in Barnsley and Hoyland Common, which is just south of Barnsley. It's the village where Barry was born. It was very simple, really. The school was the school; all the teachers who came were the teachers from the school apart from Colin Welland and Bob Bowes, who was a headmaster at Doncaster.

"I've never really been interested in going back and revisiting my characters. It's dangerously vain because it's like assuming that everybody is going to be interested in the stuff you've done in the past. I'm not sure you can make that assumption. It smacks of being self-regarding."
Ken Loach

"I was a teacher. Barry Hines was also a teacher who wrote a novel called A Kestrel for a Knave which they turned into a film called Kes. *I knew Barry well – he was a teaching colleague of mine. I was already doing a bit of acting, plus I'd been in the wrestling game and I had an Equity card. I knew what games masters were like. I'd taught with plenty. I never was a games master although Barry Hines was. It was very, very good for me, that film. It's stood the test of time. Kids still see it as a Christmas treat at schools, and it's 20-odd years old now. We shot it in '68 and it took a couple of years to get out. Everyone said the accents were impenetrable. But we did it and we were a success. It was a good film."*

– Brian Glover, 1992

1970

The Railway Children

The railway. The children… And the wonderful secret they'll share with you!

Director: Lionel Jeffries

Producer: Robert Lynn

Writer: Lionel Jeffries, from the novel by E. Nesbit

Production Company: E.M.I. Film Productions

Year of Production: 1970
(Released December 21, 1970)

Where filmed: Oakworth Station, Oakworth; Keighley Station, Keighley, Oxenhope, Haworth, West Yorkshire, from May 10 to June 12, 1970.

Credited cast: Dinah Sheridan (Mother), Bernard Cribbins (Perks), William Mervyn (Old Gentleman), Iain Cuthbertson (Father), Jenny Agutter (Bobbie), Sally Thomsett (Phyllis), Peter Bromilow (Doctor), Ann Lancaster (Ruth), Gary Warren (Peter), Gordon Whiting (Russian), Beatrix MacKey (Aunt Emma), Eddie Davies (Mrs. Perks), David Lodge (Bandmaster), Christopher Witty (Jim), Brenda Cowling (Mrs. Viney), Paddy Ward (Cart Man), Erik Chitty (Photographer), Sally James (Maid), Dominic Allen (C.I.D. Man).

Uncredited cast: Amelia Bayntun (Cook), Robert (Bob) Cryer (Mr. Cryer), Paul Luty (Malcolm), Graham Mitchell (Railwayman) and members of Haworth Band.

Extras: Ann Cryer, Jane Cryer, John Cryer, David Pearson.

People have a fascination with Jenny Agutter. Mostly it is due to her association with a timeless family film that became, on its release at the end of 1970, an instant classic: *The Railway Children*. Some actors tend to shrug off or reject the role that propelled them to fame and fortune. Agutter does not. In fact, her reaction to *The Railway Children* and her character, Bobbie, is one of continued warmth and gratitude: the film made her an overnight star at the age of just 17, led to offers to appear on stage with the likes of John Gielgud and created for her a unique niche within British cinema.

Yet the film that became *The Railway Children* occurred purely by chance. The fact that it has lasted and become elevated to the status of international classic, makes its gestation and creation all the more remarkable. Author E.

Nesbit – the 'E' stands for Edith – wrote the novel in 1905. It concerns the Waterburys, a well-to-do Edwardian family whose happiness is shattered when their father leaves their home one night accompanied by two mysterious strangers. When penury forces them to relocate to rural Yorkshire the three children, Roberta, Phyllis and Peter become fascinated by the nearby railroad. Each day they wave to the passengers on the passing trains and build a friendship with the station porter, Perks, and an elderly man they call the Old Gentleman. It is he who will eventually help them solve the mystery of their father's disappearance, and bring to an end their enforced sojourn in the countryside.

Actor Lionel Jeffries was sailing to New York on the QE2 when his eight-year-old daughter, Martha, suggested the book to him, having just finished reading it. "Daddy, this is a lovely thing," she said. "Surely it should be made into a film." Jeffries read it and was immediately smitten. On returning home from America he bought the rights for £2,000 and began work on a screenplay. Enthused by the concept of the movie, he was crestfallen when one potential financier after another gave him the brush-off. The time wasn't right for "that kind of film", they chirruped in unison. Jeffries soldiered on until he was backed by Bryan Forbes and EMI to the tune of £350,000.

Green-lit by Forbes, *The Railway Children* was rightly considered a "safe" project. Forbes knew what he was talking about. A former actor, he had successfully segued into screenwriting, moved onto producing and directing and, by 1969, headed up Associated British (EMI). "The British public is weary of the spate of violence and pornography on both the large and the small screens," he announced in a statement when the picture went into production. "There is a crying need for films which all the family can go and see." During his brief (two-year) tenure as Head of Production at EMI, Forbes oversaw only two genuinely successful pictures. *The Tales of Beatrix Potter* was one. *The Railway Children* was the other.

A book beloved by generations of parents and kids, *The Railway Children* had been twice serialised for television in the 1950s. It was remade again in 1968 and starred Jenny Agutter, Gillian Bailey and Neil McDermott as the children, with Ann Castle as the mother. For Lionel Jeffries

title page: Between takes at Oakworth Station, 1970. Jenny Agutter smiles for the camera. Bernard Cribbins has swapped his stationmaster's hat for a white Stetson.

previous page: Jenny Agutter returned to Oakworth in 2005 whilst a guest of Bradford Film Festival.

opposite: Crouching by the engine, a sound recordist hides out of sight of the camera.

right: The railway children in their kingdom. Jenny Agutter (Bobbie), Sally Thomsett (Phyllis) and Perks (Bernard Cribbins) on the platform at Oakworth. Ann Cryer and her children. All three enjoyed playing extras.

the show offered intriguing possibilities. The first was the backdrop – the series had been filmed largely on location at the Keighley & Worth Valley Railway, a preserved five-mile stretch of line that had been re-opened by volunteers following closure in 1962 during the Beeching cuts. The second was 15-year-old Jenny Agutter.

The teenage Agutter had been plucked from obscurity by no less a personage than Walt Disney to star in the 1966 drama *Ballerina*. By 1968 she had several films and TV plays under her belt; thus the seven-part series of *The Railway Children* was just another job. Jeffries considered her crucial to the casting of his movie. Another actress he had in his sights was 49-year-old Dinah Sheridan, the elegant star of a string of '40s and early '50s films who walked away from a glittering career in 1953 shortly after appearing in the smash hit *Genevieve*. Sheridan had married John Davis, head of the Rank Organisation, and had agreed to give up work to raise a family. She was as good as her word and turned down a string of offers. They included the Douglas Bader biopic *Reach for the Sky*, with her *Genevieve* co-star Kenneth More, *The Million Pound Note*, opposite Gregory Peck and *The Court Jester* with Danny Kaye.

By 1964 her marriage was in tatters and, following a bitter divorce from Davis, Sheridan went back to work. She found that the popularity of *Genevieve* opened doors and, even after a break of 11 years, swiftly found herself employed in the theatre. Then Lionel Jeffries came calling. "We met for lunch at the White Elephant in Curzon Street in London with the producer, Bob Lynn. I'd got my fingers crossed

above: Cast and crew shooting the end sequence.

under the table saying 'Oh please let him give me a definite offer. Please let it happen.' Then he said to me 'Do you know any children who could play the children in the film' and I said 'No. I haven't been doing much work in films recently'. And the producer passed a note to Lionel but let me see it as it went round. Lionel was just saying that the girl in the television series was so good. 'She was called Jenny Agutter. You don't know where she is now, do you?' And the little note from the producer to Lionel, which I saw, said 'She's sitting on your right'. I didn't know her, but there she was - sitting at the next table. Lionel jumped up with such enormous joy and pleasure that his chair went over backwards. He blurted out to Jenny 'Would you like to play Bobbie in a film of *The Railway Children*?' She went terribly pink and said 'Oh yes, I'd love it!' And Lionel immediately said 'Well, meet your mother!' And that's how I knew that I'd definitely got the part."

Many months later when the film was underway, Jeffries confessed to Sheridan that he, too, had had his fingers crossed under the table, mentally willing her to accept the part. Jenny Agutter, however, was initially reluctant to return to a role she had previously played just two short years before. But she was bowled over by Jeffries' enthusiasm for her and the film he wished to make as his directorial debut. "I was very uncertain about making the film," she remembered. "When it came up I said 'I should be looking towards doing other things.' I was 17 and feeling very grown up. But there was no question in Lionel's mind, and it's very winning when someone is so absolutely positive like that. I never looked back."

The 80-strong cast and crew of *The Railway Children* arrived in Yorkshire in May 1970. Alongside Sheridan and Agutter were 20-year-old Sally Thomsett as Phyllis and 15-year-old Gary Warren as Peter. Bernard Cribbins played Perks, the porter, and William Mervyn was the Old Gentleman. Work began on Sunday, May 10, at Oakworth Station under the watchful eye of Bob Cryer, the chairman and a founder member of the Keighley & Worth Valley Railway Preservation Society. Cryer, later to become the Labour MP for Keighley, had advised the makers of the 1968 TV series on locations and locomotives; he was to perform a similar duty for Jeffries. One of his first jobs during the autumn of 1969 was to escort director and producer on a five-mile walk along the track – an on-the-ground "recce" that provided Jeffries with an overview of what he had to work with. Cryer also helped select one of the other stars of the film: a Barton Wright tender engine No. 957 which, for the film, was named the Green Dragon. Other volunteers were hired as engine drivers and train guards; to have used actors for such skilled roles would have been to court disaster.

Jeffries monitored every aspect of the production and ran his unit like a big family. He was concerned that the illusion of innocence be maintained throughout the shoot and prohibited Agutter and Thomsett – the elder actress by three years although playing the younger sister – from driving, smoking or drinking alcohol lest they be photographed by the Press. It would ruin the mood of the piece. "Lionel Jeffries had such a particular attitude to filmmaking," recalled Agutter. "He was like a father to everybody, so the whole thing was very family orientated. It was a very small film

- very small budget – so everybody was very close. It was very friendly. He would watch out for Sally and me. Sally is a little older than myself even though she was playing younger, which was extraordinary. He used to give us half a crown if a shot had gone well, and we were all wondering if we could get a drink for half a crown!"

Agutter, Thomsett and the other actors were staying with Jeffries in the Parkway Hotel on the outskirts of Leeds. Each morning they would travel by car to the locations in Oakworth, Oxenhope (where Bents Farm doubled as Three Chimneys, the Waterburys' home) or Haworth, in which the Brontë Parsonage served as the local doctor's house. The proximity to Leeds inevitably meant that Agutter and Thomsett were tempted to enjoy a night out. One weekend they headed off to a nightclub. Said Agutter: "I remember one night Sally and I went out dancing somewhere and Lionel was actually waiting up in the hotel lobby to make sure we were back in good time. I think we were in just before midnight and he said 'I hope you'll know your lines tomorrow and be on form.' I found something rather wonderful about that. He was so careful of us. It made it so right."

Jeffries' old-fashioned approach was appropriate to the milieu he was reverently recreating. This was nostalgia for a lost age. Only 60 years had passed but the world had changed beyond all recognition. Jeffries wanted to resurrect some of that olde-worlde feel and put it evocatively on the cinema screen. He did it with dedication and passion. On June 3, the UK experienced its hottest day of the year. Temperatures soared. The cast sweltered in long, warm smocks and winter boots. Jeffries made his actors shelter under an umbrella – to shield their make-up from the hot sun. With the day's work in the can, they were rewarded with an ice cream. "I've cut the gloss," he told Merete Bates of *The Guardian*. "No make-up. Never mind if their faces are shiny with runny noses. No stuck-on moustaches. Home-grown sideboards. All the props authentic down to the last detail. That blouse there is over 80 years old. No extra lighting, so that it seems that only gas and oil lamps were used. I'm trying to get as close as possible to what Victorian England must have been like. I've kept to the story. It would be an imposition not to. After all, E. Nesbit's lasted 50 years. Maybe it's not so sugary sweet with long pathetic sequences of duckies and dearies, but otherwise it's pretty straight. And I've kept Bobbie – that's the eldest child – as voice-over, so it's as if she's telling the story."

In the finished film, two sequences stand out. The first is the moment when Bobbie, Phyllis and Peter flag down a speeding locomotive to prevent it crashing into earth and trees that have slid down into a cutting. The second was the film's emotional finale, as a tearful Bobbie is reunited with her lost father.

This is how Jeffries conceived the landslide – arguably the film's most memorable moment: "Trees … seem to be slowly walking down towards the railway line. The tree with the grey leaves bringing up the rear like some old shepherd driving a flock of sheep. The trees cease to walk; they stand still and shiver. They seem to hesitate a moment, and then the rock and trees and grass and bushes, with a rushing sound, slip right away from the face of the cutting and fall on the line with a blundering crash."

The drama of the first scene was captured on film via movie magic: a camera was ingeniously hidden inside a fake boulder. The earth and trees were made to move via a system of steel channels cut into the hillside, into which were placed short vertical tubes. Cables caught and released the tubes as necessary. Small trees were located in the outside channels; in the centre stood a faux tree made of fibreglass and crafted by technicians at Elstree Studios. Jeffries had only one chance to get his shot so the pressure was on to do it right. When he gave the signal, the landslide began. When the fake tree reached a set position it tipped forward on a hinge and, simultaneously, a controlled explosion blasted a combination of fuller's earth and gravel, hidden behind railway sleepers, across the track. When the landslide – faked in a cutting on the Oakworth side of Mytholmes tunnel – was triggered, the camera-in-a-rock bounced down with it. The resultant footage was added to shots from three other cameras to produce the final sequence.

The film's unforgettable lump-in-the-throat end scene took a great deal of time to set up. Jeffries took his inspiration straight out of Nesbit's novel. "I just put the words into pictures," he said. Having conceived the moment in his mind, he painstakingly pieced it together in the edit suite. Background noises on the day prompted him to re-dub Agutter's heart-wrenching cry of "Oh my daddy! My daddy!" but, in the end, he used the original soundtrack. Said Agutter: "I read something about E. Nesbit and I realised that her own world was nothing like the world she was conjuring up. The reason that sequence at the end is so moving is because

opposite, top: *Mother and daughter: Dinah Sheridan and Jenny Agutter.*

opposite, bottom: *The railway children in their kingdom*

right: *Friends reunited: Sally Thomsett, Iain Cuthbertson and Jenny Agutter in 1996.*

Nesbit's father died when she was four. So there was always a sense of longing in her that she could fulfil in her books. It's what she really wanted more than anything – for her father to come home. So it's an extraordinary moment: beyond anything she wants her father back, and Nesbit could never have her father back. She said something important at that time to children growing up, and to all of us: isn't it a shame that we have to leave behind all those wonderful parts of our imagination and our childhood. It's so important to bring that with you, and it's so hard for us to do so."

40 years after it was made, *The Railway Children* continues to be a magnet for film fans, drawing visitors to the now-thriving Keighley & Worth Valley Railway. Back then, the fledgling organisation welcomed film crews with wide-eyed enthusiasm. Nowadays, after hosting big-budget productions like John Schlesinger's *Yanks* and the Mel Gibson production *Fairytale: A True Story*, the K&WVR veterans are old hands at making movies. But the adventures of Bobbie, Phyllis and Peter prompted a huge interest in the line and its steam locos – the exposure generated by the film doubled visitor figures within months. The volunteers increased capacity and operated twice as many trains. It was, quite simply, a thrill.

For Jenny Agutter and Dinah Sheridan, *The Railway Children* remains a film of which they are inordinately proud. "Before the film came out I took John Gielgud to see it," said Sheridan. "He was renowned for crying at the slightest little thing – very sweet. He was sitting on my right and my right shoulder was really damp because when John cried the tears just spurted out. At the end of *The Railway Children* he

was absolutely in floods of tears, and enchanted. He really had enjoyed it. Of the films I've done, it's my favourite. It was just a gentle joy."

On April 3, 1996, to tie-in with the film's 25th anniversary, Agutter, Thomsett and Cuthbertson were reunited for the first time since making the movie. The occasion was the unveiling of a plaque at Oakworth Station as part of the celebrations of Cinema 100 – the centenary of cinema in Britain. Hundreds of film fans and steam aficionados crowded onto the station to watch the ceremony, which had been organised by the now-defunct Bradford Film Office. Said Agutter: "It's an honour to be here celebrating 100 years of the British film industry, and a quarter of a century since *The Railway Children* was made." That evening the film received a gala screening at Bradford's Pictureville cinema, with Agutter as guest of honour. Nine years later Jenny Agutter again walked the platform at Oakworth when she returned to Yorkshire for a retrospective of her work at the 11th Bradford Film Festival. Ten of her films were presented, but it was *The Railway Children*, a timeless portrait of a gentler time, that everyone queued to see.

1974

All Creatures Great and Small

James made friends with the animals at once. Some of the people took a little longer.

Director: Claude Whatham

Producers: David Susskind, Duane Bogie

Writer: Hugh Whitemore, based on the books by James Herriot

Production Company: A Venedon Limited Production

Year of Production: 1974 (Released July 27, 1975)

Where filmed: Pickering, Malton, Thirsk, Hovingham, Whitby, North Yorkshire, during September, 1974.

Credited cast: Simon Ward (James Herriot), Anthony Hopkins (Siegfried Farnon), Lisa Harrow (Helen Alderson), Brian Stirner (Tristan Farnon), T.P McKenna (Soames), Brenda Bruce (Miss Harbottle), Freddie Jones (Cranford), Christine Buckley (Mrs. Hall), John Collin (Mr. Alderson), Jane Collins (Connie), Fred Feast (Farmer in Cinema), Glynne Geldart (Joyce), Harold Goodwin (Dinsdale's Uncle), Doreen Mantle (Mrs. Seaton), John Nettleton (Head Waiter), Daphne Oxenford (Mrs. Pumphrey), Burt Palmer (Mr. Dean), John Rees (Geoff Mallock), Jenny Runacre (Pamela), Jane Solo (Brenda).

There can be few more enduring love letters to the majesty and beauty of Yorkshire than the books of James Herriot. First published in the 1970s, they remain a best-selling phenomenon, harking back to nostalgic days of blue, cloudless skies, seemingly endless sunny days and the rugged hills, verdant fields and winding roads of the Dales. His stories chronicled the day-to-day life of a hard-working young vet named James Herriot in the quaint Yorkshire town of Darrowby. To this day, thousands of foreign tourists, many of them American, flock to Thirsk and the Dales to soak up the atmosphere of a man who never truly existed.

For James Herriot was the nom-de-plume of Alf Wight, a Sunderland-born, Glasgow-raised veterinary surgeon who only turned to writing at the advanced age of 50. Within four years his books had taken the publishing world by storm. Five years later his first book was transformed into a film, followed almost immediately by another. Thus it was that Alf Wight, aka James Herriot, became one of the most successful authors in the English language. Not bad for a man whose muse was located in his local library in Thirsk. Her title: *Teach Yourself to Write*.

Born in 1916, James Alfred Wight was a bookish child. By the age of 15 he had read the entire works of Charles Dickens – no mean feat. Looking for a career, he was torn between becoming a writer or a veterinary surgeon. He chose the latter because, he said, it was probably easier to earn a sustained living. For more than 30 years he stored away incidents from the daily life of a country vet. Having finally decided

title image: Simon Ward (James Herriot) and Lisa Harrow (Helen Alderson / Herriot).

previous page: Claude Whatham directs.

above: Fact meets fiction: actors Anthony Hopkins, Simon Ward and Brian Stirner with real-life counterparts Donald Sinclair, Alf Wight (aka James Herriot) and Brian Sinclair.

above: The real "Herriots" attend the fictional Herriots wedding.

right: For It Shouldn't Happen to a Vet, *John Alderton and Colin Blakely replaced Simon Ward and Anthony Hopkins.*

next page: Simon Ward practices the Lambeth Walk.

final page: Christopher Timothy, TV's James Herriot with his alter ego filming James Herriot's Yorkshire.

to immortalise his experiences on paper, he began writing, often doing so whilst watching television. In this fashion he happened across his pseudonym. Alf had privately decided that publishing under his own name would risk breaking the Royal College of Veterinary Surgeons' Code of Conduct. He chose his pen name after watching a tremendous save by Birmingham City's goalkeeper. The heroic goalie was called James Herriot. Alf looked in the veterinary register to see if there was a vet with that name. There wasn't. At that moment, author, vet and quintessential Yorkshireman James Herriot was born. Similarly his colleagues Donald and Brian Sinclair became Siegfried and Tristan Farnon.

Alf endured a steady stream of rejections until his first book, *If Only They Could Talk*, was published in 1970. His

second, *It Shouldn't Happen to a Vet*, followed in 1972. Each sold just 2,000 copies. Somehow, both books found their way to the desk of Thomas McCormack, president of St. Martin's Press in the United States. His wife read them and persuaded her husband to do the same. His reaction was to immediately call the author. Their conversation was reminiscent of dialogue in a movie: "If you can give me three chapters where the hero gets the girl, I'll publish".

Alf did so. As good as his word, McCormack added the new chapters, combined both titles and released the omnibus book as *All Creatures Great and Small*. The hardback shifted 206,000 copies and immediately flew onto the American bestsellers list. The paperback, in a fairly short time, sold 4.1 million copies. Everyone seemed to want to read about the adventures of James Herriot and his eccentric, irascible employer-turned-partner, Siegfried Farnon.

Alf always thought his books would make an ideal television series, but not films. Together with his agent he approached the BBC once and Yorkshire Television twice, offering them full film and television rights to all books. The fee: just one pound. He was rejected every time. In the light of such disinterest the rights were sold to an American company – and for far, far more than £1!

Rising stars Simon Ward and Anthony Hopkins were cast in the first film, *All Creatures Great and Small*, shot in and around Pickering, North Yorkshire, during the late summer of 1974. New Zealander Lisa Harrow played James's love interest, (later his wife), Helen. It was a gentle, quietly autobiographical drama set in the years between the wars as James takes up a new job as a vet with Siegfried Farnon.

Director Claude Whatham took his cast and crew to Pickering, which became the base for the making of *All Creatures Great and Small*. Filming was scattered throughout the glorious landscape of the surrounding area: the village hall in Hutton-le-Hole; Malton market square; York railway station; the Worsley Arms in Hovingham; the North York Moors and 18th century Houndgate Hall, in Pickering, which became the primary location: Siegfried's house and practice. The family living in the hall were invaded by film folk for the duration of the shoot, and abandoned their home to strangers. While Ward, Hopkins, Harrow and Brian Stirner (played Tristan) occupied the ground floor the owners temporarily relocated to the upper floor. "The whole place was overrun by them."

By 1975 both Ward and Hopkins had moved on to other things. For *It Shouldn't Happen to a Vet* – the second film in the series – John Alderton became James Herriot and Colin Blakely stepped into Hopkins' shoes as Siegfried. Of the principal cast, only Lisa Harrow returned as Helen. Even the area in which James lived and worked was re-cast, with the Yorkshire Dales replacing the various locations of the previous film.

Both *All Creatures Great and Small* (dubbed All Creatures Grunt and Smell by those that worked on it) and *It Shouldn't Happen to a Vet* were hugely popular and extremely successful - so successful in fact that the BBC was forced to cough up a significant amount of money for the rights when

it finally saw the potential of a TV series. Between 1978 and 1990 the Corporation made 87 one-hour episodes and three feature-length specials, all starring Christopher Timothy (as James), Robert Hardy (as Siegfried) and Peter Davison (as Tristan). Timothy, a devotee of the books, the characters and the man who created them, even produced his own film, *James Herriot's Yorkshire*, which also became a bestseller.

Many expected Alf Wight to throw up his country life and move abroad, becoming a tax exile like Richard Harris or Richard Burton. Wight laughed it off. I have had immense fun from writing but I am a veterinarian." He remained in Thirsk for the rest of his life, even when he became very wealthy and his tax advisors suggested that he retire and move to the Bahamas. At the height of his popularity he was paying 98 pence in the pound to Harold Wilson's government and was at the time one of the very few British authors paying super tax. He said he was living in such idyllic part of the world and paying such high tax was such a small price to pay for such a privilege.

When the books were first published Alf Wight claimed he had based his stories entirely on people he had met and incidents he had witnessed. Towards the end of his life he admitted, just like his hero Charles Dickens, that he had embellished some of the drama and atmosphere of his stories. Nevertheless, he created a world that continues to entertain and enthral – a landscape of dour farmers, busy wives and border collies that, to millions of people around the world, spells out one word: Yorkshire. And didn't he do it well?

1976

The Water Babies

Director: Lionel Jeffries

Producers: Peter Shaw, Ben Arbeid

Writers: Michael Robson, Lionel Jeffries

Production Company: Water Babies Ltd

Year of Production: 1976 (Released 1979)

Where filmed: Denton Hall, Ilkley, West Yorkshire; and York and Bolton Abbey, North Yorkshire between October and November, 1976.

Synopsis: Framed for theft, apprentice chimney sweep Tom dives into Dead Man's Pool and finds there an underwater world full of magical creatures.

Credited cast: James Mason (Saul Grimes), Bernard Cribbins (Masterman), Billie Whitelaw (Mrs. Doasyouwouldbedoneby), Joan Greenwood (Lady Harriet), David Tomlinson (Sir John), Tommy Pender (Tom), Samantha Gates (Elly), Paul Luty (Sladd) and Wilfred the Donkey.

Voices: James Mason (Killer Shark), Bernard Cribbins (Eel), Lionel Jeffries (Cyril the Walrus), Jon Pertwee, Olive Gregg, Lance Percival, David Jason, Cass Allan, Liz Proud, Una Stubbs.

"Come on, Yorkshire! Give us a chance!"

Peering through the milky autumn mist that had begun to shroud Ilkley Moor, disconsolate actor-turned-director Lionel Jeffries raised his hands to the heavens and pleaded for a break in the weather.

Ninety minutes later shivering members of the cast and crew of *The Water Babies* fled the rolling moors and sought shelter where they could find it. Some retreated to Denton Hall, a rambling 36-room mansion that provided the backdrop for this unusual adaptation of Charles Kingsley's 1863 novel. Standing in 2,500 acres of land it was an imposing stately pile and provided a suitable gothic setting for Jefferies' production base. Others, like Bernard Cribbins and 12-year-old child actor Tommy Pender, clambered inside a Land Rover to play a half-hearted game of I-Spy. Young Tommy opted for 'T' which, he claimed, stood for 'terrible weather'. "Wrong," replied a smiling Cribbins. "Right," argued damp and miserable crewmen and women, standing beneath threatening black skies.

The location was reached by narrow, winding moorland roads. Hardy journalists from a variety of outlets, including *Films Illustrated* magazine and the *Huddersfield Daily Examiner,* trudged up to the top of a ridge to meet Jeffries, Cribbins and Pender. But the real star had yet to appear. His arrival was suitably dramatic, as first his anthracite black top hat, then his familiar face, emerged over the rise of the hill.

title page: James Mason as Grimes

previous page: Gloom settles on Ilkley Moor. Director Lionel Jeffries, seen at left, calls a temporary halt to shooting as he waits for the skies to clear. Next to the camera, actor David Tomlinson talks to a heavily camouflaged Billie Whitelaw

right: Usually stars are served food in their trailers by their dresser. James Mason would have none of it and insisted on queuing like everyone else.

Caked in soot, sporting several days' growth of stubble and garbed in ragged greatcoat, grubby, fingerless mittens and heavy boots, James Mason strode through the bracken accompanied by his wife, actress Clarissa Kaye. At 67, Mason's days as a matinee idol were long past, but he was unmistakeably a star and, as chimney sweep Saul Grimes, brought a touch of elegant menace to this Victorian children's fable.

Born in Croft House Lane, Marsh, Huddersfield, in May 1909, Mason had never actually made a movie in the county of his birth. Instead he had spent a 40-year career globetrotting from one exotic location to another. *The Water Babies* marked one of his few outings targeted at a youth market.

"Grimes is a classic villain," said Mason during the weather break. "He's fairly cruel and nasty to everyone. People identify me with this type of part. It's a good-natured charade. Adults are aware he's a figure of fun. The child audience will hate him because he's wicked and might even give them bad dreams. I think Grimes can be compared with Captain Hook in Barrie's *Peter Pan*. I believe it says somewhere in the book that Hook went to Eton, and because of this very high standards are expected of him. Being well-educated makes him a more terrifying villain. I am playing him with great sincerity. It was a real treat to work in Yorkshire and by the greatest piece of good luck I found I was back at Bolton Abbey."

Jeffries was delighted with the casting of Mason and Cribbins as master and scoundrel and confided that he was

looking to employ them as a double-act in another project. "James Mason has an enormous talent and is tremendously receptive. And Bernard Cribbins is, quite simply, the best screen comic character actor we have. They are the new Don Quixote and Sancho Panza of England," he confided.

Jeffries claimed to have an affinity with Yorkshire. Six years after making his directorial debut with E. Nesbitt's *The Railway Children* he was back on his old stamping ground. Once again he was helming a period drama. Once again he was working with children and animals. Wrapped against the cold in bright yellow waterproofs, sturdy Wellington boots and a deerstalker hat, he settled into his canvas director's chair and spoke of his empathy for days of yore.

"My father was born in Bradford and my grandparents also come from here, so I have very strong Yorkshire connections," he said with enthusiasm. "Yorkshire has always been lucky for me, going back six years to *The Railway Children* which was shot on a stretch of line at Keighley, about 12 miles from here. People tell me I am almost paranoiac about the Victorian period. In those days there was warmth within the family, security with strong discipline. I dislike the modern era intensely."

The idea of adapting Kingsley's tale of the poor transcending their lot fell to Peter Shaw, a young producer of documentaries who had had the project in mind from the early 1970s. Jeffries was approached but balked at the suggestion of using special effects to tackle the film's central

underwater sequences. Shaw finally came up with the idea of a cartoon segment to illustrate the story's underwater episode. It was a plan that convinced Jeffries, who then came aboard the film as director and co-writer of the script with Michael Robson. Shaw hired Polish animators at Film Polski and, for three days every fortnight, he and production designer Tony Cuthbert flew to Warsaw to check progress. The animation took 11 months to complete, with the result that the finished film was eventually released two-and-a-half years after production began. In addition, Shaw, Robson and Jeffries turned *The Water Babies* into a musical with eight separate songs.

As the weather cleared the stars came out to shine. Except, while Mason, Cribbins and Co were paragons of thespian

professionalism, one member of their acting troupe had decided that conditions were not quite right for his performance. Wilfred the Donkey was a four-legged prop slung with the tools of Grimes' trade: a variety of baskets, brushes and sweeps. He was also as stubborn as his breed is notoriously known to be. With Mason on his back the little donkey steadfastly refused to budge.

All the coaxing, cajoling, wheedling and enticement would not persuade Wilfred to hit his marks. Mason, sitting atop his mount, was slowly going nowhere. It was a marked difference to previous days, when the unpredictable beast had assisted in Mason tumbling unceremoniously to earth. Ever the gentleman, Mason merely gritted his teeth and muttered something about employing "non-professional

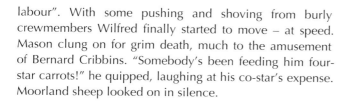

far left, top: Wilfred the donkey goes on strike.

far left, bottom: Lionel Jeffries supervises Billie Whitelaw's make-up.

left: The final transformation.

right: Bernard Cribbins, James Mason and Paul Luty on a damp and drizzly day at Denton Hall.

labour". With some pushing and shoving from burly crewmembers Wilfred finally started to move – at speed. Mason clung on for grim death, much to the amusement of Bernard Cribbins. "Somebody's been feeding him four-star carrots!" he quipped, laughing at his co-star's expense. Moorland sheep looked on in silence.

James Mason recovered his dignity enough to ruminate on his Yorkshire roots. Formerly a frequent guest at his family home, he had not visited Huddersfield since taking part in a Yorkshire Television documentary, *Home James*, in 1972, the year his father died.

"We were very close and I haven't been back to Huddersfield since then," he said, his voice taking on just a little of the hometown accent he was using in the film. "The house we lived in has been knocked down. It was the end of that world for me, as we had a very close bond. Now it is a closed era. I feel like a stranger when I return to that part of my life." The native had returned, but it was a wistful homecoming tinged with sadness.

Mason's comments were in contrast to some of the feelings he had previously voiced about the county of his birth. Back in 1972 his commentary to *Home James* revealed how he had been desperate to flee Huddersfield for the bright lights of London. As his career soared and his bank account filled up with the proceeds from big movies he was able to look back on his roots with something akin to nostalgia. While not a sentimental man, Mason did however warm to the rough-hewn charm of the town that fashioned him in the hour-long film.

"Huddersfield's character is made up of solid things – a sturdy beauty, blunt and uncompromising. Huddersfield has a reputation, not necessarily to its discredit, of keeping behind the times. It's just these qualities that make the place so attractive to me. I have become more and more won over by it. I like the old chimneys, the noise of the machinery, the smell of wool.

"To the casual traveller Huddersfield may be practically indistinguishable from half a dozen other Northern industrial towns, but when you really get to know it you find it has a personality all its own – very seductive," he said.

James Mason died in 1984 at his home in Switzerland. While he never made another film in Yorkshire he is remembered as one of the all-time great British film actors with three Oscar nominations to his credit. Today a plaque bearing his name clings to the front of Huddersfield Library – a gesture made possible thanks to the campaigning by loyal fans who continue to keep alive the memory of a magnificent international star, a fine actor and a proud Yorkshireman.

1977

A Prayer for the Dying

Director: Edward Dmytryk

Producer: Stan Walker

Writer: Edward Dmytryk, based on the novel by Jack Higgins

Production Company: Norwood Motion Pictures (U.K.) Ltd.

Year of Production: 1977
(This version of the film was never made)

Proposed Locations: Leeds, West Yorkshire.

Synopsis: An IRA hitman on the run finds sanctuary with a Catholic priest who has witnessed one of his killings.

Publicised cast: Lee Marvin.

Edward Dmytryk cut something of an incongruous figure as he surveyed the gothic majesty of a Victorian graveyard. It was May, 1977. The Oscar-winning American director was in Leeds to scout locations for a much-hyped movie of the Jack Higgins bestseller *A Prayer for the Dying*. With producer Stan Walker and cinematographer Dave Secker he toured locations in the Lawnswood and Quarry Hill Flats areas of the city and prepared to begin shooting three months later. While some dismissed the project as a pipe-dream, others looked ahead to the prospect of a Leeds premiere for a Leeds-based film adapted from a novel by a writer with significant Leeds connections. Alas, it was not to be but, for a brief moment in time, it looked as if old-time Hollywood and contemporary Yorkshire were to become partners in a remarkable scheme.

Norwood Motion Pictures had been set up by Stan Walker, a former sound recordist with a dream of turning Leeds into a centre for filmmaking to rival London and, perhaps, even Los Angeles. Based in a large terrace house in Victoria Road, Norwood Motion Pictures was a hive of activity. Working alongside Walker and Secker were camera operator Dafydd Hobson, location manager Vic Johnson, associate director Chris Clough and production secretary Ros Waddock. Clearly, Walker considered his dream to be achievable. What's more, so did Jack Higgins.

Real name Harry Patterson, Higgins had enjoyed runaway success with his 1975 novel *The Eagle has Landed*. A hit novel that became a star-studded film, the book propelled Higgins into the big time, multi-millionaire status and led

Every year, every film producer develops yet another screenplay. This could be an idea, a novel, a magazine article, a real event etc. A screenwriter will be chosen and a 1st draft screenplay will be crafted. Usually this has holes so another draft will be commissioned. This will go on until the screenplay is felt to be perfect or else abandoned because it just does not gel together as a coherent story. The producer will then try to package the film with a director and stars and set about the mammoth task of raising the production finance. With some films the funding can come from 20-30 different sources and take years to put in place involving complicated contacts and complex tax arrangements. Some producers just cannot put everything in place all at the same time.

It is thought that for every film that makes it to the screen at least 50 screenplays do not. It is a highly competitive business at every level. Even if the film is made only 1 in 10 makes a profit.

Without the support of organisations such as the UK Film Council backed by Lottery money and tax credit arrangements put in place by the Government, the British film industry would not be as healthy as it is at the time of this book going to press.

to a move to Jersey as a tax exile. *A Prayer for the Dying*, his sixth book as Jack Higgins, concerned an IRA gunman in hiding in Leeds. For Walker, it was a perfect subject for a dedicated band of first-timer filmmakers.

"*A Prayer for the Dying* is set in Leeds and it was in Leeds that Harry Patterson wanted it to be made," revealed the fledgling producer. "I heard that an American company had an option on the book but they wanted to change the story and when I heard that it had become available I flew to see Harry in Jersey and told him how we would propose to tackle the job."

Walker and Patterson/Higgins discussed the potential for the film and agreed that it could and should be shot in Leeds. Higgins, said Walker, was so delighted with Norwood's proposals that he offered up the rights for a fraction of what they were worth. A previous book had been sold for more than $300,000. On the basis of Norwood's commitment to Yorkshire, *A Prayer for the Dying* was negotiated on what Walker called "very favourable terms". Walker planned to set *A Prayer for the Dying* entirely in Leeds apart from shots of Liverpool docks and the M62 motorway as the credits rolled. There were to be ten weeks of exteriors with locations including a church, funeral parlour and cemetery. Added Walker: "We have had marvellous co-operation from the city authorities and the police over locations."

The signing of 69-year-old Dmytryk suggested that Walker and Norwood were extremely serious about their plans for the movie. A veteran of more than 50 films including *The Caine Mutiny, The Young Lions, Anzio, Shalako* and *Bluebeard*, Dmytryk had a reputation for delivering action cinema with macho stars of the calibre of Bogart, Brando, Mitchum, Connery and Burton. Pleased with the feel of the all-action story, he was planning to return to his Malibu home to work up the script whilst Walker sought funding at the Cannes Film Festival. The icing on the cake was the proposed casting of none other than *Dirty Dozen* star Lee Marvin, still a box office draw at the age of 53, as the IRA killer, Fallon.

Walker's dream would never materialise. A decade would go by before *A Prayer for the Dying* hit cinema screens, and by then Dmytryk, aged 79, had been long retired. The film finally emerged in 1987 with Mickey Rourke as the hitman, Bob Hoskins as the priest who witnesses a murder

and Alan Bates as the crime kingpin. It was not a good film and made the headlines for all the wrong reasons. When it was re-edited director Mike Hodges asked for his name to be removed from the credits.

Several major Hollywood stars have made movies in Yorkshire over the years including Bette Davis, Sophia Loren, Paul Newman and Morgan Freeman. Lee Marvin, one suspects, would have made the biggest headlines of the lot. I wonder which Leeds pub would have become his local…

title page: Lee Marvin

previous: Edward Dmytryk and Stan Walker scout locations in a Leeds graveyard. They hoped their version of Jack Higgins' novel would bring Oscar-winner Lee Marvin to Yorkshire.

above: Hollywood tough guy: Lee Marvin in 1977.

1977

Agatha

A fictional solution to the real mystery
of Agatha Christie's disappearance

Director: Michael Apted

Producers: Jarvis Astaire, Gavrik Losey

Writers: Kathleen Tynan, Arthur Hopcraft

Production Company: Casablanca Filmworks/
First Artists/ Sweetwall

Year of Production: 1977 (Released 1978)

Where filmed: Harrogate and York North Yorkshire
between November 7 and 28, 1977.

Synopsis: Distressed by her cold-hearted husband's
open affair with his secretary, best-selling novelist
Agatha Christie flees to the elegant northern spa town
of Harrogate. Her disappearance sparks a massive
manhunt while she, under a nom-de-plume, escapes
identification. Then a tenacious American journalist
tracks her down.

Credited cast: Dustin Hoffman (Wally Stanton),
Vanessa Redgrave (Agatha Christie), Timothy Dalton
(Archie Christie), Helen Morse (Evelyn), Tony Britton
(William Collins), Timothy West (Kenward), Celia
Gregory (Nancy Neele), Alan Badel (Lord Brackenbury),
Paul Brooke (John Foster), Carolyn Pickles (Charlotte
Fisher), Robert Longden (Pettelson), Donald Nithsdale
(Uncle Jones), Yvonne Gilan (Mrs. Braithwaite),
Sandra Voe (Therapist), Barry Hart (Superintendent
MacDonald), David Hargreaves (Sergeant Jarvis), Tim
Seely (Captain Rankin), Jill Summers (Nancy's Aunt),
Christopher Fairbank (Luland), Liz Smith (Flora),
Peter Arne (Hotel Manager), D. Geoff Tomlinson
(Hotel Receptionist), John Joyce (Hotel Waiter), Hope
Johnstone, John Ludlow (Royal Baths Clerks), Ray
Gatenby, Hubert Rees (Officials at Literary Luncheon),
Howard Blake, Jim Archer, Reginald Kilbey (Hotel Trio),
Ann Francis (Jane).

Extras: Brian Berry, Rhoda Brooks, Sally Cordell, Joan
Holgate, Arnold Kellett, Pat Kellett, George Kenton-
Muir, Ralph Lindley, Paula Reeves, Olive Richardson,
Albert Whiteley and the Harrogate Pierrots.

"Missing from her home Mrs. Agatha Mary Clarissa Christie, aged 35: height 5ft 7"; hair red, shingled, part grey; complexion fair; build slight; dressed in grey stockinet skirt, green jumper, … left home by car at 9:45 Friday night." – Police circular from Saturday, December 5, 1926

It is one of the most enduring mysteries of the modern age – the type of puzzle that has detectives baffled and crime writers struggling to recreate it in print. When Agatha Christie vanished on Friday, December 4, 1926 she was the toast of literary London. Her car, found abandoned in a wooded glen close to her Berkshire home, contained a fur coat, a pile of rumpled clothes and a briefcase containing personal papers. Close by were a scarf and a shoe, badly scuffed. Of Mrs. Christie herself there was no sign whatsoever.

Her disappearance provoked a frenzy and a flurry of increasingly alarmist reports hinting at her fate and any number of reasons why she may have driven off into the night. Gossip fed on gossip until rumour became accepted fact. Mrs. Christie had been kidnapped. She had been murdered. As his men dragged a small lake known as The Silent Pool the police chief tasked with finding her predicted she would be located "somewhere in these woods". Newspaper editors offered huge rewards for information leading to her whereabouts. Thousands of people - among them dog handlers, Boy Scouts, pilots, mystic diviners and macabre day trippers - turned out to comb the rolling Berkshire Downs in what was the greatest manhunt in English history. There was no trace. It truly was a mystery as intriguing and bizarre as any of Mrs. Christie's whodunnits.

title page: Vanessa Redgrave as the Queen of Crime Fiction

previous page: Dustin Hoffman had to get used to looking up at Vanessa Redgrave. He is 5ft 6ins; she is 5ft 11ins.

above: Harrogate is transported back to the 1920s – except for the cheeky '70s youngster on the left.

opposite: Hoffman and Redgrave rehearse in the ballroom of Harrogate's Old Swan Hotel – scene of Agatha Christie's discovery in 1926.

photographs published in national newspapers. The police were notified and her husband, World War I flying hero Colonel Archibald Christie, travelled alone to Harrogate where, sitting in the hotel lounge, he waited for his wife to come down for dinner. It was the evening of Tuesday, December 14. As she emerged, dressed in silky salmon pink ninon, he immediately identified her as his wife. The couple returned home the next day.

The discovery was as dramatic as the disappearance, and the Press went berserk. Some accused the Christies of cooking up an elaborate hoax to drum up publicity and sales for her latest book, *The Murder of Roger Ackroyd*. The colonel, meanwhile, issued a flat statement: his wife was suffering from a form of amnesia brought on by overwork and the effects of a suspected concussion. "She does not know who she is," he said. Not many believed him, and the Press began to smell a rat when it was revealed that Mrs. Christie's Harrogate pseudonym was, in reality, the name of her domineering husband's secretary and mistress. Colonel Christie rejected any notion of marital discord. His wife remained silent. For the next 50 years, until her death on January 12, 1976, she refused to discuss her disappearance. In her autobiography she dismissed it in three lines and interviewers were strongly warned not to broach the subject. Whatever was truly the reason for her sudden and ambiguous flight to Harrogate, she took it to her grave.

Less than two years later filming began on the $1.5 million production of *Agatha*. The imaginative script, written by former *Observer* and *Sunday Times* journalist Kathleen Tynan, wife of the acerbic theatre critic Kenneth Tynan, provided a scenario that offered up a believable, if imaginary, solution to the authentic mystery. Her screenplay took Agatha Christie (played by Vanessa Redgrave) to Harrogate to research electrical wiring, currents and methods of murder – or suicide. Hot on her trail is an (entirely fictional) ex-pat American newspaper columnist, Wally Stanton (Dustin Hoffman), who, antennae twitching, actually locates the woman the entire country is seeking. But, instead of revealing her whereabouts, he befriends her. By the film's end he has lost his heart. Sadly for him, it is a one-way love affair. "I'm not saying it's the solution," pointed out Kathleen Tynan. "Much of it is conjecture and imagination. It fits all of the facts, but not enough of them are known to be sure how close I came to the truth. In that sense, it's fiction."

Eleven days later, Agatha Christie was revealed to be staying incognito in the North Yorkshire spa town of Harrogate, hundreds of miles from her home. She had registered at the Hydro Hotel under the assumed name of Mrs. Neele and had spent the time as many who journeyed to Harrogate did: taking the sulphurous waters, enjoying electrical massages and healing baths, and generally relaxing as a health tourist. Sometimes she sat alone; sometimes she mingled and danced with other guests. No-one had suspected a thing, even though 'Mrs. Neele' had arrived from 'South Africa' with just one small attaché case. She was rumbled by Bob Leeming and Bob Tappin, saxophonist and banjo player with the Hydro Dance Band, who became suspicious of 'Mrs. Neele' when it was rumoured that Mrs. Christie might have been in Harrogate. They also noticed a resemblance to

"To understand what happened to Mrs. Christie in 1926, you have to see her as she was: a repressed, romantic, old-world kind of person from a small village where values of marriage and family were very strong," said director Michael Apted. "Yet, as a brilliant mystery writer, she enjoyed a very active fantasy life. Perhaps, in a moment of crisis, those existences overlapped - it's happened to other writers before – and she cast herself as the focal character in a thriller of her own invention."

It was natural for Apted to want to make *Agatha* as realistic as possible, and that meant filming in and around the places where her story had taken place. Top of the list was Harrogate, the fashionable spa town that had been a magnet for health buffs for 200 years. There had been many changes in the half century since Agatha Christie had, momentarily, put Harrogate on the world stage. However Apted and his crew were delighted to discover that their principal location, The Hydro Hotel (re-christened The Old Swan Hotel), needed only a few cosmetic changes to take it back to the 1920s. A false wall had been built over the glass façade and cast-iron columns of the Winter Gardens Ballroom where Agatha Christie had danced. The ballroom itself had been turned into what Apted described as "a pseudo-modern restaurant". With Shirley Russell, the film's costume and production designer who would return to Yorkshire 20 years later to make *Fairytale: A True Story*, Apted sought and received permission to restore the hotel to the grandeur of Christie's stay. The roof was taken down to reveal a splendid glass framework and the room was decorated with hanging lamps, palms and wicker furniture. In an instant the clock was turned back half a century.

One mystery that stumped even the staff of the Old Swan Hotel was the vexed question of Mrs. Christie's room. During World War II the hotel had been requisitioned and its various records, including guest books, were placed into storage in a nearby house. Ironically the house was hit by one of only two bombs that fell on Harrogate during the war, and all the papers were destroyed. Later alterations and the re-numbering of the hotel's rooms meant the makers of *Agatha* were unable to positively identify which room Mrs. Christie had stayed in.

They should have asked Rosie Coles. In 1926 the young Rosie was a chambermaid at the Hydro and clearly recalled that Mrs. Christie stayed in Room 105 – on the third floor. "They had a funny system here in those days," she recalled.

above: The Old Swan today.

left: Cinematographer Vittorio Storaro sets up a shot.

opposite: Three views of Dustin Hoffman. A fastidious actor with a reputation for awkwardness, Hoffman was charm personified with the people of Harrogate.

"The best rooms were at the front of the hotel with a nice view. They were all numbered 'one' and the rooms at the back, near the kitchen, were numbered 'two' and 'three' no matter which floor they were on."

After filming scenes of Agatha's disappearance in Weybridge cast and crew began converging on Harrogate at the beginning of November. Location shooting officially began on Monday, November 7, 1977. Arriving at 1.30am that first day was statuesque 5ft 11ins Vanessa Redgrave, playing Agatha Christie. She had a few hours sleep, went into the hairdresser's at 6.30am and was on set all day. Her scenes involved dancing the Charleston with Dustin Hoffman, the intense 5ft 6ins star playing the American journalist who cracks the story.

Hoffman was intrigued by the concept of a hard-boiled newspaperman falling for the subject of the story that could turn him into an international figure. As with most of his characters, Hoffman had researched the background of the man he was playing.

"He's successful, but he's sold out to his fame, not unlike some of the Algonquin crowd of the '20s," Hoffman told *Yorkshire Post* writer Reg Brace during a snatched interview. "He tries to find Mrs. Christie's whereabouts, meets her and finds himself taken with the sense of artistry that comes from her. He realises that he is talking to a writer, someone who has accomplished what he hoped to accomplish. In a way she represents his own failure to himself. I try to find a kinship. It's not just a matter of uncovering the truth. There is an emotional link between Mrs. Christie and the character I am playing. Not only do I want to find out why she is here, and what she is doing but I would like to have her see a side of me I don't permit anyone else to see. It's a romance from my point of view."

A packed schedule was arranged for Harrogate shoot. Nov 7 at the Old Swan (aka The Hydro) in Swan Road. Nov 12 in Crescent Road. Nov 13 at the Royal Baths on Parliament Street. Shooting progressed apace and Harrogate went quietly mad with the excitement of it all. For the intricate dance sequence in the Old Swan's ballroom 300 extras were hired and each paid £8 a day. They included keen amateur actors, sales engineers, policemen, fashion models, singers and dancers. Their day was due to begin at 8am but filming was delayed until noon, first due to problems with Redgrave's period wig and secondly when a hotel window

was dramatically shattered by gale force winds. Meanwhile Hoffman, unshaven at breakfast, got down to learning new lines in his re-written script.

Problems of a more serious kind had arisen before filming began. Julie Christie, the Oscar-winning star of *Darling, Doctor Zhivago* and *Don't Look Now*, had been cast as Evelyn Crawley, a woman who befriends Agatha during her all-too-brief sojourn in Harrogate. But, just days before she was due to join the production, Christie broke her wrist and the role had to be re-cast. Her replacement was a 30-year-old actress, Helen Morse, who accepted the role with just 11 days notice. A rising star in her adopted home of Australia following her performance in Peter Weir's *Picnic at Hanging Rock*, Morse accepted the last-minute offer and found herself frantically preparing to make her English movie debut. "I had three days with the script before I left Sydney, and five days here," she told reporters visiting the set. "I read it on the 'plane but when I arrived in London my agent gave me one which was almost a complete rewrite. I'm not complaining about the rush. It is a marvellous opportunity. I get scenes with Vanessa and Dustin. I even get chance to Charleston with him."

Among those participating in the dance sequences was 74-year-old Albert Whiteley who, 50 years previously, had been a banjo player in the Hydro Band at the very time the missing celebrity was discovered in Harrogate. His verdict: "Very authentic, except that the woman I learned was Mrs. Christie always sat alone, in the shadows. We other members of the band didn't know a lot about it until afterwards. The two who noticed her kept it to themselves."

There were more scenes shot in Harrogate. A troupe of white-faced Pierrots sang endless jolly choruses of "One finger, one thumb, one arm, one leg – keep moving! We'll all be merry and bright" while a cluster of fastidiously attired extras looked on and vintage cars chugged by. The sequence, filmed in Crescent Gardens opposite the offices of Harrogate Council, was shot on a frigid, cheerless afternoon that paralleled the inner turmoil of the heroine. The attention to detail involved dressing nearby Farrah's Toffee Shop with 400 authentic old-style 1920s cakes supplied by upmarket confectioner's Betty's. Another sequence focused on Hoffman as he sprinted towards The Royal Baths where his quarry was headed. It provided excitement on a grand scale and scores of people braved the icy temperatures to watch the stars.

left: Redgrave and Hoffman in a posed shot for reporters and photographers visiting the set of Agatha.

above: The Charleston dance.

Unlike the Old Swan Hotel, The Royal Baths had been extensively re-modelled. While its imposing gothic façade was unchanged (a look that was assisted by the temporary removal of five modern lamp posts close by the entrance) the heart of the building, which once exemplified the pampered ways of wealthy Victorians, had been turned into a concert hall. Consequently interiors were filmed in Bath. Hoffman and Redgrave shot further scenes at York Station's Victorian terminal, where the Flying Scotsman, a unique steam locomotive, was hauled from retirement for a sequence that formed the climax of the film.

For 40-year-old Dustin Hoffman the excitement was in the sensationalism of the story and the intelligence of the screenplay that attempted to rationalise it. "In terms of

excitement and the focus it got, [the American equivalent] has to be the Patty Hearst story," he said during a filming break. "I'm told that to this day it is the greatest manhunt England has ever seen. Agatha Christie was a celebrated person, and when she disappeared it was big news. I can't think of a writer in my country who would arouse that kind of interest, no matter who took off."

opposite: The ever-patient, forever cheerful Harrogate Pierrots.

above: A thoughtful Dustin Hoffman pictured at York railway station.

1978

Yanks

They fought the same war. They spoke the same language. They were Allies. But they hated each other. And loved each other.

Director: John Schlesinger

Producers: Joseph Janni, Lester Persky

Writers: Colin Welland, Walter Bernstein

Production Company: J.L VIC Films Limited

Year of Production: 1978 (Released November 1979)

Where filmed: Keighley, Silsden, Steeton, Marsden, Halifax, West Yorkshire between April and August, 1978.

Synopsis: In the run-up to the D-Day invasion, thousands of American GIs arrive in towns across the north of England. In the sleepy town of Stalybridge, three couples find themselves thrown together by war, love and circumstance.

Credited cast: Richard Gere (Matt Dyson), Lisa Eichhorn (Jean Moreton), Vanessa Redgrave (Helen), William Devane (John), Chick Vennera (Danny Ruffelo), Wendy Morgan (Mollie), Rachel Roberts (Mrs. Moreton), Tony Melody (Mr. Moreton), Martin Smith (Geoff), Philip Wileman (Billy), Derek Thompson (Ken), Simon Harrison (Tim), Joan Hickson (Barmaid), Arlen Dean Snyder (Master Sergeant Henry Mallory), Annie Ross (Angie, Red Cross Lady).

Uncredited cast: Julian Belfrage, Caroline Blakiston, Nick Brimble, Lynne Carol, John Cassidy, Kenneth Cope, Bill Davidson, Patrick Durkin, Anne Dyson, Jenny Edwards, Joe Gladwin, Pearl Hackney, George Harris, Nat Jackley, Paul Luty, Al Matthews, Kevin Moreton, John Morton, Francis Napier, Jeremy Newson, Lesley Nightingale, Tom Nolan, Andy Pantelidou, Lynne Perrie, Donald Pickering, Joe Praml, John Ratzenberger, Julie Shipley, Pieter Stuyck, Stephen Whittaker.

Extras: Tina Capstick, Clive Crowther, Amanda Hopps, Brian Hopps, Paul Jennings, Ian Kerrison, Claire Louise Lootes, Lynda Lootes, Stephen Lootes, Nick Mullen, Mike North, Jill Pitts, Jane Procter, Tim Rowbotham, Jane Sanderson, Paul Seeley, Frances Smith, Patricia Smith, Brian Thompson, James Westwood and hundreds more.

It was the biggest invasion Keighley had ever seen. The movies had come to town and, for the hundreds of people who took part, the filming of *Yanks* would provide memories they would remember for a lifetime. It was spring, 1978, when locals began spotting adverts calling for extras. When the time came for their collective moment of glory more than two months later, the movie had already been in production for 12 weeks. Three more weeks were required to capture the film's finale: a mass exodus of American troops from a marshalling yard and railway station that involved director John Schlesinger handling more than 800 extras.

For Schlesinger the making of *Yanks* represented both the culmination of a stubborn dream and the return to a location he knew well and was appreciative of. Sixteen years after shooting the majority of *Billy Liar* in Bradford, he was back on his old stamping ground with another new star-in-the-making: 28-year-old Richard Gere. "I like the great feeling of space up here," he told Reg Brace in the *Yorkshire Post*. "There is something remarkable about the way industry is cheek by jowl with such wonderful landscape. I have always found it beautiful to look at since the days when I worked her on TV films. There is almost a division as one crosses over the moors between the red brick of Lancashire and the grey stone of Yorkshire."

Division or not, Schlesinger cunningly created a wholly fictional town from a patchwork of locations scattered across West Yorkshire, Lancashire and Cheshire. The entire centre of Stalybridge, between Huddersfield and Manchester, was

title page: Richard Gere and Lisa Eichhorn on Buckstones Edge, Marsden.

previous page: Director John Schlesinger surveys the world of war as he marshalls hundreds of extras in the old railway goods yard in Keighley.

above, left: Gere and co-star Chick Vennera during the final moments of Yanks.

above, right: Extras Tim Rowbotham and Frances Smith get into the spirit. "It was a challenge," said Frances, playing a London tart. "They said they wanted 'specials'. I asked what they were and they said 'ladies of the night'. I went in dressed like that because I was determined to get the part. The casting director just looked at me and grinned. He said 'This one'. If you want a part in a film you have to dress for the part. And I got it. I went on the bus all the way home. Everyone was staring at me."

redressed to recreate the atmosphere of 1943/44. Affluence was replaced by austerity. In Steeton, just outside Keighley, a disused ordnance camp again became a living organism with some 50 acres used for a newly created parade ground, barracks, Nissen huts and cold showers. And, before any of it could begin, a convoy of trucks, tankers, workshop vehicles, weapon carriers, jeeps and ambulances converged on the north from all across the country.

The old wartime accusation that the Yanks were "overpaid, oversexed and over 'ere" was fully resurrected, and how. Maybe it was something to do with the uniforms. Colin Welland certainly thought so. The actor-turned-scriptwriter had based his story on his own experiences of life in Warrington, where the Burtonwood air base was situated. Looking back on the making of the picture he smiled as he recalled some strangely familiar scenes. "It's incredible. When we were filming in Keighley Station, the American and British extras were necking with each other. And at Stalybridge the shopgirls were leaning out of the windows and waving. It must be the American uniform, because it seemed to work as well for the English extras wearing GI uniforms as for the Americans. The Yanks don't know how to march but, by God, they know how to make a uniform look extremely sexy."

To tell the story of the making of *Yanks* is to tell the stories of the ordinary people who queued up to be in it. Their words have a familiar ring for anyone who has ever volunteered to be an extra: it all boils down to brief interludes of movement and excitement punctuated by long periods of ennui. And all for £15 a day. Many young men were hired

to play GIs complete with helmets and rifles. They flocked to Keighley's Springfield Mills where they were accepted or rejected based on their age and their looks. Mike North sacrificed his hair to a US army crew cut for four days on the film. "I booked two days off work. The other two were over a weekend. My then-wife was a bit peeved as she wanted a part but couldn't get time off like me. The proviso was that if I was to be a soldier in the film I had to have my hair short, and long hair was all the rage. The guy who cut it must have been a sheep shearer. When she saw it she nearly died. She said 'You are not going anywhere with me looking like that!' It took all summer to grow back."

Paul Seeley was on a contractual break from his regular job as repetiteur for the D'Oyly Carte Opera Company. He played

above: John Schlesinger with his youngest extra, six-month-old Claire Louise Lootes.

above: A rehearsal for another farewell, as Lisa Eichhorn says goodbye to fiancé Ken, played by Derek Thompson. John Schlesinger eyes the scene.

one of the hundreds of khaki-clad troops in the embarkation sequence filmed in the old goods yard opposite the Victoria Hotel – now the site of Sainsbury's car park. He cheekily sent a note to John Schlesinger suggesting that, as a professional musician, he might be able to assist with the film's score. He received a friendly note in return saying that Richard Rodney Bennett had already been commissioned. Nothing ventured, nothing gained. Another GI who almost got lost in the crowd was James Westwood, a 20-year-old second year university student enjoying his summer holidays. "There was a column of soldiers marching in the background," he recalls. "Everybody ended up jostling for position to get in the shot. I succeeded, and you can see about two seconds of me with Richard Gere. It was fascinating. I really enjoyed it and it's something I still think about."

For many extras, it was a fast turnaround. Westwood was notified of his involvement by letter on June 8, and filming took place between June 26 and July 14. After the goods yard scenes the other major sequence was the movie's heart-stopping finale. Almost the entire town turns out to

*right: Filming the grand finale from the
bridge at Keighley Station.*

above: A training exercise filmed near Marsden. John Schlesinger, in hat and goggles, sits behind the camera.

left: The old ordance camp at Steeton was transformed into a fully functioning US Army barracks, circa 1943.

wave the Americans off as they head south and onto France to face an uncertain future on the beaches of Normandy. Among the faces on Keighley Station was 30-year-old Tim Rowbotham, his hair cut to regulation length and his beard neatly trimmed to play a British sailor. His abiding memory provides a perfect vignette of the life of an extra.

"Imagine the scene. I am standing on Keighley Station with a lot of extras. There is a man in a light-coloured suit and he is getting up everyone's noses. At one point he tries to get two non-smokers to smoke like troopers. It does not go down well. My friend was driving Big Jim, the locomotive from the Keighley & Worth Valley Railway. He had to stop it within an inch or two of a certain point on the platform. The man in the light-coloured suit calls the driver over and tells him where to stop. He shouts at him a lot. The driver throws his blackened, half-eaten bacon buttie into the fire box, beckons to the man to stand on the footplate and rolls the engine into the tunnel. After a lot of clanking, a thick black cloud rolls out of the tunnel, and then comes the engine. Suddenly the man's suit isn't light-coloured anymore. Hundreds of extras cheer and he storms off the set. He had had us doing the thing so many times he had lost the sympathy of the extras. Half an hour later John Schlesinger arrives. What a difference. Everything soon runs smoothly until the first take, when the train arrives and 400 extras surge forward only to find the carriage doors locked. We rehearsed it until we were all sick of it."

Ian Kerrison and Paul Jennings were part of a crowd that cheered a boxing match between the Yanks and the Limeys. Filming lasted a week. "You can see me on screen for a split second," says Jennings, playing an RAF flyer in a scratchy uniform. "I was allocated what you'd call an English 'floozy' and, at a given moment, we had to stand up and cheer the English guy. She took it really seriously. You would have thought she was going to be a Hollywood star." Kerrison remembers a lot of talk about Richard Gere, sitting with the rest of the hollering crowd. "I didn't know who he was at the time although I heard later that he was an up-and-coming American star. He was pleasant enough and I passed a few words with him. We all used to go to the canteen together to get sandwiches." Further scenes were shot in Southowram, Halifax, and Pule Hill, Marsden. The latter involved training sequences in which GIs scrambled from wooden landing craft onto moorland as they prepare for the D-Day invasion.

Sadly, Yorkshire missed out on hosting the northern premiere of Yanks. Instead of Keighley, United Artists chose to present a special preview in Stockport, prior to a Leicester Square premiere in London on November 1. The decision provoking much local disgust. *The Keighley News* stepped in and arranged for 400 readers to see the film at the Davenport Cinema on October 18, 1979. The Stockport event was given a suitably '40s backdrop courtesy of wartime vehicles and a shimmering white Compton cinema organ that rose from the floor to begin the show. "If it pleases the people of Stockport, it will please anybody," said the town's mayor. Two hours and twenty minutes later, spontaneous applause proved that he was right.

And what of the reaction of its quiet, laconic American star? "Playing a character from another time allows you to get outside yourself a bit," said Gere, adding: "I doubt I'll ever have another year *that* enriching."

below: Troop extras prepare to move out of the goods yard. The train the background is transporting artillery to the front - the various guns were all made out of timber.

Extras' snapshots

left, top: Filming in Dobcross as the American trucks leave for the station. Director John Schlesinger, in green t-shirt, watches the action as local people look on.

left, bottom: Richard Gere and Chick Vennera wait in the truck in the old goods yard, Keighley, in a sequence towards the end of the film.

below: Filming of the final sequence of Yanks. Extras stand on the roof of the tunnel at Keighley Station, waiting for their call to action.

above: Chick Vennera and Richard Gere on location.

below: Extras gather in the old goods yard opposite the Victoria Hotel.

right, top: The artificiality of a boxing match that took a week to capture on film. Lisa Eichhorn, Richard Gere and Wendy Morgan are surrounded by supporting actors and local extras.

right: A weary John Schlesinger during filming of the boxing match.

right, bottom: Extras cheer the boxers – but without the main cast.

1983

The Dresser

Director: Peter Yates

Producer: Peter Yates

Writer: Ronald Harwood, based on his play

Production Company: Goldcrest Films

Year of Production: 1983 (Released March 20, 1984)

Where filmed: Alhambra Theatre, Bradford and Halifax, West Yorkshire; York, North Yorkshire during June and July, 1983.

Credited cast: Albert Finney ('Sir'), Tom Courtenay (Norman), Edward Fox (Oxenby), Zena Walker (Her Ladyship), Eileen Atkins (Madge), Michael Gough (Frank Carrington), Cathryn Harrison (Irene), Betty Marsden (Violet Manning), Sheila Reid (Lydia Gibson), Lockwood West (Geoffrey Thornton), Donald Eccles (Mr. Godstone), Llewelyn Rees (Horace Brown), Guy Manning (Benton), Anne Mannion (Beryl), Kevin Stoney (C. Rivers Lane), Ann Way (Miss White), John Sharp (Mr. Bottomley), Kathy Staff (Bombazine Woman), Roger Avon (Charles), Christopher Irvin (Evelyn, the Airman), Stuart Richman (Evelyn's Friend), Sandra Gough (Actress on Station), Joe Belcher (Arthur), Johnny Maxfield (Electrician), Paul Luty (Stallkeeper), Lori Wells (Barmaid), Alan Starkey (Train Guard).

Anyone even remotely interested in the British theatre of the 1950s will immediately remember the so-called 'big three': Laurence Olivier, Ralph Richardson and John Gielgud. In theatre, movies and television their names shone brighter than anyone else's when it came to superlative character performances in the classical tradition. Yet most people are hard-pressed to recall Donald Wolfit, an actor-manager of the old school who dragged a company around the provinces and made occasional forays into film and television.

The theatre creates its own stars, and Olivier, Richardson and Gielgud were in the vanguard. Strange, then, that it was Wolfit whose life inspired Oscar-winner Ronald Harwood to write a play that has lasted over 3 decades and which continues to be produced all over the world in many different languages. The play was *The Dresser*, and a touring theatre in Bradford was to provide the backdrop for what was to become one of the most fêted and atmospheric movies ever made about the stage and the people who claim it as their own.

Ronald Harwood was just 19 when he was employed by Donald Wolfit. It was 1953 and Wolfit, a grandiose thespian with big ambitions, was leading a season at the King's Theatre, Hammersmith. Harwood, a small-part player, had little to do. In some plays he had no lines at all. So he watched and listened, observing the sometimes deafening tirades and righteous anger of a mighty, egomaniacal actor battling against the odds to present great plays to often indifferent audiences. Wolfit died in 1968, never truly accepted by his peers or the acting establishment. He was considered a poor relative of Oliver, Richardson and Co. John Gielgud, asked to contribute a tribute on Wolfit's death, demurred. "I couldn't," he said with characteristic bluntness. "You see we always considered him as something of a joke."

Joke or not, Wolfit provided Harwood with a wealth of material for a play about 'Sir', a grandiloquent actor-manager leading a rag-tag band of performers on a tour through wartime England. Harwood presented his biographical tale as a look behind the scenes at life and relationships in a traditional touring stage company against a backdrop of air raid sirens and falling bombs. 'Sir' has given his soul to the theatre and is close to cracking under the strain. His closest companion is Norman, his effete dresser, utterly

dedicated to his master but wryly aware of his frequently unreasonable demands.

One scene sums up the mood of *The Dresser* and the character of the man at the centre of it. What's more it is based entirely on Harwood's own experiences with the magisterial, mercurial Wolfit. "I was on the crew that did the storm for King Lear," recalls Harwood more than 50 years later. "It was never loud enough for Wolfit. He wanted the storm so loud - BANG, BANG, BANG! He called a special rehearsal and it still wasn't loud enough. We were cracking drums and thunder sheets and Christ knows what. Then one of the carpenters said 'I've got a big water tank downstairs, Mr. Wolfit. If we hang that from the flies and somebody bangs it, that'll increase the sound.' So this was brought up.

title page: Tom Courtenay as Norman, on location in Halifax. Summer, 1983.

previous page: Norman (Tom Courtenay) not only dresses Sir (Albert Finney), he also has to bath him.

opposite: Norman as The Storm.

right: Norman shopping for Brown & Poulson's Corn Flour which Sir uses as part of his make-up regime.

He looked round and said 'Harwood!' They sawed off a bit of broomstick, wrapped it in padding, I put my head in the thing and thumped. He said 'That'll do'.

"That night we did the play and I was reeling after. You can imagine my head inside this tank, banging away. The reverberations were appalling! Later I was out in the corridor having a cigarette and Wolfit came down for his next entrance - also having a cigarette - as Lear. He said 'Were you on the storm tonight, my boy?' I said 'Yes, I was, sir.' He said 'You're an artist.' Then he made me his dresser. Years later I had the idea to write a play about a dresser and an actor. It had to be about King Lear because I wanted the wartime company to mirror Shakespeare's Lear: the giving up of the kingdom, the reduction of the retinue, the three women – his daughters were mirrored in the play."

Rich in comedy and compassion, *The Dresser* first captivated audiences in London and New York in 1980. Three years later it briefly drew the attention of Orson Welles before finally going before the cameras in London, Bradford, Halifax and York. It would return reluctant film star Tom Courtenay to the movie screen, create a memorable partnership between him and co-star Albert Finney and eventually be nominated for a clutch of Academy Awards. Most importantly for Yorkshire, it completely rejuvenated the fading Alhambra Theatre, in Bradford – a majestic venue opened in 1914 that had seen better days.

The success of *The Dresser* all around the world led to a bizarre 'phone call from Orson Welles, who asked Harwood to meet him in Paris to discuss a film adaptation. Harwood

below: Star Tom Courtenay, right, with director Peter Yates, whom writer Ronald Harwood said "was the most decent and gentlemanly director I've ever worked with".

opposite: Sir as Lear.

never heard another word and, instead of collaborating with the-then gargantuan Welles, he found himself on a dream project with a perfect triumvirate of partners: Tom Courtenay, Albert Finney and writer/director Peter Yates, who had made his name with *Bullitt*. Courtenay, says Harwood, "was a given for the movie" having performed the play hundreds of times on both sides of the Atlantic. "No-one took over from him." Albert Finney was cast as Sir, edging out the excellent Freddie Jones who had introduced the part on stage. Finney, a tried and tested film star, had box office clout. He also had the showier role. In essence the film rested on his shoulders.

Initially Finney was reluctant to accept the role. At 47 he felt he was too young to tackle a man in his late 50s or

early 60s. Happily he was subsequently persuaded to do it. "Albert has a gift that I don't know in any other actor: the moment he comes on stage or on screen, the audience goes towards him," says Harwood. "He just is extraordinarily magnetic. It's something in his personality to which people warm. From the moment he said yes, we were on. Then we made the movie."

Curiously, Courtenay and Finney had never previously worked together. A Yorkshireman and a Lancastrian from similar backgrounds, both men had made their reputations in the 1960s. Crucially, both had played the same role: Billy Liar. When Finney left the part in 1961, Courtenay took over. Their relationship in the film was as equals – vital to the end result.

"It's difficult to grandstand in a movie," muses Harwood. "You can do it on the stage because there are technical things that you can do. You can go upstage; you can get into light… all kinds of things. But on a movie that's impossible. Sometimes you just strike very, very lucky with the personalities of your actors and these two complemented each other. Albert and Tom are both very, very conscientious men. They did the play. Not only did they act the parts but they wanted to contribute to the centre of the play."

The other key element was Yates, who Harwood describes as "the most decent and gentlemanly director I've ever worked with". Yates fundamentally understood *The Dresser*. Like Finney, Courtenay and Harwood a one-time Royal Academy of Dramatic Art graduate, Yates had directed for the London

willing extras. Parts of the building were 'doubled' with the Wimbledon Theatre, which stood in for some backstage sequences. Everything else was shot in Bradford. Says Harwood: "Albert did the big curtain speech in one take. The extras who were there, the Bradfordians, cheered him. It was very moving. Peter was very clever with the extras. We couldn't fill the house with extras because we couldn't afford it, so you only see half the auditorium at any time. Then he changed them all round. It's shot in such a way that you wouldn't know."

Yates shot other scenes in Halifax's Piece Hall – a memorable scene in which 'Sir' has the beginnings of a breakdown – inside the Cock and Bottle pub in Bradford and in York railway station. It was another moment taken directly from life as 'Sir' bellows "Stop that train!" and a giant locomotive lurches to a halt. The scene was a last-minute addition and, to Yates, an epiphany. Despite the casting of Finney and Courtenay, Yates had been concerned that the end result would still be overly theatrical – that The Dresser would not comfortably translate from stage to screen. 'I don't want to just make a film of the play. I want to make a film of the film,' he revealed to Harwood. The two tossed around various ideas. Suddenly Harwood remembered the incident with the train - a typical Wolfit story. "Peter's eyes lit up and he said 'That's fine. Let's do it'. It made it into the film."

On release The Dresser was a critical smash. The film was nominated for five Academy Awards – Best Picture, Best Director, Best Writing and Best Actor for both Finney and Courtenay, who cancelled each other out. The Oscar went to Robert Duvall for Tender Mercies. The picture also signalled the re-emergence of Tom Courtenay after a self-imposed break from movies of more than a decade. While working on the film the choosy star quipped: "Why don't you put on the bill 'And re-introducing Tom Courtenay!'"

The Dresser is rightly regarded by many as the quintessential film about the British theatre. For Harwood, who initially thought the play would be a flop, its success on stage and on film has been comforting. For the first time in his career he had made it in financial, and critical, terms. He was 48 years old. It also pleases him that the awareness created by the play has helped to bring the unpopular and tyrannical Wolfit in from the cold. "None of the others liked him. Gielgud didn't like him. Olivier couldn't bear him. Wolfit and Richardson didn't mind each other but Ralph Richardson was a more generous man than the other two.

and New York stage and was renowned for being able to communicate with actors. What's more, he was passionate about the subject. "If I can make a film which will get people to go to the theatre, I will feel I have achieved something," he said from the set. "I don't think there has ever been a film which shows just a piece of the theatre's tradition and presents it in an attractive and palatable way. I hope with The Dresser we've changed that."

Prior to the start of shooting Yates had made a special recce to Yorkshire to scout potential locations. Top of his shopping list was a realistic and bonafide theatre of the type that had welcomed companies like Wolfit's in the years between the wars and after. He found it in the Alhambra. "Peter came back and said 'We've found it, there's no question. The Alhambra gave the film authenticity. That was the crucial factor, because it was a touring theatre. All the great actors had played there, including Wolfit. Bradford was considered to be a good date back then because it was a wool town. There was money in the town in the old days."

Yates, Harwood, Finney, Courtenay and a fine ensemble that included Edward Fox, Eileen Atkins, Michael Gough, Zena Walker, Lockwood West, Cathryn Harrison, Donald Eccles and Llewelyn Rees arrived in Bradford like an old-time touring company. Booked into a local hotel where they enjoyed lavish breakfasts laden with black pudding, the Alhambra became their second home.

The Alhambra presented Yates with a perfect milieu – a genuine Georgian stage and stalls that he could pack with

When it came out most of the Wolfit family were outraged. They didn't want to see me again and cut me off. I told Ralph this and what he said was very interesting: 'You know, Wolfit's a lucky fellah. When we're all dead he'll still be remembered because of your play.' I think not a day has passed since I wrote that play that it hasn't been performed somewhere, all over the world."

opposite: The Piece Hall, Halifax loved by many filmmakers for its visual elegance.

above: Kathy Staff had a small but memorable role in The Dresser. *She is pictured here between scenes with Tom Courtenay.*

1984

A Private Function

Director: Malcolm Mowbray

Producer: Mark Shivas

Writer: Alan Bennett

Production Company: Handmade Films

Year of Production: 1984 (Released November 1984)

Where filmed: Ilkley, Ben Rhydding, Bradford, West Yorkshire; Bolton Abbey, North Yorkshire during May, 1984.

Synopsis: Yorkshire, 1947. A small village is preparing to celebrate the wedding of Princess Elizabeth. Chiropodist Gilbert Chilvers and his social climbing wife Joyce find themselves hopelessly embroiled in a secret plan: to fatten a pig that will then be devoured on the big night.

Credited cast: Michael Palin (Gilbert Chilvers), Maggie Smith (Joyce Chilvers), Denholm Elliott (Dr. Charles Swaby), Richard Griffiths (Henry Allardyce, the accountant), Tony Haygarth (Leonard Sutcliff, the farmer), John Normington (Frank Lockwood, the solicitor), Bill Paterson (Morris Wormold, the meat inspector), Liz Smith (Joyce's Mother), Alison Steadman (Mrs. Allardyce), Jim Carter (Inspector Noble), Pete Postlethwaite (Douglas J. Nuttol, the butcher), Eileen O'Brien (Mrs. Sutcliff), Rachel Davies (Mrs. Forbes, Wormold's landlady), Reece Dinsdale (PC Penny), Philip Wileman (Preston Sutcliff), Charles McKeown (Medcalf, a butcher), Susan Porrett (Mrs. Dorcus Medcalf), Donald Eccles (Dorcus' Father), Denys Hawthorne (Grand Hotel Manager), Don Estelle (Barraclough, a butcher), Eli Woods (Ernest), Amanda Gregan (Veronica Allardyce), Paula Tilbrook (Mrs. Turnbull, a Chilvers neighbour), Bernard Wrigley (Painter), Lee Daley (Painter's Boy), Gilly Coman (Dorothy, Allardyce's secretary), Maggie Ollerenshaw (Woman), Josie Lane (Mrs. Beavers), David Morgan (Marvin).

A *Private Function* should be a peculiarly autobiographical film for Alan Bennett, given that his father was a butcher and that the film focuses on the efforts of a small group of middle-class Yorkshire folk to quietly fatten and kill an illicit pig to celebrate the 1947 royal wedding. It was Bennett's first film and arguably remains his most popular. Yet while it features all the established Bennett touches that his admirers adore, it was in fact based not on anything in Bennett's early life but on a childhood memory of Malcolm Mowbray, the man who would later direct the film.

Mowbray and Bennett had met after the filmmaker had directed a BBC2 Playhouse film, *Days at the Beach* and received a letter of congratulation from an admiring Bennett. Seizing the opportunity, Mowbray asked Bennett

to collaborate with him on a feature film script. Bennett, an established writer of television plays, had penned a number of feature film scripts that for various reasons had never been made. However he had an idea about a chiropodist, while Mowbray was fascinated by memories of post-war Britain – an austere period where black market goods and severe rationing went hand-in-hand. Says Bennett: "Malcolm wanted to do a film about a pig and I wanted to do a film about a chiropodist. So that's how it came about, more or less". The screenplay took two-and-a-half years to deliver. Its original title: *Pork Royale*.

Bennett's father was a butcher in, Leeds. There were two others on the same street. "Both of them said I was a twit," he recalls. "My vision of my father is at night. He's sat at

the table in the kitchen going through the things you cut out of ration books – coupons, etc – trying to work out how he is going to make ends meet. We got delivered a certain amount of meat and we had to make that fit the number of customers we'd got. I have vivid memories of the misery of that time but the actual pig is part of Malcolm Mowbray's time, not mine. His wife's in-laws were butchers near Bradford. They had kept a pig, killed it and had it in the bath. One night the police knocked at the door over some other trivial matter and they saw the pig in the bath. That was the idea that started off the film. He had this vision of a camera panning over a toilet room filled with talcum powder and shampoos and then panning down to this farm animal which turned out to be a pig."

Backing for the film came from George Harrison's company Handmade Films despite the former Beatle's business partner Dennis O'Brien's constant worry that it would not play in America and would therefore not recoup its budget. Filming began in Ilkley in May, 1984. On May Day, 70 members of the Ilkley Players auditioned for parts and 30 were selected to attend costume fittings. Their big scene involved queuing for a meagre ration of meat outside Barraclough's butcher's shop in Ben Rhydding. The sequence took 13 hours, during which a crowd gathered, policemen diverted traffic and church bells were silenced. And, of course, star-spotters got their money's worth by watching Maggie Smith, Michael Palin and Denholm Elliott at work. Their personalised director's chairs gave them away.

Like the enthusiastic extras, some of Britain's brightest acting talent fell over themselves to work on a Bennett project. The three stars were Smith, Palin and Elliott, but in support the film can boast Alison Steadman, Pete Postlethwaite, Richard Griffiths, Jim Carter, Bill Paterson and Liz Smith who, on eyeing a script she described as "a magical read with the words dripping off my lips", sent a postcard to Bennett's London home begging to be in it. She got the part.

Bennett spent a great deal of time on location. He laughingly claims he turned up to keep Maggie Smith from becoming bored. "I was there to chat to Maggie Smith in her dressing room – a kind of social cement. She's very well-behaved but she has a reputation. If she gets bored she behaves very badly." In truth he wanted to observe how his comedy translated to the big screen and to tinker with the script if it didn't work as he had intended. "When we were filming in Bradford I'd often not seen the location and the language didn't quite fit. You've got to tailor it. I don't quite understand how writers don't want to be there or avoid it. It seems to me that you have to be there if you care about what you write."

It was a happy shoot with Maggie Smith arriving a day before the rest of the cast and crew… to ensure she had the best room. "I often go past the road where the house is and think about it," reveals Bennett. "I have very happy memories of it. There was a good atmosphere. Everyone had such a wonderful time, especially Richard Griffiths. If you watch the film, you can see that it cuts away just as he is about to break out laughing. Every time they put in the fart noises for the pig he suddenly started to laugh hysterically." One local boy who pestered the crew to be allowed to work on the film landed a job when the pig's

above: Alan Bennett and Michael Palin at a retrospective screening of the film at the 2008 Bradford Film Festival. Bennett presented Palin with a Lifetime Achievement Award, stating that for over 40 years he'd always admired Palin for his 'bounce'.

constant messing on the set began to slow down production. Handed a plastic bucket, he was ordered to clamp it over the porker's backside at the first sign – or sound – of an emission. Thus he proudly achieved a credit unique in the annals of cinema: Bucket Boy.

The pig proved to be the biggest star of *A Private Function*. An unpredictable beast, it never did what anyone expected it to do. To encourage it, the animal was fed constantly. Pig handlers would announce feeding time by banging a bucket. Sometimes it worked. Sometimes it didn't. On one occasion Mowbray was directing a night sequence in woods above Bolton Abbey for the moment in the film when the pig is stolen. The script said the pig would amble through the woods and into a car. Tasty morsels were laid to tempt it. The pig ignored them. Then someone realised that the woods were covered in wild garlic, which was all the pig could smell. The scene as written should have lasted between three and four minutes. On screen it lasts around two. Bennett remembers it as a minor failing. "If we had had more money we would have shot it again. We had to finish at midnight because of overtime rates," he says.

As one of the Pythons, Michael Palin had experienced his fair share of unusual televisual moments. Yet an episode on *A Private Function* eclipsed all others. This is how it happened. "The scene where I have to get the pig into the car turned out to be far more surreal than anything I had ever done with Python. The pig was huge and the 1940s car was not. The props boys had smeared the interior with fish oil but the pig was just not budging so in the end we had people out of sight pushing the pig's backside into the car.

"Eventually it was inside but not for long as it leapt for door and got its trotter in my crotch. I had to let the brake off while holding his trotter away from my privates. Unfortunately for me, it became very alarmed by all of this, which resulted in vast amounts of shit going everywhere: over the car, me, the men pushing. It was a nightmare. The man who owned the vintage car was a Yorkshireman and he said 'Who is that up there?' pointing to Alan. 'Oh, that's the writer,' I said. The man nodded his head a bit, looked at the pig being pushed into his car, the shit, the commotion and everything and said, 'He's no Ibsen, is he?'"

above: Liz Smith, Michael Palin,
Richard Griffiths and Alison Steadman.

1986

Rita, Sue and Bob Too!

Thatcher's Britain with her knickers down

Director: Alan Clarke

Producer: Sandy Lieberson

Writer: Andrea Dunbar

Production Company: Umbrella Entertainment Productions

Year of Production: 1986 (Released May 1987)

Where filmed: Bradford, Baildon Moor, Haworth, West Yorkshire, during September and October, 1986.

Synopsis: Teenagers Rita and Sue, best friends from a tough Yorkshire housing estate, embark on a shared affair with the same married man.

Credited cast: Michelle Holmes (Sue), Siobhan Finneran (Rita), George Costigan (Bob), Lesley Sharp (Michelle), Kulvinder Ghir (Aslam), Willie Ross (Sue's Father), Danny O'Dea (Paddy), David Britton, Mark Crompton, Stuart Goodwin, Max Jackman, Andrew Krauz, Simon Waring (Rita's Brothers), Maureen Long (Rita's Mother), Joyce Pembroke (Lawn Mower Lil), Patti Nicholls (Sue's Mother), Jane Atkinson (Helen), Bryan Heeley (Michael), Paul Oldham (Lee), Bernard Wrigley (Teacher), Dennis Conlon (Taxi Driver), Joanna Steele (Sylvia), Joanna Barrow (Judy), Rachel Shepherd, Paula Jayne (Schoolgirls), Alison Goodman (Hilda), Marie Jelliman (Gym Mistress), Nancy Pute (Mavis), Ken Hainsworth (Billy), Niall Costigan (Simon), Sinead Parkinson (Jenny), Paul Hedges (Hosepipe Harry), Laura Devon (Neighbour on Balcony), Charles Meek (Taxi Driver) and Black Lace (Themselves).

It is difficult to grasp the level of outrage and indignation that greeted the release of *Rita, Sue and Bob Too!* Previewed at Brighton's Cinema '87 film festival, the low-budget autobiographical portrait of life on the breadline in Bradford shocked some in the film world. Overnight it transformed working class playwright Andrea Dunbar into a reluctant quasi celebrity.

An unapologetically authentic look at life on a rough council estate as seen through the eyes of two randy teenage girls, the film was excoriated for plumbing the lower depths of crudity and profanity while, at the same time, appearing to present two fingers to the watching world. The world of Rita and Sue, the raucous, foul-mouthed baby-sitters who gleefully opt to be the sexual playthings of a bored married

title page: Siobhan Finneran, George Costigan and Michelle Holmes, the ribald trio at the heart of Rita, Sue and Bob Too! Said Finneran: "Michelle and I both look like the pits of the earth in the film, not two sex queens on a night out."

above: A posed scene that typifies the mood of the film. Left to right: Patti Nicholls, Siobhan Finneran, Willie Ross, Michelle Holmes, Lesley Sharp, George Costigan. Much of the Buttershaw Estate has undergone extensive re-development since the film was made in 1986.

left: *Director Alan Clarke films an interior with Michelle Holmes and, back to camera, Kulvinder Ghir.*

below: *It is traditional on all feature films to have a photograph taken with the entire cast and crew. This frequently causes problems with actors as it is so rare that all the actors are working on the same day.*

RITA, SUE *and Bob Too!* BRADFORD, SUMMER 1986

man, was not a familiar one to most audiences. It focused on low-lives, low morals and primitive behaviour. But it was the world in which Andrea Dunbar – single mother and victim of domestic abuse - had grown up and one she bluntly embraced.

Dunbar was that rare creature – seen as a combination of dunderhead and guttersnipe - whose energy and raw talent saw her whisked to London and that rarefied centre of edgy and avant-garde theatre, the Royal Court. She was just 17 when *The Arbour* – named after her Brafferton Arbour home on Bradford's Buttershaw Estate – was accepted by the Royal Court. It earned her the George Devine Award for Young Playwrights and propelled her into an entirely new spectrum of experience. Her second play, *Rita, Sue and*

above: Producer Sandy Lieberson (standing), Executive Producer Oscar Lewenstein (in chair) and writer Andrea Dunbar observe filming on the Buttershaw Estate, Bradford. Said Lewenstein: "Maybe it is not a typical northern estate, but it is a particularly demoralising one."

left: George Costigan and Michelle Holmes on location in 1986. The scene behind them typifies the look of the Buttershaw Estate.

above: Director Alan Clarke with actors George Costigan and Michelle Holmes. Clarke, who died in 1990 aged only 54, has often been compared to Ken Loach in his style and approach. He is rightly considered one of the great losses to British cinema.

Bob Too! was commissioned in 1982 by Max Stafford-Clark, who had directed The Arbour for the stage. Four years later Dunbar was asked to write the script for a £850,000 film that took as its inspiration the streets and boulevards of the run-down estate that had been Dunbar's home for years. The film took both plays as its inspiration.

The movie, produced by Sandy Lieberson and directed by Alan Clarke, became a bit of a cause célèbre. In some quarters it was denounced and dismissed as deliberately misleading and negative. A few people criticised Dunbar, as the author, for bringing into disrepute a city considered to be on the up. Those behind the film leapt to its defence. Lieberson praised Dunbar's unique voice and defended her right to be heard. "I read many scripts and plays. This came across as something strong with a savage humour," he said. Filming began in September 1986. Actresses Siobhan Finneran and Michelle Holmes were cast as Rita and Sue. Bob was played by George Costigan. Kulvinder Ghir played Aslam, a two-fisted Pakistani who, temporarily, becomes Sue's boyfriend. The Buttershaw Estate – a bleak wasteland of old motorbikes and wrecked cars, grimy homes, shrewish mothers and drunkenly incoherent fathers – played itself.

Some critics claimed the film was an exaggeration and did no favours for Dunbar or Bradford. The response from Hilary Mantel, writing in The Spectator, was typical: "It ought to be funny, but it isn't. It is hard to think of a film where so many comic set pieces have been played through without raising a smile. The film asks us to like them and pity them, to find them funny and to find their lives funny, but in fact the girls appear desperate and pathetic:

a hopeless pair of greasy-faced witches, with no virtue in their shrieking camaraderie."

Looking back on the reactions to his production, Sandy Lieberson recalls it as an '80s social realist throwback that presented authentic situations and real characters through which a sense of comedic tragedy emerged. "What critics found hard to understand was that the real-life characters felt no sense of self pity," he argues. "That's what Alan Clarke reflected in his attitude to the storytelling. Alan was extremely respectful to the play and Andrea. They worked together closely. Andrea brought Alan into her world of the Buttershaw Estate. They liked each other and he spent a great deal of time with Andrea, her family and friends.

"The film was made entirely on location. Our life was on the Buttershaw Estate. It became a 'family' like experience. We got to know the residents, drank in the local with Andrea, her friends and family. It was a tough shoot because of the short schedule but one of the most enjoyable I have experienced. I loved the attitude of the people of Bradford. Once they knew you were not a bullshitter they completely accepted and trusted. The residents of the estate loved the fact the film was being made there. It was probably the most exciting thing to happen there. They cooperated fully. They enjoyed eating from the catering wagon - the food was better than they were eating, and it was free."

There was a sense of middle-class missionary zeal about some elements of the filming. Top casting director and co-producer Patsy Pollock, speaking from the heart. "Some of the people on the Buttershaw Estate live below the bread line. I think their lives are appalling, sterile, loveless and hard. Drinking and sex are the only luxuries in a world where unemployment has bred a level of poverty I had never seen." she said. Her comments provoked disbelief from a few residents of the estate who felt they were being maligned – tarred by the same damning brush. It was left to Dunbar to smooth things over.

"I don't write about the haves and have-nots. That doesn't interest me," she told Jim Greenhalf, a writer with the *Bradford Telegraph & Argus*. "I don't go out of my way to say 'We haven't got this' and 'We haven't got that'. It's relationships between people that's more important than anything else. I am not moaning and groaning. I wouldn't condemn anybody. I am writing out of experience I know about. It might be laughter or tears; but to me the laughter and the tears and the friendship matter a lot." Dunbar, only 26 when the film was made, would be dead at 29 from a brain haemorrhage. Her supporters, of which there are many, believe this intelligent and vibrant young woman suffered cruelly at the hands of detractors and took attacks on the film (and her) far too personally.

"We were particularly surprised by reviews that suggested we portrayed the residents of Buttershaw unfairly," reveals Sandy Lieberson. "The residents themselves felt the film reflected life as it was. Reviews claimed we portrayed 'the working class' unfairly. The truth was that most of the residents were unable to find work! Reviewers had no real idea what life on Buttershaw was like and the conditions people lived under."

The area along with large parts of Bradford has since been rejuvenated and redeveloped by successive councils and the city is on it's way to becoming one of Yorkshire's success stories.

Leeds and Bradford are often compared to each other due to their close proximity. In many aspects Leeds has the upper hand, interestingly when it comes to film locations, Bradford wins hands down. At the time of this book going to press the Bradford area is a whisker ahead of Sheffield as Yorkshire's No. 1 filmmaking location.

1988

A Chorus of Disapproval

The ladies of the cast have a great new performer

Director: Michael Winner

Producer: Michael Winner

Writers: Alan Ayckbourn, Michael Winner, from the play by Alan Ayckbourn

Production Company: Curzon Films

Year of Production: 1988 (Released 1989)

Where filmed: Scarborough, East Yorkshire during May, 1988.

Synopsis: Transferred by his company to Scarborough, timid widower Guy Jones joins the local amateur drama group to "have fun and meet friends". Soon he is conducting an affair with the director's repressed wife and enjoying a fling with a leggy married swinger.

Credited cast: Anthony Hopkins (Dafydd Ap Llewellyn), Jeremy Irons (Guy Jones), Prunella Scales (Hannah Ap Llewellyn), Jenny Seagrove (Fay Hubbard), Gareth Hunt (Ian Hubbard), Richard Briers (Ted Washbrook), Barbara Ferris (Enid Washbrook), Patsy Kensit (Linda Washbrook), Lionel Jeffries (Jarvis Huntley-Pike), Sylvia Syms (Rebecca Huntley-Pike), Alexandra Pigg (Bridget Baines), Pete Lee-Wilson (Crispin Usher).

No murder. No mayhem. Just tea room tussles.

One of Hollywood's favourite directors of macho posturing was hard at work. But the man famed for his tough-talking, blood-spattered thrillers and revenge westerns starring the likes of Brando, Bronson and Lancaster wasn't calling "action" on death and destruction. Instead Michael Winner was concentrating on small-town life, petty squabbles and a genteel scene of discord with an underbelly of earthy humour. Outside the weather was blowing a gale. This was far from the slums of Los Angeles or New York – the milieu most familiar to those accustomed to Winner's oeuvre. Instead, in a Victorian hotel dining room overlooking the North Sea, an ill-at-ease trio – Prunella Scales, Irons and Jenny Seagrove – endured an awkward meeting over tea

and cakes while the darkening skies threatened even more rain and blustery winds. Scarborough out of season was bleak, cold and not particularly welcoming. It showed on the actors' faces. For Jeremy Irons, engaged in his own personal battle of wills with a famously autocratic director over the delivery of a scene, the sound of a clicking camera shutter, from a photographer not connected with the film, was the last straw. Winner responded with all the taciturn style for which he is notorious. "Off!" he commanded, and the errant snapper was banished from the set.

The photographer, innocently believing he was capturing the mood of a rehearsal, had inadvertently strayed into a crowd scene. Irons complained. Winner spoke. Exit

one photographer, loudly protesting. When he had the temerity to return – like the Mountie, he was aiming to get his man or, in this case, his picture – Winner's response was priceless. "Have I to get you carried off?" The photographer retreated, none too happy. Order was restored. The film continued.

The scene continued until it was, as movie types say, "in the can". Winner, a veteran of more than 20 films in England, Europe and the United States, kept plugging away until he got what he wanted. Inside the Castle Community Centre in East Sandgate, he ruminated on the making of motion pictures, the vagaries of acting and the volatile nature of the men and women who perform for a living.

"What you need in the movie business above all else, my darling, is patience," smiled Winner, drawing on a cigar, "And I've got it. You are talking about a scene that could have been ruined by the clicking of a camera. Let me tell you a story. When I was making *The Big Sleep*, Barry Norman and a TV crew waited all day outside Knebworth House for Robert Mitchum. Bob came out eventually, Barry went up and introduced himself and Bob said 'Get lost!'. It's just that some actors don't want to break off and re-concentrate. It's totally understandable. I'm a fast worker who makes quick, positive decisions without jeopardising quality. I also have a reputation for never being over budget or over schedule. Touch wood, we are going okay with this one."

Big Bob Mitchum would have been a tad out of place in Scarborough. Yet while the burly, boozy brawler wasn't

around, another actor who had gained a well-earned reputation as a hell-raiser was in the cast as a screaming despot: Anthony Hopkins. The Welshman, soon to achieve overnight stardom after three decades in the industry with *The Silence of the Lambs*, came fresh from a triumphant season with the National Theatre. Jeremy Irons, another serious player, arrived in Scarborough after his own success at the Royal Shakespeare Theatre.

Hopkins, still glowing from the reviews he received for *King Lear and Antony* and *Cleopatra*, was all geared up to play Dafydd Llewellyn, a Welsh solicitor directing a ham-fisted provincial version of *The Beggar's Opera*. He liked the project, appreciated the change of pace and spoke highly of Winner. "When you get a good writer like Ayckbourn you can ride on the lines. But never analyse. If you start looking for meanings, you are dead. Fortunately, Winner just shoots it. He's brisk, and I like his speed."

Between them Hopkins and Irons would lead the cast of a sparkling comedy by Alan Ayckbourn which won all the major awards when it premiered at the National in 1985. A transfer to the commercial West End stage followed, and finally the film version set up shop in Scarborough. It was the first of his plays - an acerbic look at small-town morals - that the acclaimed and prolific Ayckbourn had allowed to be filmed. Initially Winner seemed an odd choice as the man with the metaphorical megaphone, yet *A Chorus of Disapproval* actually took him back to the observant British comedies of the '60s with which he had made his

left: The Chorus ensemble: left to right – Lionel Jeffries, Prunella Scales, Alexandra Pigg, Richard Briers and Patsy Kensit.

above: A vision at the window. Could anyone resist the charms of Jenny Seagrove?

reputation. Years before 1972's *Death Wish*, Winner had lensed *The Jokers*, *I'll Never Forget What's'is name* and *The System*, the latter another seaside-set story. "This is the first film I've made in years where all the cast are alive at the end," laughed Winner. "I slipped into action films when I bought a western script in 1968. When I got that the American majors said I couldn't do a western - I was a comedy director. Now they say I'm an action director!"

Ayckbourn himself was rarely, if ever, on the set, preferring to work at his desk within the Stephen Joseph Theatre. One day he drove, quite accidentally, into the midst of an exterior scene while en-route to collect his cat from a cattery. Yet, aside from an early period of collaboration with Winner - who served as director, producer, co-writer and editor, the latter under the nom-de-plume Arnold Crust - the playwright's involvement was marginal.

"Michael is a nice man. Very honest. Sort of Yorkshire in the sense that he doesn't pussyfoot around. He just says it with sometimes brutal frankness. It's an extraordinary business being a film director. In the theatre a director can go more gently. In films everything is time; everything is money. If it is anything it is now Michael Winner's play, not mine. I worked on the screenplay with Michael, and I had a lot of casting approval. But it is the director who makes a decision when it is being shot. Although I am here if he wants me, my work was done before filming started. It's an odd feeling because *A Chorus of Disapproval* started its life here in Scarborough. I can remember the first read-through. Now it has come home again in a different guise with a multi-star cast. Obviously I will go along to see the finished product but I don't see any point in being involved in between. They would feel a bit inhibited if the guy who put it on first time was hanging around making quiet sighs. One feels rather remote. It's like someone else driving your car."

Winner had his own thoughts on Ayckbourn, who he first discovered in the late 1960s when he took Burt Lancaster to see one of his plays. When he saw *A Chorus of Disapproval* he felt at once that it would make the perfect transition from stage to screen. "Alan's much more than the writer on this," stressed Winner. "He's helped in every stage of the production, casting, location hunting, in every way. That's as it should be. No point in buying an Ayckbourn play and turning it into something else."

1990

Robin Hood: Prince of Thieves

For the good of all men, and the love of one woman, he fought to uphold justice by breaking the law

Director: Kevin Reynolds

Producers: Pen Densham, Richard Barton Lewis, John Watson

Writers: Pen Densham, John Watson

Production Company: Warner Bros. Pictures

Year of Production: 1990 (Released July 19 1991)

Where filmed: Aysgarth Falls and Hardraw Force, North Yorkshire during 1990.

Synopsis: Robin Hood returns from the Crusades to find his father murdered and his home in ruins. He vows to seek revenge on the evil Sheriff of Nottingham and rallies local peasants, hiding in Sherwood Forest, to assist him in his fight for justice.

Credited cast: Kevin Costner (Robin of Locksley), Morgan Freeman (Azeem), Mary Elizabeth Mastrantonio (Marian Dubois), Christian Slater (Will Scarlett), Alan Rickman (Sheriff of Nottingham), Micheal McShane (Friar Tuck), Brian Blessed (Lord Locksley), Michael Wincott (Guy of Gisborne), Nick Brimble (Little John), Daniel Peacock (David of Doncaster), Walter Sparrow (Duncan), Harold Innocent (Bishop of Hereford), Jack Wild (Much the Miller's Son), Geraldine McEwan (Mortianna) and Sean Connery as Richard the Lionheart.

Far away from home, and a stranger in a strange land, a noble Moor gazes upon a scene of verdant, tranquil beauty. It is in stark contrast to the land of his birth and, in open-mouthed wonder, he gives voice to his thoughts: "In my dreams alone have I imagined such a place."

What follows is an inventive telling of the story of Robin Hood, here transformed into a quasi western tailored to the talents and '90s appeal of Kevin Costner, fresh from the Oscar-winning epic that was *Dances with Wolves*. His companion, an unlikely Saracen, is Morgan Freeman. Sitting quietly on a horse with Robin's elderly, blind servant, he watches events unfold. Costner's Robin Hood is soon in the thick of combat with Little John, self-styled "best man of the woods", for the freedom to cross a series of waterfalls.

The scene was shot in the winter of 1990. Costner, the hero, gamely plunged into the icy waters of Aysgarth Falls while his audience, a jeering band of miscreants, shouted their glee from the banks. The setpiece sequence set up the mood of the rest of the movie - a medieval romp.

Robin Hood: Prince of Thieves, a $68 million blockbuster, was shot all over the UK with key scenes filmed at Hadrian's Wall in Northumberland, at Hardraw Force near Hawes in Upper Wensleydale and at nearby Aysgarth Falls. Almost 20 years later Morgan Freeman remembered his flying visit to Yorkshire with crystal clarity. "I've been in your neighbourhood," said a voice on the other end of a telephone line somewhere in New York. "We had to spend a lot of time travelling through a lot of England looking for greenery. We couldn't use Sherwood

title page: Director Kevin Reynolds with Kevin Costner and Morgan Freeman. North Yorkshire, 1990.

previous page: "In my dreams alone have I imagined such a place." Morgan Freeman wasn't the first foreigner to be charmed by the beauty of Aysgarth Falls.

above: Morgan Freeman as the Saracen, Azeem.

Forest – it was brown! From Hadrian's Wall all the way back down to Aysgarth Falls it was gorgeous. What do I remember? It was winter and it was cold, cold, cold! Thankfully I had a very nice, warm, comfortable costume to wear."

Director Kevin Reynolds took his cast on a game of geographical leap-frog through glorious English settings. Arriving at Dover following a four-month journey from the Middle East, Locksley kisses the Sussex shingle and heads off on foot to his father's castle via Hadrian's Wall and the limestone cliffs of the broad acres. In Hollywood, nothing is sacred. Sherwood Forest is a world of lush greenery and unexpected oases of sparkling, fast-flowing rivers and picturesque waterfalls that tumble over broad limestone steps. It is there that an out-of-shape Robin Hood – his double chin was blamed on too much ale and Yorkshire Pudding – takes on the man who will become his good friend, Little John. Except, of course, that Pen Densham's peculiar screenplay rewrote Robin as the Lone Ranger with Freeman as a scimitar-wielding Tonto. "It would be terrible if I was not capable of doing the action," said a defensive Costner from the location. "The fact is, I love firing arrows, riding horses, swinging from trees and getting involved in fights. But if I thought it was going to be very dangerous, then it would be crazy to go ahead because too much is sitting on this film."

The scene where Robin bathes in the icy cascade of a waterfall was filmed at Hardraw Force, at 100 feet the highest unbroken waterfall in the UK, though for insurance reasons, because of the force of the water, Costner could not bare his backside for the cameras. Instead a body double braved the blast of the water. It is his buttocks gleaming in a veil of white spray as Maid Marian watches in wide-eyed appreciation.

The film came at a point in Freeman's career when he was flying. In 1987, just shy of his 50th birthday, he had landed a best supporting actor Oscar nomination for playing a vicious pimp in *Street Smart*. Two years later he landed the role of black chauffeur Hoke Colburn in *Driving Miss Daisy*. Another Oscar nomination followed – this one for best actor. In 1991 he was hand-picked by Clint Eastwood to co-star in *Unforgiven*. Three years later there came *The Shawshank Redemption* and another best actor Oscar nod. Not a bad tally considering he was 49 before stardom beckoned. He finally won in 2005 for *Million Dollar Baby* – his second collaboration

with Eastwood – Freeman was seemingly cast as Azeem because he epitomises dignity and integrity. He gets to play detectives, scientists, generals and presidents. In *Bruce Almighty* he was God – the ultimate role. Even his bad guys – like his bank robber in 1998's *Hard Rain* – seem to have honour at their core. "That's the perception – that I have this wisdom, this gravitas, this dignity. I don't know what it is that infuses the roles that I do. So I'm pretty much stuck with it. And, of course, who did they choose to play God?" he laughed.

above: Morgan Freeman: "What do I remember? It was winter and it was cold, cold, cold!"
Yorkshire cold? surely not!

1991

Emily Brontë's Wuthering Heights

Emily Brontë's immortal classic of love and vengeance on the Yorkshire moors

Director: Peter Kosminsky

Producer: Mary Selway

Writer: Anne Devlin, based on the novel by Emily Brontë

Production Company: Paramount Pictures

Year of Production: 1991 (Released October 16 1992)

Where filmed: Grassington, Aysgarth Falls and Boss Moor, Hetton, North Yorkshire; Shibden Hall, Halifax, and East Riddlesden Hall, Keighley, West Yorkshire between September and October, 1991.

Synopsis: Denied his true love, embittered Heathcliff vows vengeance on the family that prevented his happiness.

Credited cast: Juliette Binoche (Cathy/Catherine), Ralph Fiennes (Heathcliff), Janet McTeer (Ellen Dean), Sophie Ward (Isabella Linton), Simon Shepherd (Edgar Linton), Jeremy Northam (Hindley Earnshaw), Jason Riddington (Hareton Earnshaw), Simon Ward (Mr. Linton), Robert Demeger (Joseph), Paul Geoffrey (Mr. Lockwood), John Woodvine (Thomas Earnshaw), Jennifer Daniel (Mrs. Linton), Janine Wood (Frances Earnshaw), Jonathan Firth (Linton Heathcliff), Jon Howard (Young Heathcliff), Jessica Hennell (Young Cathy), Steven Slarke (Hindley Earnshaw, 16), Trevor Cooper (Doctor Kenneth), Rupert Holliday Evans (Vicar), Dick Sullivan (Parson), Sean Bowden (Young Hareton) and Sinéad O'Connor as Emily Brontë.

"First I found the place. I wondered who had lived there, what their lives were like. Something whispered to my mind, and I began to write. My pen creates stories of a world that might have been - a world of my imagining. And here is one I am going to tell. But take care not to smile at any part of it…" - opening narration

A lone, cowled figure wends its way across a bleak and desolate moor. In the distance, silhouetted starkly against the stark horizon, two massive stones point like fingers towards the darkening sky. They stand like silent witnesses to the drama that is about to unfold – a dreadful saga of hatred, revenge and obsessive love that continued through life to death and beyond. The figure is revealed as Emily Brontë, and she climbs a lonely, rutted path to an imposing

gothic house high on a windswept scar. It is derelict and deserted. Gazing around its decaying majesty, she begins to imagine what might have been…

Beginning a modern interpretation of Emily Brontë's epic story of love and loss by introducing the author herself is about as audacious as filmmaking can get. Yet *Emily Brontë's Wuthering Heights* challenged many established conventions, not least in daring to tackle the entirety of the novel (and its two interlinking storylines) and then by casting a French actress as the book's tempestuous heroine.

For Mary Selway, a revered casting director who had made the leap into film production, the opportunity to cut her teeth on a film adaptation of a literary behemoth was beyond

daunting. And always, lurking in the back of everyone's minds, was the classic William Wyler version of the story filmed in 1939. The star-studded cast included Merle Oberon and Laurence Olivier as Cathy and Heathcliff with other key roles filled by David Niven, Geraldine Fitzgerald and Flora Robson. Selway was bullish about what her new version, budgeted at $9 million, hoped to achieve.

"You had to really understand and admire the Olivier film, which I thought was absolutely wonderful, but it was so much of its time. The Olivier film was made in 1939. People do Shakespeare plays all the time. What's so different about film? The most daunting thing was to try and take Emily Brontë's book in its entirety and film it all. That proved the hardest thing of all because you are, in effect, telling two stories over a generation. If you hadn't done the whole book, which was a terrific challenge, then really you're left with the Heathcliff/Cathy love story, which is less than half the book. Then you are really up against the Oliver/Merle Oberon film, and then they have to be very untruthful to the book. The only thing Simon Bosanquet kept saying to me during the filming was 'We are not making the book. We are making a film'. You have to honour the book and honour the writer's intention of what she wanted to achieve in the book but make that in film terms. The story absolutely lends itself to a mini series – the size of it is so vast – but it needs the largeness of the screen filled with the Yorkshire moors. I'm glad we stuck with our decision."

The scope of the story meant that the screenplay, by Irish writer Anne Devlin, encompassed 27 turbulent years – from spring 1775 when the 12-year-old Heathcliff enters the Earnshaw household, until his death in 1802. And unlike the Olivier/Oberon version, this 1990s adaptation did not end with Cathy's death but followed the chronology of the book to include Cathy's daughter, Catherine Linton (also played by Binoche) growing to adulthood. Devlin also introduced an eerie prologue and epilogue in which the figure of Emily Brontë, played in an uncredited cameo by Irish singer Sinéad O'Connor, opens and closes the film.

Controversy dogged the production from the off. To direct the picture Selway selected Peter Kosminsky, an award-winning documentary-maker who had never before tackled a feature film. Then the filmmakers ditched Haworth for Grassington, near Skipton. The reason was that Haworth was too modern and would be too expensive to re-dress, such as removing TV aerials. Grassington, with its rolling landscape,

limestone pavement and bleak views, was deemed perfect. Unit publicist Sue D'Arcy said: "Haworth is fascinating but we couldn't possibly have filmed there. It is not as remote as when Emily Brontë was writing about it. You see pylons and pockets of population everywhere. Our chosen site is more authentic to the spirit of *Wuthering Heights*. We went over Yorkshire with a fine tooth comb but there was such a wonderful vista here, we felt there was nowhere else more perfect."

But arguably the most sacrilegious decision was the casting of French actress Juliette Binoche as Cathy, the elemental wild child of the heather. Kosminsky, and Selway, herself a casting director with 30 years' experience, saw, read and tested 200 British actresses but all were considered unsuitable.

"Cathy just isn't a modern part," asserts Kosminsky. "She's capricious and sexually manipulative. She flaunts her sexuality and she uses it. She's precocious and she's elemental. And she shines like a kind of beacon in this tiny, isolated moorland community of 200-odd years ago. She's the kind of character who comes along maybe once in ten generations in a place like that. But the British actresses I saw, especially the attractive ones, had a kind of cool, a kind of distance – possibly the result of having to fend off admirers. There was a sort of hauteur about them that was utterly inappropriate for the playing of Cathy. Some were great actresses. But they all had, as part of their persona, this kind of aloofness – an overlay of civilisation and style that they just couldn't strip away."

title page: Juliette Binoche and Jason Riddington on the moors above Grassington.

opposite title page: moody shot of the fake standing stones erected on Boss Moor, near Grassington.

opposite: The paraphernalia of filmmaking at Shibden Hall, Halifax.

next spread: Ralph Fiennes and Juliette Binoche by the River Ure.

He found his Cathy after spotting Juliette Binoche in an American TV movie – playing a prostitute. They met and initially Binoche baulked at conquering the accent. Kosminsky used all his charm to persuade her to accept. Eventually, after screen tests and a strenuous regime of voice coaching, Binoche took the role. Kosminsky was delighted and clung to his belief that his judgement had been vindicated – that Binoche was the only actress who encompassed the spirit of Cathy. "I don't think any French actor or actress has ever done a better job of eliminating his or her accent. Juliette was worth all the trouble. I'd always believed that capturing the emotional quality of Cathy was more important than the occasional slurred vowel."

Making his film debut alongside Binoche was 28-year-old Ralph Fiennes, a smoulderingly handsome actor of the same breed as Laurence Olivier and James Mason. "I didn't expect him to have the depth of understanding of the darkness of Heathcliff," says Selway. "He surprised us all." RADA-trained, Fiennes had enjoyed a rapid rise through the ranks of British theatre actors and had made his mark with the Royal Shakespeare Company. Prior to *Wuthering Heights* he had played TE Lawrence in *A Dangerous Man*. Immediately after he was cast as the monstrous Nazi Amon Goeth in *Schindler's List*. Interviewed during filming, Fiennes brushed off concerns about the rigours of filming and the limiting preconceptions adopted by some people about the character of Heathcliff. "Every job is tough, but I'm not going to be put off by any preconceived notions people may have about Heathcliff. It has to take on its own identity," he said.

Production began in late September, 1991. It was the beginning of a fevered 10-week schedule – five weeks of location work following by a further five weeks at Shepperton Studios. Unit base was set up at 70-room Broughton Hall near Skipton, which was "cast" in the film as Thrushcross Grange, home of Edgar and Isabella Linton. The house has been in the same family, the Tempests, since it was built in 1597. It was suggested to the filmmakers by Ralph Fiennes, who went to art school with the wife of the present owner, Roger. Artistic licence allowed Wuthering Heights itself to evolve from the remote farmhouse of the novel to a five-storey castellated mansion high on a scar and exposed to wind and driving rain.

The 80ft-high mock house was built at Yarnbury, a mile or so north of Grassington, from plaster, plywood and fibreglass. The production also installed *faux* graves and imported rocks and skeletal trees to add requisite gloom to the site. Enveloped in mist, the house looked every inch the home of a glowering brute. However locals soon began taking bets on whether the structure and its scaffolding would survive the 60 mph hour winds, lashing horizontal rain and sleet. An animal outhouse was converted into Gimmerton Chapel.

For Peter Kosminsky, the major challenge in filming *Wuthering Heights* was to make the movie a visual metaphor for the choice between head and heart - what he considered to be one of the central themes of the book.

"So you have, on the one hand, Wuthering Heights itself – an uncomfortable building on a hill, exposed to the elements, dark, partly disused, an architectural mish-mash of different styles and periods. It's a very elemental place, almost pagan. It's the place of the heart. And it's where Heathcliff, who's passion personified, lives. The Grange is completely different. It's big, bright and comfortable. It's sheltered in a valley, not windswept out on the moors. It's built to one architectural style. It's a renaissance, age-of-reason kind of place."

Kosminsky also filmed for a day at Shibden Hall, the 15th Century folk museum near Halifax, and at East Riddlesden Hall on the outskirts of Keighley. On the moors he found a limestone pavement. Wild open Boss Moor provided the site of the standing stones. And Aysgarth Falls (also a setting for *Robin Hood: Prince of Thieves*) provided the backdrop for Heathcliff and Cathy's declarations of love.

During their Yorkshire sojourn both Binoche and Fiennes would live in cottages rather than hotels to assist with their assimilation in Yorkshire ways. On an average day they would be picked up at 5.45am and would be in make-up by 6.30am. Filming would begin no later than 8am and might finish at 10.30pm. Fourteen and fifteen-hour days were not uncommon. Both stars allowed themselves to be subsumed in the atmosphere. Said Juliette Binoche: "When you go into the house, to the little room of Emily Brontë's there's a cemetery on one side and the moors on the other. It was as if I didn't need to understand the book because it was there – freedom on one side, reality on the other."

Wuthering Heights was the first production green-lit by Paramount Pictures newly revamped European division.

Rumour has it that the project was pitched as a "chick flick" geared towards the same female audience that had enjoyed the previous year's *Pretty Woman*. Mary Selway was always disappointed by it's lack of success at the box office.

"Paramount were looking for a love story to make and decided on *Wuthering Heights*. They knew and understood that the star of the film is Wuthering Heights. It's the title: everybody knows, in whatever country, when you see the words *Wuthering Heights* you know the type of film you're getting. They understood perfectly well: Wuthering Heights – England.

"Where the audience for the film lies is without question from kids up to 25/30, and mostly girls. Kids adore this film.

Emotionally, they absolutely love it. They come out crying. Everybody can understand it. It's dense but I don't think it's intellectual. That's where the audience is. The audience is the same in America. The audience that adored *Pretty Woman* is the same as here. I think most people would agree that it looks a lot more than nine million dollars on the screen. It looks really rich and big and good, and I'm very proud of that. It was marvellous to have filmed it in Yorkshire. Emotionally what it gave to Juliette and Ralph was terrific."

With so many films being released at the box office each week, just a few can succeed financially. For the filmmakers whose films fail it is a blow after all the years of hard work they have devoted to the project.

"Peter Kosminsky saw me in a Shakespeare play, in a very un-Heathcliff part, but decided he would like me to do a screen test for Heathcliff. Originally I was considered as possible casting for Edgar Linton. It's been quite a change for me because most of the roles I've played in the theatre have been 'honourable men' and I've always been quite keen to keep away from the sort of 'Edwardian collar' type of role. The Edgar Linton perception of me was something I was expecting. I was surprised and delighted that it worked out another way.

"Most of my work had been in the theatre up until I got this part, so working with the medium of a camera was completely different. It's a whole new set of problems to get your mind around. In the theatre you rehearse for six or seven weeks and then you play the whole thing in its entirety for two or three hours every night. In this it was new to me to play things in the wrong order and have to have a sense of continuity in where you come from and where you're going to. To keep that level of concentration up for ten weeks was just a whole new ball game.

"We were on location for five weeks. On the whole we had a good mix of weather. We were blessed with a few very bright, very sunny days. I loved it when the weather was really bad. I thought that was more in keeping with the spirit of the book – blustery, dark and cold days.

"The emotional range of the part was more daunting than anything else. It was a part and book that everyone knows and has their own expectations of. I didn't know the book that well and the Olivier film hadn't played a big part in my cinematic education. When I read the book I liked Heathcliff and I liked the fact that often I was unsympathetic towards him. I wanted to be as uncompromising as possible in being as true to Emily Brontë as I understood her creation.

"I took the decision with the make-up designer that Heathcliff probably shaved once every three days and therefore had continual stubble on his face. I also had dirty hair and dirty cuffs. I don't think he has great sartorial priorities. I didn't find the accent difficult. I had to find that happy medium where the Yorkshire was implied but not so strong that it would create a problem for Juliette. If I had a very strong Yorkshire accent against the accent that Juliette had then it would have looked incongruous.

"The role as it was written in this script, where Heathcliff goes on living after Cathy's death, was wonderful for any actor to play: the journey from the underdog at the beginning right through to this man in his late '30s harbouring this bitter canker of hatred and resentment. It gives you a lot of imaginative fuel to carry on playing the latter stages. I enjoyed the challenge of playing a character as black and as dark as Heathcliff – you have to bring your own darkness to it. I'd like to have gone even further with him. Once you've played a character like that, part of it lies dormant in you for the rest of your life."

- Ralph Fiennes

previous spread: Juliette Binoche and Ralph Fiennes shot at Shibden Hall, Halifax.

above: Ralph Fiennes as Heathcliff in Broughton Hall.

With DVD, airlines, ferries, hotels, TV and download sales this production of *Wuthering Heights* should have performed a lot better. Paramount Pictures has a world-wide distribution network and television output deals with all the world's leading broadcasters.

Timothy Dalton and Anna Calder-Marshall in the 1970 version of the film.

Whither Wuthering Heights?

"Sam Goldwyn's classic 1939 version of Wuthering Heights *got no closer to the bleak wilderness of Yorkshire than sunny Conejo Hills, California. The film was entirely shot on cowboy star Joel McCrea's 450-acre hillside range 40 miles outside Los Angeles. A reconstruction of the Earnshaw family's Yorkshire farmhouse was built there and movie lore has it that tumbleweed was dyed purple in an attempt to recreate the look of moorland heather.*

Thirty years later American International Pictures announced a $3 million remake with 23-year-old Timothy Dalton as Heathcliff and 22-year-old Anna Calder-Marshall as Cathy. "I've found Catherine's character absorbing, although I doubt we would get on together were we to meet in real life," said the young actress. "There is something selfish about her."

Like Mary Selway and Peter Kosminsky, director Robert Fuest rejected Haworth as a viable location because it was spoiled by TV aerials, telephone wires and pylons. What's more, the sky above the village was too frequently criss-crossed with the vapour trails of jet aircraft to lend an authentic traditional feel.

"We are anxious that the film should remain faithful to the novel," said Fuest as he revealed that filming would be switched from Haworth to Ilkley, Otley and Bolton Abbey. "We've heard that some Haworth people have been really upset about this; we scouted for sites there, but always there was some difficulty which would have marred the picture, like housing estates in the distance or damn pylons. It's a shame. If anyone in the Yorkshire Electricity service will chop down the pylons 300 yards on either side of Haworth we might just get away with filming there."

Redshaw Farm, near Blubberhouses on the outskirts of Harrogate, doubled for Wuthering Heights while 17th Century Weston Hall, near Otley, served as Thrushcross Grange. A cemetery was custom-built on the moors to accommodate Catherine's grave. One American observer described the locale as "like Boot Hill in Yorkshire". The film began shooting in April, 1970.

The film's screenwriter Patrick Tilley added: "In our production we are aiming at a film about people living a very hard, isolated, austere life in a wild Yorkshire moorland landscape. They are people who blend into that landscape. They are the product of a harsh environment. We have to remember life was tough, brutish and short. It was a time when children were still being hanged for stealing crusts of bread and when, for equally trivial and inhuman reasons, adults were being strung up from gibbets and left to rot."

American International was so confident of the film's success that it planned a similar production, also to be shot in the West Riding, on the lives of the Brontë sisters. Dramatist Christopher Fry wrote a script that was to have been filmed with Glenda Jackson as Charlotte, Mia Farrow as Emily and Hayley Mills as the fragile Anne. Branwell was to have been portrayed by John Hurt. "It will definitely be made in Yorkshire," said an enthusiastic AIP spokesman in May 1971. Alas, the less than stupendous box office takings for Wuthering Heights *effectively scuppered what could have been the definitive portrait of the Brontë family. "*

1995

Brassed Off

A comedy that hits all the right notes

Director: Mark Herman

Producer: Steve Abbott

Writer: Mark Herman

Production Company: Channel Four Films/Miramax Films/Prominent Features Inc.

Year of Production: 1995 (Released November 1996)

Where filmed: Piece Hall, Halifax and the National Coal Mining Museum, Wakefield, West Yorkshire; and Grimethorpe, Barnsley, Doncaster and Rotherham, South Yorkshire between October and December, 1995.

Synopsis: As their colliery faces closure, coalminers in a small Northern town look to their brass band as the only positive focus for their lives.

Credited cast: Pete Postlethwaite (Danny), Tara Fitzgerald (Gloria), Ewan McGregor (Andy), Stephen Tompkinson (Phil), Jim Carter (Harry), Philip Jackson (Jim), Peter Martin (Ernie), Sue Johnston (Vera), Mary Healey (Ida), Melanie Hill (Sandra), Lill Roughley (Rita), Peter Gunn (Simmo), Stephen Moore (McKenzie), Kenneth Colley (Greasley), Olga Grahame (Mrs. Foggan), Toni Galacki (Gary), Sky Ingram (Kylie), Luke McGann (Shane), Christopher Tetlow (Craig), Bernard Wrigley (Chapman), Ken Kitson (Heavy 1), Adrian Hood (Heavy 2), Sally Adams (Ward Sister), Tubby Andrews (Bus Driver), Katherine Dow Blyton (Nurse), Adam Fogerty (Miner), Vanessa Knox-Mawer (Mother 2), Sally Anne Matthews (Waitress), Jacqueline Naylor (Mother 1), Bob Rodgers (Halifax Judge), Max Smith (Nightwatchman), Ronnie Stevens (Albert Hall Judge), Peter Wallis (Elderly Man) and the Grimethorpe Colliery Band.

November, 1995.

It is a freezing day. A chill winter wind whips along Grimethorpe's main street where, against a backdrop of thunderous traffic and noisy children, the cast and crew of *Brassed Off* labour to complete a pivotal scene. Inside an old shop, re-fitted by the film's designers to become In Cod We Trust, the town chip shop of fictional Grimley, actors Ewan McGregor and Tara Fitzgerald shoot a climactic confrontation.

He is Andy, a pessimistic young miner and a member of Grimley's brass band. She is Gloria, his girlfriend and fellow bandsman, the local lass who left the restrictive confines of Grimley for London and returned with a new look, a new accent and a new job. But Andy has been betrayed. Like the rest of Grimley he is waiting for the axe to fall on pit which feeds, clothes and sustains the close-knit community. Then he discovers Gloria is working for the Coal Board.

McGregor, fresh from completing a supporting role opposite Gwyneth Paltrow in *Emma*, is clad in a scruffy green jumper, sleeves rolled up, revealing the tattoos on his arms. He is unshaven, and wears an earring. Fitzgerald, the husky voiced star of *Sirens* and TV's *The Camomile Lawn*, wears a light blue woollen top, black trousers and high, patent leather black boots. Her hands are adorned with silver rings. Behind them, extras ready themselves to tuck into warmed-up plates of fish and chips. A set decorator sprays condensation onto the shop windows. Writer/director Mark Herman calls "action".

title page: Making music: Ewan McGregor and Tara Fitzgerald as Andy and Gloria.

previous: Ewan McGregor, Jim Carter, Peter Martin, Stephen Tomkinson and Phil Jackson covered in 'make-up' coal dust.

above: Bradford-born producer Steve Abbott on location. "There'll be a vacuum left behind us when this circus leaves town. If you've got a conscience, those aspects are very difficult."

opposite: Writer / director Mark Herman directs Pete Postlethwaite, playing conductor Danny Ormondroyd, in a scene set in the Piece Hall, Halifax.

Later during a break in filming, McGregor says: "I thought the message was very important and that people ought to know that the pit closures didn't just happen in 1984 – they've been closing them ever since. It's become easy for us to say 'Oh, another pit's gone', it's desperate; you're not just sacking people, you're destroying communities."

Fitzgerald agrees: "We're very cosy and safe down south. As an intellectual idea it's horrific, but it stays that. It's one thing to see it on the news or read about, but when you actually witness the physical effect of it, it really bangs it home."

The remains of Hatfield Colliery doubles as Grimley Pit. Just seven months elapsed between the closure of the real colliery and the site being levelled. Today it is a wasteland, a barren moonscape where occasional pieces of wrecked pit machinery jut from the ground, pointing disconsolately towards the azure sky.

"Someone said a few weeks ago that it's too late to be making this film," says 40-year-old Herman, "but it's exactly the right time because we are now seeing the devastating effects of the pit closures. Whether the pit closures were economically right is not the point. It's the social things that have gone wrong that are important. People were just not taken into account. That fear was already there back in the 1980s; now it's been confirmed."

Herman, a supporter of the miners' 1984 strike, along with his friend and producer Steve Abbott, had long harboured

ambitions to encapsulate the plight of the coal industry on film. The problem was finding a peg on which to hang it. He found his peg in a traditional colliery brass band, but realised such a subject did not have the commercial capability to attract an audience on its own. Instead, he used the story of the band struggling to play on against overwhelming odds as an allegory for the local community fighting to survive as its livelihood is swept away.

"The script has universal appeal, even to the Americans," says Abbott. "Over there, there have been disadvantaged communities. Look at Pittsburgh and Detroit. The hearts of the communities have been ripped out. Half of our backing is coming from US distributor Miramax, and clearly their hope is that they will be able to tap into that emotion and

that the film will appeal to the blue collar audiences in the States."

Busy British character actor Pete Postlethwaite plays Danny, leader of Grimley Colliery Band. *Ballykissangel* star Stephen Tompkinson, making his film debut, plays his son, Phil. Both men are fired up about the film. Tompkinson describes the script as "a gift, covered in gold and studded with diamonds. It shows what awful, criminal acts went on, and what devastation can be caused by the stroke of a pen. Punches are not being pulled on this." Postlethwaite calls it "a story that must be told".

"This story was written for the people of the urban areas of England which have been completely raped by the powers

that be over the last 16 years," says Postlethwaite. "My feelings are not very far away from what the basis of the story is, which is that it's not fair to treat a community like this. Not only does it strike an emotional chord with me, but it strikes a very angry chord. When people ask me why I'm not in Hollywood making another film like *The Usual Suspects*, it's because I'd much rather be doing something like this."

Brassed Off was shot on location across the North, including Halifax's Piece Hall, Doncaster and the pit villages of South Yorkshire. In Grimethorpe, Herman, Abbott and the actors initially faced suspicion from locals who, after a TV documentary had misrepresented the town, the pit and its miners, feared the film would be a hatchet job. That resentment was dispelled when first the authentic Grimethorpe Colliery Band, and then many of the townspeople themselves, were recruited for supporting roles in the film. The movie, a temporary visitor, also brought its own permanence to the town by completely revamping an upstairs room at The Grimethorpe, the main pub, and turning it into Gloria's cheap but cheerful bedsit. Twelve months on, the room remains in use.

"What's most frustrating is that ours is a fictional film but, if it can be paralleled with Grimethorpe, then the community is the star if our film," says Abbott. "You can't say that to people without sounding patronising or as if you are using them. I always feel like there's this double-edged sword, that we are providing employment and putting money into the community but equally it's not money that's necessarily going to stay. There'll be a vacuum left behind us when this circus leaves town. If you've got a conscience, those aspects are very difficult."

Perhaps the final word should go to the people whose lives are mirrored by the movie. Former miner Gary Smith, now licensee of The Grimethorpe, wants only two things from the picture: honesty and integrity. "Grimethorpe Colliery, and the band, were well respected. The band was that good we didn't class them as workers, we classed them as ambassadors," he says with pride. "They must have prestige when the American president can ask them to play in the White House for him and his dignitaries. I hope the film will be a success, but mostly I want it to show us in a good light. We've been knocked enough."

opposite: The camaraderie between the central cast is evident from this candid shot of McGregor, Fitzgerald and Postlethwaite. Everyone bought into the concept. "When people ask me why I'm not in Hollywood, it's because I'd much rather be doing something like this," said Oscar nominee Postlethwaite.

above: Phil (Stephen Tompkinson) increasingly desperate attempt to earn more money as the children's performer Mr Chuckles.

1996

Fairytale: A True Story

Believe

Director: Charles Sturridge

Producers: Windy Finerman, Bruce Davey

Writer: Ernie Contreras

Production Company: Icon Entertainment International

Year of Production: 1996 (Released February 13 1998)

Where filmed: Ramsgill, Kilnsey, Allerton Park, North Yorkshire; Keighley Railway Station, West Yorkshire between May and June, 1996.

Synopsis: Cousins Elsie and Frances cause a worldwide sensation when they claim to have photographed fairies at a stream close to their Yorkshire home. Soon a controversy is raging over their pictures: are they real or an elaborate hoax?

Credited cast: Harvey Keitel (Harry Houdini), Peter O'Toole (Sir Arthur Conan Doyle), Paul McGann (Arthur Wright), Phoebe Nicholls (Polly Wright), Florence Hoath (Elsie Wright), Elizabeth Earl (Frances Griffiths), Bob Peck (Harry Briggs), Bill Nighy (Edward Gardner), Tim McInnerny (John Ferret), Peter Mullan (Sergeant Farmer), Don Henderson (Sydney Chalker), Willie Ross (Old Print Worker), David Calder (Harold Snelling), Anna Chancellor (Peter Pan), Benjamin Whitrow (Mr. Binley), and Mel Gibson as Frances's Father.

Extras: Jack Allen, Sarah Austin, Claire Bannister, Ian Bannister, Richard Beckett, Jason McCuish, Christopher Morend, Rachel Studholme, Sabrina Walton.

The story of the Cottingley fairies is the stuff of legend. In 1917, while the Great War was raging in Europe, two little girls, working with a borrowed camera, claimed to have captured fairies on film. Their story was a simple one. The end terrace house they shared in Cottingley, on the outskirts of Bradford, looked out onto a beck which, according to the girls, was home to an array of fairies and other supernatural creatures. Over time they produced a number of photographs, all of them showing the girls in contact with fairies. The fact that the two girls were just 15 and nine was astonishing. It caused a sensation.

To a land seared by the daily scourge of warfare, the prospect of fantastical creatures existing in the modern world was cause for celebration – and more than a hint of cynicism. Some bought wholeheartedly into the girls' story, content to accept their photographs as evidence that fairies were indeed real and that they could (and did) live happily near the doorsteps of Man. Among them was Sir Arthur Conan Doyle, creator of Sherlock Holmes and, since the death of his son in France, a committed believer in spirituality. Fairies were merely an extension of his beliefs in 'the other side'.

For Elsie Wright and Florence Griffiths, such patronage was astonishing. Their controversial photographs – shot on glass negatives with a Midg quarter plate camera – were the subject of mighty debate. Were they faked? If so, how? And how could two young girls with no knowledge of camera trickery be able to fool the world's experts? Such was the

title page: Portrait of a character actor:
Bob Peck as Harry Briggs.

previous page: Charles Sturridge with actor Paul McGann
on Keighley Station.

above: No small detail goes unnoticed. A costume assistant
makes sure a hat is worn correctly for the period.

opposite: Phoebe Nicholls as Polly Wright.
Bob Peck as Briggs. Charles Sturridge and
cinematographer Mick Coulter.

premise behind *Fairytale: A True Story*. Almost 80 years later, in the spring of 1996, the film came to Yorkshire.

Perhaps the biggest mystery surrounding the Cottingley Fairies was why no-one had bothered to turn the story into a film until the twilight of the 20th century. A quintessentially English tale involving Sir Arthur Conan Doyle and Harry Houdini, the story had begged for the big screen treatment for eight decades. It inspired documentaries and television plays but it took the support of American producers Wendy Finerman and Bruce Davey, and '90s superstar Mel Gibson, to turn the myth into movie reality.

For their £9 million period fantasy, originally known as *One Golden Afternoon*, hatpins and fake paper fairies gave way to digital effects and heavyweight stars, to wit Harvey Keitel as Houdini and Peter O'Toole, who played Conan Doyle. Still, it seemed an unlikely story for Hollywood to tackle. Over the previous 79 years the story of how Elsie and Frances saw and photographed fairies dancing and frolicking in a leafy dell had captivated millions. The pictures were adjudged authentic by Kodak and completely fooled Sir Arthur Conan Doyle, who first published them in *The Strand* magazine and then wrote a book, *The Coming of the Fairies*, about the girls' experiences. More than 60 years later the-then Elsie Hill admitted that the gossamer-winged sprites were really elaborately-drawn cardboard cut-outs, created as an excuse to escape a scolding when Frances got her clothes wet in the dell's beck. But during the fairy myth heyday of the 1920s, the girls stuck to their story. It stimulated a fierce and often bitter debate between dismissive sceptics and devout believers which continues to this day.

Even the actors were divided. In his trailer near the old railway station in Keighley, which had been dressed to resemble Bradford Station circa 1917, Paul McGann admitted he was not convinced by the famous, fuzzy, glass-plate images. In the film McGann played Arthur Wright, father of Elsie and the amateur photographer whose camera captured those remarkable images. Said McGann: "Arthur developed the plates, but he remained highly sceptical. Once the thing snowballed he got carried along by it. Looking at the photographs now, it's hard to believe that anyone got taken in by them because they are so obviously faked. However, one of the plates, the Fairy Bower, is the weird one. It's spooky, because it looks distinct from the others. It looks *real*."

Bill Nighy, on the other hand, was a believer. He played the theosophist Edward Gardner who passed the glass plates onto Sir Arthur Conan Doyle. Gardner was the national secretary of the Theosophical Society which claimed that fairies worked inside the stems of flowers, tinted petals and gave a warm, green colour to the leaves. They were visible only when they were relaxing. "The girls thought Gardner was the only one who truly believed in the fairies," revealed Nighy. "He believed they would only see fairies together, because between them they created an etheric field which allowed the fairies to metabolise subtle amounts of ectoplasm into their bodies, thus making them visible and allowing the girls to capture them on film. Gardner spent a lifetime in a sceptical world, but he was a true believer. He was well-used to being dismissed and he knew the world's view was that he was a laughable figure, but in his own circles he was a very eminent man."

The real Cottingley Beck still exists but it lacked the requisite magical beauty for a feature film. Writer/director Charles Sturridge found another location near the village of Ramsgill, in North Yorkshire. "It's a beautiful place. We filmed in a bluebell wood, with a waterfall, by a brook, where the girls take me to show me the fairies," added Nighy. "They tell me to hide behind a tree while they herd the fairies back my way. Mr. Gardner gets very, very excited because, if he actually sees a fairy, all his life's work will be vindicated. I'm now a firm believer in fairies. I was on the fence before but now I'm convinced."

On the railway platform – once used by John Schlesinger for *Yanks* – Charles Sturridge shot a number of scenes involving McGann, Nighy, and fellow actors Phoebe Nicholls, Bob Peck and Florence Hoath and Elizabeth Earl playing Elsie and Frances. In one, Arthur bade farewell to his daughter and niece as they headed off to London for a meeting with Conan Doyle while Briggs, his incredulous employer (Leeds-born Peck) looked on. In another, his wife Polly (Nicholls) persuaded Gardner to take the girls' pictures to London.

A quiet, intense and disciplined figure, Sturridge, the filmmaker behind 1981's TV spectacular *Brideshead Revisited* (partly filmed at Castle Howard), ably manipulated the crowds of extras in WWI garb. After each take he would scrutinise the fresh footage on a video monitor with Michael Coulter, the Oscar-nominated cinematographer who made *Sense and Sensibility* and *Four Weddings and a Funeral*. Off camera, a group of young men in military uniform, replete with rifle and pack, sat around waiting for their cue. The 100-plus extras had been on call for more than eight hours. Among them was a group of amputees from the Chapel Allerton Prosthetic Centre, in Leeds, hired to play wounded Tommies fresh from the Western Front. Around them the giveaway signs of modern-day life had been disguised. A custom-built newspaper stand features authentic picture postcards and realistic billboards. 'Red Baron Raids Again', announced one.

Despite rumours to the contrary neither Harvey Keitel nor Peter O'Toole was in Keighley for the location filming. All their scenes would later be shot in London or at Pinewood Studios. The two stars enjoyed pivotal roles in the movie. Houdini and Doyle were friends who famously fell out over the authenticity of the pictures. The escapologist was a confirmed sceptic while the writer was a devout spiritualist.

It fell to veteran costume designer Shirley Russell to dress the performers in the film. She scoured costume houses for the right look, and based the girls' clothes on the white dresses worn by Elsie and Frances in their photographs. Keitel and O'Toole were, however, rather more tricky. "Harvey said he wanted this big black hat he'd seen in some old footage of Houdini. I'm having it made, but there's nowhere in the film where he can wear it!" she laughed. "Conan Doyle was a big, ordinary man, and we've got a very flamboyant, rather languid, elegant, over-the-top actor who doesn't look a bit like him. I've tended to tone Peter down. He wanted a big, floppy bow tie, and I gave him a little one. I'm trying to keep him simple and Conan Doyle-like."

The release of *One Golden Afternoon* – briefly re-named *Illumination* and changed again to become *Fairytale: A True Story* upon release in 1998 – re-opened the controversy over whether the pictures were real or faked. It also turned the spotlight once again on Conan Doyle, the man most maligned by his association with them. The author's reputation was irreparably damaged by his unshakable belief in the supernatural. People failed to understand how the creator of such a rational detective as Sherlock Holmes could become so completely wrapped up in spiritualism. In some quarters he became a laughing stock, and gossip-mongers claimed he was discarded for a peerage because of his involvement with psychic matters.

After three weeks on location in Yorkshire, including a stint at Allerton Park, near Knaresborough, Sturridge and Co moved to the studio to film climactic scenes involving the fairies. Details of the creatures themselves were kept strictly under wraps, but Shirley Russell offered a few tantalising clues as to their appearance. "They are very hard thing to do. I've had loads of goes at them but we're still working on how they're going to be. There's a lot to contend with. Obviously we have to try and make some of the fairies look like the ones the girls saw or imagined, but some of them are going to be a bit more exotic and strange."

opposite: Ready for 'action':
extras dressed as WWI
Tommies wait for their call.

1996

Monk Dawson

Guided by faith. Blinded by hope. Betrayed by love.

Director: Tom Waller

Producer: Tom Waller

Writer: James Magrane, from the novel by Piers Paul Read

Production Company: De Warenne Pictures

Year of Production: 1996 (Released July 31, 1998)

Where filmed: Leeds, West Yorkshire; Pickering and Malton, North Yorkshire during July and August, 1996.

Synopsis: A disillusioned Roman Catholic monk loses his faith and embarks on a new career as a journalist, but he is destined never to find contentment in a life dominated by sex, religion and death.

Credited cast: John Michie (Eddie Dawson), Benedict Taylor (Bobby Winterman), Paula Hamilton (Jenny Stanten), Martin Kemp (David Allenby), Kate Steavenson-Payne (Theresa Carter), Rhona Mitra (Mollie), Rupert Vansittart (Fr. Timothy), Frances Tomelty (Mrs. Carter), Geoff Nuttall (Sir Hugh Stanten), Mark Caven (Henry Poll), Daniel Brocklebank (Young Dawson), Toby Hadoke (Brother Simon), Tristan Sherwood-Roberts (Furness), Tola (Party Dancer).

Tom Waller had fire in his belly. A graduate of the class of '95 at Leeds's Northern School of Film & Television, he wanted to make a feature film but figured most people wouldn't take him remotely seriously. He had a point: he was just 22, had no money and, crucially, had never made a film before. Nevertheless he ploughed ahead with his vision and came up with an inspired plan: to raise the £250,000 he needed to finance the picture he would write to the 500 men and women featured on the *Sunday Times* 'rich list'. Perhaps inevitably he received an avalanche of rejection letters. But one man signalled his interest and offered to invest in the project. At that moment, *Monk Dawson* was born.

The film, based on the 1969 novel by Piers Paul Read, tells the tragic story of Eddie Dawson, a young Benedictine

Monk from a remote North Yorkshire monastery school who discovers the sins of the flesh in 1970s London. After being expelled from his order, Dawson arrives at a new parish in Chelsea where he has a passionate affair with a rich temptress and fathers a child. He is eventually betrayed, in life and love, by his best friend. Dawson's journey also takes him to Northern Ireland at the height of the Troubles and to an involvement with the outrage surrounding the assassination by Republican terrorists of Shadow Northern Ireland Secretary Airey Neave in 1979.

Perhaps it was merely coincidence that led Waller to Read's racy novel. Like Waller, Read was an alumnus of the exclusive Ampleforth College, near Thirsk – a highly regarded Benedictine school in the Roman Catholic

tradition led by the monks of Ampleforth Abbey. The book was certainly considered contentious by the Catholic establishment. Waller, born in 1974 in Bangkok to a Buddhist mother and a Roman Catholic father, was convinced it had its roots in life at the school. "The book fascinates me. It is a fictional work, but obviously the author and I both went to Ampleforth, and were influenced by our time there," he said. "It is a sort of rites of passage story, but I was tremendously excited by the fact that he had such an understanding of how a Catholic priest could fall from grace. As a first-time filmmaker, who had had quite a privileged education, it reflected my knowledge without having to tell my own story. If anything, my own character is nearer that of the priest's friend, who works in the media."

The remarkable tale of how the movie made it to the screen is the stuff celluloid fairytales are made of. For Waller, the end result was never in any doubt: he just had to figure out the route. A few short months later he and his crew were in the midst of a brisk six-week shoot, filming on the streets of Headingley and Burley, two Leeds suburbs that were transformed, albeit temporarily, into strife-torn Ulster. It was a remarkably effective metamorphosis: narrow streets of brick-built terrace houses, burned-out vehicles, an imposing armoured car and a checkpoint manned by RUC officers and British troops. Uncanny and unsettling, it was also 100 per cent authentic. Other scenes were filmed at Constable Burton Hall, near Leyburn in Wensleydale, and Howsham Hall School, near York, both of which together became the fictional Kirkham Preparatory School.

The imaginative use of inner city locations was not the only impressive part of the making of *Monk Dawson*. From the outset Waller had accepted that his youth and inexperience might prevent most people from taking him seriously, so he decided against being part of the casting process. "My strength is tenacity rather than ability so I hired a casting director. I was quite inexperienced, and slightly overawed at employing well-known actors, but I wanted to surround myself with as many talented people as possible."

Darkly handsome John Michie was cast as the turbulent priest. Benedict Taylor came on board as the friend who ultimately betrays him. And statuesque former model Paula Hamilton landed the crucial key role of the seductive Sloane Ranger who first infatuates, and then corrupts, the naïve and trusting Dawson. The film enjoyed its world premiere as the closing night film of the 1997 Leeds Film Festival. But while Waller enjoyed the experience, he was convinced the good monks of Ampleforth would show their discontent by boycotting his movie. "The school is very isolated and a lot of the monks are cut off from the real world. Even today with mass media many don't have access to film or radio and in some sense are living in the past," he said.

He was wrong. Whilst the Abbot was unavailable, several members of staff – some in clerical collars, others "in mufti", as one put it – journeyed from Thirsk to Leeds to see it for themselves. Perhaps Waller shouldn't have been worried. Controversy or no controversy, the monks of Ampleforth had been watching movies for more than 60 years. The tradition dated back to the 1930s when movie mogul Sam Goldwyn met one of the Ampleforth community in Ireland. Goldwyn was asked if he would supply films for the monastery's own bijou cinema and agreed. From that day on Ampleforth often hosted exclusive screenings of the latest films, often weeks or even months before they hit the local commercial circuit. Whether, six decades later, they ever went as far as playing *Monk Dawson* is quite another matter…

title page: Police and burned out cars on the streets of Leeds – doubling for 1970s Ulster.

previous page: A remarkable effective recreation of The Troubles.

opposite: Actor John Michie, playing the titular Monk Dawson, is stopped at an RUC checkpoint. Only the figures of watching children give the game away.

top: Director Tom Waller in baseball cap on location.

above: Street filming in Leeds.

1997

Elizabeth

Declared illegitimate aged 3. Tried for treason aged 21. Crowned Queen aged 25.

Director: Shekhar Kapur

Producers: Alison Owen, Eric Fellner, Tim Bevan, Mary Richards, Liza Chasin, Debra Hayward

Writer: Michael Hirst

Production Company: Channel 4 Films/Polygram Filmed Entertainment/Working Title Films

Year of Production: 1997 (Released October 2 1998)

Where filmed: York Minster, York and Bolton Castle, Leyburn, North Yorkshire during September and October, 1997.

Synopsis: The early years in the reign of Elizabeth I, the Virgin Queen, tracing her progress from malleable young woman to strong-willed monarch.

Credited Cast: Cate Blanchett (Elizabeth I), Geoffrey Rush (Sir Francis Walsingham), Christopher Ecclestone (Duke of Norfolk), Joseph Fiennes (Robert Dudley, Earl of Leicester), Richard Attenborough (Sir William Cecil), Fanny Ardant (Mary of Guise), Eric Cantona (Monsieur de Foix), Vincent Cassel (Duc d'Anjou), Kathy Burke (Queen Mary of Tudor), Edward Hardwicke (Earl of Arundel), Emily Mortimer (Kat Ashley), John Gielgud (The Pope), Liz Giles (Female Martyr), Paul Fox (Male Martyr), Terence Rigby (Bishop Gardiner), James Frain (Alvaro de la Quadra), Jamie Foreman (Earl of Sussex), Kelly Macdonald (Isobel Knollys), Wayne Sleep (Dance Tutor), Sally Gray (Lady in Waiting), Kate Loustau (Lady in Waiting), Elika Gibbs (Lady in Waiting), Sarah Owen (Lady in Waiting), Lily Allen (Lady in Waiting), Daniel Craig (John Ballard).

For passing tourists it was like stepping back in time. Outside York Minster, the noise and bustle of the 20th century carried on as normal. Inside something magical was happening: the coronation of Elizabeth I was being conducted with all the panoply accorded to a 16th century monarch. Familiar faces were scattered around the Minster's magnificent nave. For most of those observing the proceedings perhaps the biggest name was that of Richard Attenborough – veteran actor, producer, director and lord of the realm – playing the pivotal role of Sir William Cecil. Standing reverently watching his young queen, he personified the grace and majesty of the new Elizabethan age.

But the real star of the show was the red-headed woman in the neon yellow dress walking with queenly grace down the 200ft red carpet that stretched the length of the nave. This was 28-year-old Australian beauty Cate Blanchett, and curious visitors who looked on in respectful silence cannot have known that they were witnessing a breakthrough performance and the birth of an Oscar-winning movie star. Ten years later Blanchett looked back on that momentous period and recalled her feelings at making her first important movie in York. "It was a really high moment for me, as it was for *Elizabeth*, in a strange way. It was amazing. We did a couple of shots, just after the coronation, which actually didn't end up in the film."

A combination of technical wizardry and ingenious camera angles allowed York Minster to double as Westminster Abbey, scene of the coronation of Queen Elizabeth I on

Elizabeth *was filmed amid some of the most spectacular historical sites in the UK. The $25 million picture represented a location-driven production, with two of the three-month schedule being shot entirely on location. After an intense scout the producers settled on the north of England as the main focus for the shoot. The enormous task of finding the right settings - 12 in all - fell to location manager Sue Quinn. "The overview on the locations for* Elizabeth *was to create an indeterminate ambience as a backdrop to the diversity of scenes both exterior and interior," she explained.*

Principal photography began on September 2, 1997, at Haddon Hall in Derbyshire, which represented Hatfield House, home of the young Princess Elizabeth. Other key northern locations included Bolton Castle, in Leyburn, where Mary, Queen of Scots "entertained" while en-route to her execution, Raby Castle and Durham Cathedral in County Durham, and the combination of Alnwick, Bamburgh, Chillingham, Aydon and Warkworth castles, all in Northumberland. The filmmakers also shot scenes at Dorney Court, at Windsor, and St. Alban's Church in Middlesex.

The film's opulent look and grand style was rewarded with seven Academy Award nominations in 1998, for best picture, actress (Blanchett), art / set direction, cinematography, costume design, score and make-up, winning only for the last category. The film also scooped six out of 12 BAFTA film awards, including best film and best actress.

January 15, 1559 – 438 years earlier. For more than 1,300 years worship had been offered in the Minster, the largest medieval cathedral in northern Europe. *Elizabeth* was the first feature film to obtain permission to film there and, for two days, the main cast joined 300 costumed local extras recruited as courtiers, churchmen and guards clutching pikes to witness the ceremony. Standing by the throne Bishop Carlisle (actor Michael Beint) waited, crown in hand. Christopher Ecclestone, playing the Duke of Norfolk, made cinema history by becoming the first actor to film on camera in the Minster.

Scene 353 was played out repeatedly. Director Shekhar Kapur would call 'Action'. Blanchett, Attenborough and Ecclestone would enact the physical elegance of a coronation. After each take, Kapur would patiently watch the sequence on a monitor, sometimes joined by members of his cast, sometimes not. One budding actress who burst the bubble of history and tradition was Lily Allen, still only 12 and a long way from becoming a pop sensation. "Look, our bums are wiggling down the aisle!" she giggled, chewing gum as she watched a monitor with three other teenage ladies in waiting. Moments later, wad of gum hastily removed, she was back in the nave for yet another take as the search for cinematic perfection continued.

title page: Jamie Foreman and Cate Blanchett both gave breakthrough performances in Elizabeth.

precious page: Sir William Cecil (Richard Attenborough) leads Elizabeth (Cate Blanchett) and the ladies-in-waiting through the nave of York Minster. Among the young girls is Lily Allen, ten years before she became an overnight pop success.

opposite, top: Cate Blanchett and Jamie Foreman share a musical interlude.

opposite, bottom: Richard Attenborough was an immensely popular figure during filming of Elizabeth *at York Minster.*

right: Christopher Ecclestone as the ambitious Norfolk.

1997

Among Giants

Some heights can only be reached by the heart

Director: Sam Miller

Producer: Stephen Garrett

Writer: Simon Beaufoy

Production Company: Kudos Productions Ltd

Year of Production: 1997 (Released June 11 1999)

Where filmed: Sheffield, Doncaster, South Yorkshire; Burbage Edge, Derbyshire, during July and August, 1997.

Synopsis: When he's not climbing Yorkshire's cliffs and peaks, middle-aged Ray runs a gang of workers who paint massive electricity pylons. Ray hires aloof Australian Gerry to help out, and falls for her. Unfortunately, so does his best friend, Steven.

Credited cast: Pete Postlethwaite (Ray), Rachel Griffiths (Gerry), James Thornton (Steve), Lennie James (Shovel), Andy Serkis (Bob), Rob Jarvis (Weasel), Alan Williams (Frank), Emma Cunniffe (Barmaid), Steve Huison (Derek), Sharon Bower (Lyn), David Webber (Billy), Alvin Blossom (Steve's Dad), Sam Wilkinson (Ray's Son), Jo Wilkinson (Ray's Daughter).

Tightly gripping the rope that anchors him to a perilous crag, Pete Postlethwaite effortlessly scales 30 feet of sheer rock. Above, belaying the rope, co-star Rachel Griffiths sings Light My Fire and tells him to watch his knees. Postlethwaite pauses to glance back at the landscape laid out before him, and then continues his journey. "Made it, Ma. Top o' Tescos!" he announces, self-deprecatingly paraphrasing James Cagney's famous final line from *White Heat,* as he reaches the top. And, from where he sits on a ledge of rock overlooking the haunting beauty of the Peak District – Derbyshire doubling as Yorkshire - he can certainly claim to be on top of the world. He makes the climb three times. He is rewarded with applause and a hug from an admiring Griffiths. Next week they will be climbing a bigger crag – a formidable 200ft cliff. What's more Pete, Rachel and their pals will do it themselves.

Among Giants celebrates the mavericks and free spirits who roam the world seeking out the ultimate adrenaline rush. The script – the first to be written by *Full Monty* creator Simon Beaufoy and quickly put into production after the success of the earlier film – combines romance, earthy sexuality and macho bravado while once again honouring the look, feel and atmosphere of the Yorkshire backdrop that inspires him. "I was fascinated by this whole sort of 'cowboy' culture – these climbers who would live out of the back of a van like cowboys lived out of wagons – then take on black economy jobs, real dodgy jobs for which they didn't have any qualifications. A lot of them worked as electrical pylon painters. Then they'd all be off to Patagonia, India and Nepal mountaineering and they'd come back to Sheffield three months later," he revealed.

Casting the film's extraordinary location was as important as the performers who, alongside Postlethwaite and Griffiths, include newcomer James Thornton, Andy Serkis and Steve Huison. It fell to location manager Mark Herbert, now a successful film producer, to scout the area around Sheffield and Doncaster. He found what he wanted at Burbage Edge, seven miles above Sheffield and just over the border into Derbyshire. A windswept, sun-dappled plateau looking out onto rolling hills scattered with boulders and carpeted with fern, it seems to sum up the freedom and adventure of Beaufoy's screenplay.

It was sufficiently impressive to attract expert climbers Gavin Ellis and Dave Connelly, who turned down the chance to work on Steven Spielberg's *Saving Private Ryan*

title page: Rachel Griffiths and Pete Postlethwaite, the lovers at the heart of Among Giants.

previous spread: Pete Postlethwaite's grin sums up the happiness of the Among Giants *shoot during the summer of 1997.*

opposite: Mugging for the camera. Pete Postlethwaite and Rachel Griffiths endured high winds while filming their climbing scenes at Burbage Edge, just over the Yorkshire border into the Peak District.

above: Director Sam Miller (in white trousers) discusses his next shot at Burbage Edge.

above: Rachel Griffiths and Pete Postlethwaite: lovers on screen, great friends in real life.

opposite: Pete Postlethwaite on the end of a rope. He did all his own climbing in Among Giants.

to do *Among Giants*. Producer Stephen Garrett, keeping a close eye on the proceedings, is another avowed fan of the spectacular locale. He calls it Tolkien scenery. "What makes this film cinematic is the landscape in which this drama unfolds. Mark Herbert is a climber and knows this area like the back of his hand. What's remarkable is that he's always wanted to find a film that could play out a drama in this landscape. This is the first one that's come along."

Combining moments of high comedy with profound drama, *Among Giants* is not an easy film to define. Not part of any obvious tradition, and far from being an "English" movie, it falls into no particular genre. Garrett describes it as "love on a pylon top". The big scene of the day is a break-up between lovers Postlethwaite and Griffiths, filmed on a rocky promontory with the stunning scenery of the Peak District stretching off to the horizon. As director Sam Miller prepares to call action, both stars prepare for the intensity of one of the film's climactic moments.

Griffiths, in scruffy, paint-spattered jeans and boots, talks to herself, continually repeating her lines. She jumps around to get into character. Opting for momentary isolation, Postlethwaite climbs to the top of a square stone cairn. He adopts a different position every time to start the scene. Griffiths hops from foot to foot. Garrett watches quietly from the sidelines. Earlier she had been comforted by Miller and Postlethwaite for the intensity of her performance. Says Garrett: "The great thing about Rachel is that if she has to be angry then she works herself up and gets mad with everybody." When the camera rolls, it captures undistilled, raw emotion. The scene builds to its climax and suddenly the energy evaporates. "That was very 'over', that one," says Griffiths as Miller calls cut. "It's all downhill from here."

The intensity of the scene is matched by the laid-back nature of the filmmakers. Occasionally strolling walkers pause to watch before moving on. Crewmembers hold up traffic in the road nearby and ask passing ramblers to be silent. Not easy when you have kids about. Between takes Postlethwaite gets a make-up touch-up. Later he jumps from rock to rock as he prepares to shoot another scene. When they come to film Postlethwaite's close-up Griffiths returns to give him something to act opposite. "We were really 'into the moment'," says Postlethwaite later. "Rachel did it this morning. It was supposedly only a two-minute scene of four or five lines, but she hit it in such a way that it burned. We got something completely ravenous. When it happens to you, it's great. But when you see it happen to another performer, it's brilliant."

1997

Solo Shuttle

Director: David Cohen

Producer: Nick Cohen

Writer: David Cohen

Production Company: Psychology News

Year of Production: 1997 (Released 2002)

Where filmed: Sheffield, South Yorkshire during August, 1997.

Synopsis: A young woman working as an immigration officer on the Eurostar dumps her boyfriend and becomes involved with a man who smuggles foreigners through the Channel Tunnel.

Credited cast: Virginie Aster (Juliette), Jean-Yves Berteloot (Georges), John Shrapnel (Cain), Sean Hughes (Grigby), Alex Jennings (Chris), Kulvinder Ghir (Frank), Claire Price (Mel), Valerie Stroh (Liane), Bryan Murray (Frank's Mate), Alexandra London (Junkie/Café Girl), Chloe Davies (English Girl), Maria Andrews (Girl on Train), Wilbert Johnson (Nigerian), Mike Shannon (French Boss), Mike Rogers (Cop), Nick Cohen (Junkie), Rene (Rene, the Waiter), Pascal Ngunzi (Taxi Driver).

Summer, 1997. The narrow streets of Sheffield were transformed into London's Camden Town and even French Paris by an enterprising film crew when they descended on the city to shoot the Anglo-French thriller-romance *Solo Shuttle*. The low-budget movie was the latest in a string of films to use Sheffield as a backdrop and followed on from the one picture that was to truly put Sheffield on the international filmmaking map: *The Full Monty*. But *Solo Shuttle* was the first to turn Sheffield's terraces and dilapidated former engineering works into plausible Parisian apartments.

The film, starring French actors Virginie Aster and Jean-Yves Berteloot, Brits Kulvinder Ghir and John Shrapnel, and Irishman Bryan Murray, was built around a triangular love affair between Juliette, a French woman working on the Eurostar, her married boyfriend and a young English-born Asian. Aster, Berteloot and Ghir played the main triumvirate. The plot revolved around Frank (Ghir), a smuggler of illegal immigrants through the Channel Tunnel. Events took a darker turn when Juliette became embroiled in Frank's idealistic law-breaking scheme and comes into contact with Kane (Murray), a small-time hood.

Writer/director David Cohen used the abandoned Clarence Works, near Sheffield Wednesday's Hillsborough ground, to double for Juliette's plush Paris flat, while Café Jacques, a short distance across town in London Road, became a rendezvous for a clandestine meeting set in Camden Town. Cohen, who had previously directed the low-budget hit *The*

title image: Kulvinder Ghir and Virginie Aster.

previous page: Director David Cohen, seated right, coordinates a scene in Café Jacques, Sheffield. Actor Bryan Murray stands with back to camera.

top: Virginie Aster has her make-up touched up by Scott Beswick.

above: Kulvinder Ghir and Bryan Murray – two villains made for each other.

opposite: The creative process at work: David Cohen directs Kulvinder Ghir.

Pleasure Principle, remarked: "Presenting Sheffield as Paris and London is not easy, but we are enterprising."

Solo Shuttle attracted an eclectic array of Yorkshire talent. Actor Kulvinder Ghir was born in Leeds while make-up designer Scott Beswick came from Upton, near Pontefract. Beswick looked around him at the breeze blocks and splintered wood that littered the set and smiled. "It's not always glamorous," he said by way of an apology for the off-camera mess. "Basically, working in films is what you make it. Standing around in pigeon muck, like today, is about as far from Hollywood as you can get. It's also long hours, lots of hanging around and sometimes poor pay. Then again, I'm going to Mexico soon to work with Bob Hoskins and Michelle Pfeiffer, so it's not all bad."

For restaurateur Jonathan Cummings, chef-patron of Café Jacques, the glamour of the film business meant shutting down his business for three days. His reward: a modest daily pay cheque of just £100. The loss of trade was compensated by his bistro's guest role in the movie. On the night in question Cohen, his cast and crew crammed themselves into the tiny eaterie which had been packed with lights, cameras and all the paraphernalia of filmmaking. There was time for a rehearsal or two, a quick check of the script and then the scene was shot. It was brisk, efficient and very quick. Cohen couldn't afford to hang about.

A taste of the action ran thus: actor Brian Murray, star of TV's *Perfect Scoundrels* and *The Irish RM,* strode onto the set as the chief villain. He shouted and screamed in a south London accent, swapping and changing the oaths and curses in the dialogue to suit the mood. After each outburst he would look to Cohen for affirmation – a nod of the head – or rejection. Then the process would begin again: more noise, more swearing, more aggression. The shouting and shooting went on for hours. Outside, the streets fell quiet. Inside, creativity reigned. It would be a long night.

1997

Little Voice

Director: Mark Herman

Producer: Elizabeth Karlsen

Writer: Mark Herman, based on the play *The Rise and Fall of Little Voice*, by Jim Cartwright

Production Company: Scala Productions

Year of Production: 1997
(Released February 8, 1999)

Where filmed: Scarborough, East Yorkshire, during October and November 1997.

Synopsis: Fading talent agent Ray Say thinks he's hit the big time when he happens across a shy young woman with a secret gift: she can belt out old-time songs like Judy Garland. But can he persuade her to perform before an audience...?

Credited cast: Brenda Blethyn (Mari), Jane Horrocks (LV), Ewan McGregor (Billy), Philip Jackson (George), Annette Badland (Sadie), Michael Caine (Ray Say), Jim Broadbent (Mr. Boo), Adam Fogerty, James Welsh (The Bouncers), Karen Gregory (Stripper), Fred Feast (Arthur), Graham Turner (LV's Dad), George (Pawnbroker), Virgil Tracy (Loan Advisor), Dick Van Winkle (Money Lender), George Bradley, Geoffrey Emmerson, Barry Gomersalt, Angela Harrison, Jean Hotton, David Kemp, Aiden Lawrence, Michael Lynskey, Peter Marshall, Peter Minns, Christine Quick, Len Rangely, Bob Scott, Melanie Simpson, Doug Stewart, Peter Thomson, Stan Wright (Mr. Boo's Band), Howard Grace (Talent Scout), Alex Norton (Bunnie Morris), Melodie Scales (George's Girlfriend), Sean Hadland, Roger Neville, Michael Prior, Paul Swan, Carl Whittaker (Take Fat), Kitty Roberts (Brenda Bailey), Fred Gaunt (Wild Trigger Smith), Alita Petrof (Elaine), Jonathan Clark (Fireman).

October, 1997. On a freezing Scarborough cliff top, shrouded in mist and soaked in drizzle, a star is about to be born.

Inside the Club Rendezvous, filming on the big screen version of *Little Voice* is progressing apace. As writer/director Mark Herman prepares to set up a shot of the stage, star Jane Horrocks dashes through the throng wearing a thick coat over her thin pink dress. Herman, the prodigiously talented and multi award-winning filmmaker behind *Brassed Off*, is about to shoot one of the key scenes of *Little Voice*, the film version of the West End smash *The Rise and Fall of Little Voice*, in which Horrocks returns to the role that made her famous. Watched by co-stars Michael Caine, Brenda Blethyn, Ewan McGregor and dozens of dinner-suited diners on to the stage above which the words "Little Voice" glow

title page: Ewan McGregor as 'Telephone Bill'.

above: Philip Jackson, Ewan McGregor and Jim Broadbent outside the Scarborough set of Mr. Boo's.

in too-bright lights and prepares to belt out a song. Outside, the neon sign for Mr Boo's – the club's name in the film – blinks through the gloom.

Herman has been filming in Scarborough for a month. The previous night he shot a tricky scene with Caine, Blethyn and Jim Broadbent where Blethyn, in a too-tight top, micro mini skirt and four-inch high heels, tottered down a cobbled alley as she screamed drunken abuse at Caine's sleazy seaside impresario in a biting comic scene. It's all part of the rich fabric of life that makes up *Little Voice*.

Blethyn, Oscar-nominated for her performance in Mike Leigh's *Secrets and Lies*, is making her first movie with Bridlington-born Herman. She's full of praise for his quiet manner. "This is not a musical. It's like a play - a black comedy with singing in it. I love it," she reveals. "Mark has written it too, and it's been joyful. I always like working with the writer, even if he's not the director, because you can ask him what the intention is. They're always there to help. A lot of actors don't like that, but I do. I like to be able to question things, or ask 'How do I go about this?' I think you should always listen and take direction. You can argue a point, certainly, but you should always listen. Mark's great at that."

Sitting huddled in the corner of the packed, smoky Leeds Hotel, she looks every inch the tart. Sporting long nails, too much make-up and far too much cleavage, she sips from a polystyrene cup during a break in filming. Looking at the woman before me, and then hearing the voice of the actress within is a real shock to the system. It's like saying hello to the Queen and hearing her answer like an East End fishwife. But that's acting. In *Little Voice* Blethyn loses herself in Mari Hoff, a middle-aged widow who's throwing herself into life with vigour in the deeply-hidden knowledge that she's past it. She's flabby. She's loud. She's brassy, garrulous, foul-mouthed and drunk. She's certainly not sexy. And that's just how Blethyn likes to play it.

"Mari is a widow with a grown-up daughter. She's very brash and abrasive. She wouldn't say she was tarty, but I would! She's very dominant and just doesn't stop speaking when she starts. Nobody can get a word in edgeways, so her daughter just goes into her shell. She's very funny but it's also very dark. She's not sinister but she's very jealous. They're all desperate people really but it's written very tenderly and accurately, so it's very funny as well. I usually play

sympathetic characters and Mari is quite unsympathetic, so it's a bit of a breakthrough for me to get this one. She's not a villain; just a working class, hard-done-by woman who's struggling. She lacks a partner and would like one. She's mourning the loss of her looks and does her very best to look glamorous. She dresses far too young for herself. She's just one of those - she's losing it."

For movie fans one of the coups is in having the youth idol Ewan McGregor in Scarborough. His part of shy BT telephone engineer Billy was beefed up when he became a star in *Trainspotting*, but it's still only a supporting role. McGregor took the part after collaborating with Herman on *Brassed Off*. He is not on call when we speak and immediately begins talking about Caine, one of his heroes.

"I don't actually have a scene in the film with him at all, and I've only met him once," he says. "He's like royalty to me in terms of actors. They don't come much more serious than him. I grew up watching his films and it was unbelievably good stuff. I was watching *Zulu* one day and two days later I heard he was going to be doing this. I was saying 'What part? What part?' I'd love to do something else with him. He's a pillar in the action world, isn't he, so it's such a treat to be working with him." Spoken like a true fan.

Inside the smoky pool room of the Leeds Hotel, renamed The Seabirds for the film and perched atop a perilously steep alley, Caine, Broadbent and Blethyn run through a scene. It will last barely two minutes on screen but it's a slow process. "This is Little Voice's mum," says Caine in his instantly recognisable south London accent as he opens the scene. Mark Herman, sitting on the fringes of the set and watching the action on a monitor, isn't happy and calls for another take. As the scene is re-set, Caine jokes with Blethyn while, in the cramped conditions, extras jostle for space, drink alcohol-free Kaliber from the beer glasses and try to avoid the cables trailing across the floor. Minutes later, a voice shouts: "Background action – come alive, everybody", and the whole process begins again with the extras laughing, clinking glasses and switching channels on the television. Then it stops. Jim Broadbent, as Mr. Boo, has blown a line. Herman calls action once more, only for Caine to mess up by referring to Broadbent as "Mr. Boot". It could be a long night…

If writer/director Mark Herman feels the pressure, he doesn't show it. Two years have passed since he made *Brassed Off*

above: Brenda Blethyn as Mari Hoff, a loud, brassy, garrulous drunk. "She wouldn't say she's tarty, but I would!" she said.

above: "It's rather corny, but it's the first time I've
ever actually watched a star being born."
– *Michael Caine on Jane Horrocks.*

and the experience has changed him. He's less intense, far more relaxed, and content to let matters take their course. "I'm very confident about the script and the cast. That all helps," he says. "Most of my work is done in the writing anyway. *Little Voice* is actually a much more difficult film to make than *Brassed Off*. There was a magic in the theatre piece that we have to try to retain for the screen and that's a difficult thing to do. Whereas *Brassed Off* was purely narrative and the passion in it was all part of that, here it has the tragedy, passion and music but also a magical angle. It's difficult to achieve that in film." Herman rattled off the script for *Little Voice* in just five months – the film had a start date before the screenplay was even begun. "It was through-the-night stuff, you know? A few people had a bash at this screenplay but it was always a little bit theatrical. That was the failing. I think I was brought on to try and turn it into a film, add a bit of cinema to it."

The second scene of the night tests everybody. It's 10.30pm and it is freezing. Michael Caine, oblivious to the locals gathered watching nearby, wraps up against the cold in a big anorak. He takes it off only for the scene with Blethyn and Broadbent where all three stagger down the alley from the pub to his gaudy American car. As soon as Herman calls "Cut" the coat is back on again and Caine stands alone, talking to no-one and ignoring the crowd. Caine took the part of Ray Say after a self-imposed four-year break from making movies. Director Herman said he was "desperate to do it". "He was like a drama student who had got his first job. He's been waiting for a part like this for years, to get him away from the normal Caine stuff."

Caine agrees: "When I saw the script I knew straight away it was something I had to do. It was a perfect way for me to come back to films, having reinvented the parts I play, and it also looked like it would be great fun, which it was. The first time I saw Jane sing, my character, Ray, is supposed to be thinking 'I'm gonna make a fortune. I'm going to get out of this rotten town'. I was supposed to be playing happy. But I had tears in my eyes. I remember saying to Brenda Blethyn: 'It's rather corny, but it's the first time I've ever actually watched a star being born'."

"I've been involved in this for about two years or so. I did a thing called Tales from the Crypt *with Jane Horrocks and we said we'd love to work with each other again. She said she had something in mind, which I guess turned out to be this. I love it. It's a lovely play, and it's a great script. I saw the play down in London, but Mark Herman's written a brilliant script. It's really sweet with great dialogue.*

"My character, Billy, is a BT engineer and a pigeon fancier. That's really all he cares about: his pigeons. He's a very shy guy, not a very communicative person, except when he's with his birds or talking about them. I'm very fond of racing pigeons myself. We've been doing all the pigeon coop stuff this week and I've become quite into them in the last couple of days. They're beautiful birds. I can tell you lots of things about them if you like...

"I finished Star Wars *about four weeks ago. It was amazing but it was massive. There were about 600 people on the crew, and it's really nice to come back to a small crew. It's quite a relief, actually - a much more intimate experience. When you're away on location somewhere like this, you can have a lot of fun. You're all together, away from home and you tend to have a right laugh.*

"I love Scarborough. It really is a great town. There's something really magical about these seaside towns when it's off-season. There's plenty to keep you occupied during the day as well. I'm having a great time up here.

"I'm not really worried about the loss of anonymity. In London, nobody really bothers about what you do. Everybody lets you get on with your business. You get more stuff like that in Scarborough, because it's a small town. People know more about what's going on and because they know the film's here they know that we're about. You get the occasional arsehole but on the whole it's all been very pleasant. "
– Ewan McGregor, 1997

1994/1998

Sweet Surrender/ Fanny & Elvis

Finding your perfect partner
is just a matter of chemistry...

Director: Kay Mellor

Producers: Brian Daniels (1994)/Laurie Borg (1998)

Writer: Kay Mellor

Production Company: Surrender Films Ltd (1994)/
Scala (1998)

Years of Production: 1994 (unfinished) and 1998

Where filmed: Leeds, Farsley, Rodley, and Otley,
West Yorkshire during June and July, 1994.
Hebden Bridge and Halifax, West Yorkshire, from
September 20 to October 10, 1998.

Synopsis: A thirtysomething wife whose body clock is
ticking receives a shock when her husband runs off with
his lover.

Credited cast – Sweet Surrender: Jenny Agutter (Kate),
Peter Howitt (Rob), Gaynor Faye (Samantha), John
McArdle (Dave), Gareth Tudor Price (Dr. Langford).

Credited cast – Fanny & Elvis: Kerry Fox (Kate),
Ray Winstone (Dave), Ben Daniels (Andrew), David
Morrissey (Rob), Jennifer Saunders (Roanna), Colin
Salmon (Alan), Gaynor Faye (Samantha), William Ash
(Rick), Gareth Tudor Price (Dr. Langford), Bridget
Forsythe (Nurse Lynne), Eileen O'Brien (Midwife), Nick
Lane (Car Salesman), Richard Moore (IVF Consultant),
Sarah Parks (Receptionist), Ron Blass (Jeweller),
Michael Medwin (Registrar), Yvonne Mellor (Harassed
Mother), Joyce Kennedy (Dave's Mum), Robert Maxfield
(Postman), Dan Riley (Samantha's Young Man), Mike
Kelly (Stall Holder), Maureen Lunt (Dr. Barker's Patient),
Paul Gibbon (Red Indian), Rachel Egan (Cassy), Rita
May (Rick's Mother), Harriet Andrews (Kirsty), Abbie
Craven (Shelly), Katie Hodgson (Chloe), Richard Stacey
(Daniel), Andrew Nixy (Paul), Grace Francas-Mellor
(Crying Girl), Elliott Francas-Mellor (Crying Boy).

There was something about the way he was throwing glasses about which made people keep away from Ray Winstone. The burly Londoner was propping up the bar of a moorland inn – and aiming glasses at other drinkers – as one of the characters in *Fanny & Elvis*, the first movie to be written and directed by actress, playwright and TV dramatist Kay Mellor.

Winstone joined co-stars Kerry Fox, Neil Morrissey and former *Coronation Street* regular Gaynor Faye for the film, which was on its final day of shooting at the remote Mount Skip Inn, high on the hills above Hebden Bridge. The movie, a romantic comedy set in the North of England at the tail-end of the millennium, revolved around 30-something fledgling novelist Kate Dickson, played by New Zealander

title page: Jenny Agutter and Kay Mellor on the first incarnation of the film, 1994.

above: Filming in Rodley on Sweet Surrender, *the film that never was. Jenny Agutter is about to prang her battered car.*

Fox, whose ordered life takes an unexpected turn when her husband runs off with a student on the same day she is told she has just 12 months to get pregnant. With time rapidly running out, her biological clock kicks into overdrive and she begins dealing with sperm counts, ovulation and IVF treatment in her hunt for the ideal sperm donor.

Shooting on the film had begun on September 27, 1998, in London, before moving onto location work in Yorkshire. Yet the movie was actually Mellor's second stab at the story. Four years before she had begun the project under a completely different name with a completely different cast. Jenny Agutter and former *Bread* star Peter Howitt – now a successful film director himself – were recruited to shoot 12 minutes of footage as test material for the final movie, then known as *Sweet Surrender*. The film was made in the grounds of Wharfedale General Hospital, in Leeds city centre and on the slopes of Otley Chevin with Mellor, her cast and a largely volunteer crew working only for expenses.

The project was the brainchild of Mellor and her producer Brian Daniels, in reality a Leeds-based recruitment consultant, who bankrolled the project to the tune of £50,000. He considered it to be a good investment: by touting the completed 'teaser' around distributors, film companies and local businesses, Daniels hoped to drum up the final budget of £1.8 million. The buzz words were sponsorship and product placement. "I think it's the commercial way forward to help the British film industry," said Daniels on location in Otley, "because obviously you need to raise the capital from somewhere. The best way is for somebody to use the film to advertise. It's a novel way of advertising. If you look at the cost of making a two-minute television commercial, the cost is probably £20,000 plus the airtime when it's shown. With one successful film, if you get it right, the product exposure is going to be terrific."

Jenny Agutter, like everyone else, was roughing it. This was British filmmaking at its most basic. No bloated budgets. No Winnebagos. Just energy, enthusiasm, dedication and sheer hard graft. On the day in question she had filmed a scene in a doctor's surgery at which she is given the grim news: get pregnant in a year or lose the opportunity. Clutching the draft of her first novel – completed that morning – she watches it tumble to the floor thanks to the meddling hands of a smiling toddler. "On no. There's nine months' work there!" she cries, looking at the scattered pages of her book

below: Kay Mellor, actress daughter Gaynor Faye and Ray Winstone during the making of the new version, re-named Fanny & Elvis.

opposite: Ray Winstone as Dave.

and, then, straight up at the swollen belly of the child's very pregnant young mum. Never was a truer word said. Days before she and pony-tailed actor Gareth Tudor Price (in a dual role as the doctor and a fantasy, Heathcliff-esque lover) had played out a romantic love scene against the rising sun on The Chevin – part of a dream sequence that would open the film. Early morning walkers could have been forgiven for thinking they had strayed into a modern-day version of *Wuthering Heights*. For the pub where Kate is dumped, interiors were shot at The Jester, in the Leeds suburb of Alwoodley, and exteriors at The Stanhope, in Rodley.

"It's just lovely to be involved with a group of people that is actually doing something," said Agutter. "If it comes off it'll be because there's the energy behind getting it done as

opposed to talking about it. The trouble with the industry is that there's a lot of people talking and they just don't have the energy or the belief or get enough people behind them to make it happen. There's no question in my mind that, given an opportunity to be part of something developing, that's great as far as I'm concerned. Hopefully we'll just get the money very fast and get on with the rest of it. If I looked and said 'It's a waste of time because it's never going to go anywhere' then one wouldn't get involved, but it looks like something that someone's going to pick up.

"Kay's name had been coming up a lot recently with plays and all sorts of things going on. I read the script and I thought it was wonderful; a terrific character, a terrific story, very funny, very moving. Then we met and I was really thrilled.

I said 'When can we do it?' I do like the energy behind independent films."

For Kay Mellor, writing a feature film script was the natural progression from writing for TV and the theatre. She had already starred in her own TV series, *Just Us,* and her play *A Passionate Woman* was about to transfer from the West Yorkshire Playhouse to London's West End. It was a heady time; there was so much to play for.

"This is my directing debut," revealed Mellor. "I've directed in the theatre before but I've never directed either television or feature films. I've never written a feature film, so this is a whole new area for me. But a good story is a good story with a beginning, a middle and an end. If you're writing a children's drama it's got to be a story well-told. It's just whatever medium you choose to make it in. This I've always seen on the big screen. This has got an epic quality to it. It's set on the moors around Otley – which in itself is a very visual place to be and very special to me because I'm a Yorkshirewoman."

Flash forward four years and *Sweet Surrender* had metamorphosed into *Fanny & Elvis*. By then Jenny Agutter, Peter Howitt and John McArdle were working on other things, so the project was re-cast with Kerry Fox, David Morrissey and Ray Winstone as wife, errant husband and unlikely sperm donor. Of the original players, only Gaynor Faye and Gareth Tudor Price returned to pick up their roles from 1994. But four years was a long time in movies. Not only had the cast changed, so had the budget, jumping from £1.8 million to £3 million with a little help from the National Lottery. Thus it was that Mellor, new producer Laurie Borg and a quartet of stars arrived in Hebden Bridge to begin location work on the film. They had been preceded a month earlier by location scouts who scoured the town for local shops, houses and a central square for the story's end sequence, a wintry millennium party.

"We searched the north of England for just the right setting, and Hebden Bridge was it," said Borg, the man behind a string of hits including Ang Lee's *Sense and Sensibility.* "The town has everything we are looking for: romantic scenery, wonderful character and a feel hat's absolutely right. We want to involve the townspeople, who have so far been brilliant and more than helpful and co-operative. That's part of the pleasure in filming in a place like Hebden Bridge. It's not only the town which is lovely but the people, too."

With comments like that, he was bound to win friends, and he did. *Fanny & Elvis* was blessed with a huge amount of support from locals, many of whom were signed up as extras following an open casting session.

It seemed like the entire town turned out for the major final sequence: a market with fireworks, fun and frivolity held on millennium eve. Movie magic transformed St. George's Square into a perfect winter wonderland replete with inch-deep artificial snow. It looked fabulous, adding a touch of festive fantasy to a town that not only served as a backdrop for a quirky romcom, it became the focus of the film: *Fanny & Elvis* was based squarely in Hebden Bridge, making the town as big an attraction as the stars.

far left, top: Turning St. George's Square, Hebden Bridge, into a snowy Millennium Eve party.

far left, middle: Writer / director Kay Mellor, producer Laurie Borg and other crew members scout locations in Hebden Bridge. "The town has everything we are looking for," said Borg.

far left, bottom: Mother-and-daughter team Kay Mellor and Gaynor Faye.

below: An atmospheric shot of the Mount Skip Inn, Hebden Bridge. Inside, Kay Mellor is directing a scene of domestic disquiet. Outside, the moorland mist rolls in.

1998

L.A.
Without a Map

Director: Mika Kaurismäki

Producers: Sarah Daniel, Julie Baines, Pierre Assouline

Writers: Richard Rayner, Mika Kaurismäki, from Rayner's novel *Los Angeles Without a Map*

Production Company: Dan Films/Euro American Films S.A./Marianna Films

Year of Production: 1998
(Released September 17, 1999)

Where filmed: Bradford and Elland, West Yorkshire during January, 1998.

Synopsis: An undertaker from Bradford falls for a free-spirited American tourist and finds himself en-route to Los Angeles to pursue his dream of becoming a scriptwriter.

Credited cast: David Tennant (Richard), Vinessa Shaw (Barbara), Julie Delpy (Julie), Vincent Gallo (Moss), James Le Gros (Takowsky), Cameron Bancroft (Patterson), Saskia Reeves (Joy), Steve Huison (Billy), Jean-Pierre Kalfon (Jean-Mimi), Lisa Edelstein (Sandra), Joe Dallesandro (Michael), Matthew Faber (Joel), Tony Peers (Vicar), Margo Stanley (Mrs. Blenkinsop), Malcolm Tierney (Joy's Dad), Margi Clarke (Bradford Woman), Kevin West (Spielberg Man), Lisa Edelstein (Sandra), Michael Campbell (Young Porter), Brent Morris (Aviator Shades Cop), Mista Taboo (Rapper), Dijon Talton (Kid), Joey Parillo (McCrea), Amanda Plummer (Red Pool Owner), Dominic Gould (Music Store Clerk #1), Andre Royo (Music Store Clerk #2), Jerzy Skolimowski (Minister), Don Ranvaud (Man with Script), Debra Carrol (Waitress), Tootie (Lippy Blonde), Christa Lang (Woman on Bus), Michael Franco (Barman), Nathalie Huot (Tall Woman), Joseph Arsenault (Jealous Man), Kenneth Hughes (Smoking Guest) plus Anouk Aimée, Robert Davi, Johnny Depp, Monte Hellman and the Leningrad Cowboys as themselves.

Uncredited cast: Andy Bradford (Corpse in coffin), Mika Kaurismäki (Michael Bambihill), Darren Rhodes (Gravedigger), Valentin Siroon (Bartender).

A bright winter sun glints off dewy grass and damp gravestones as pallbearers bear a coffin on its final journey. Looking down on the scene from a nearby slope, Finnish director Mika Kaurismäki watches Scottish actor David Tennant break from the formality of the funeral procession and make his way purposefully to where a pretty blonde girl stands, out of place among ostentatious monuments to long-dead Victorians. Kaurismaki calls 'cut' and the crew of *L.A. Without a Map* begins setting up the next shot – a moment of black comedy in which Leonard Blenkinsop, recently deceased, tumbles from his coffin and is hurriedly re-located. For David Tennant, filming in Bradford's vast Undercliffe Cemetery represents a reality check: just a few short days before, he was basking in the heat of California. Yorkshire in January means the temperature has dipped to the opposite end of the scale. But while it's cold, it's not wet. At least not wet enough for the disappointed Kaurismäki, forcing a hurried re-think that has meant shooting the film's finale rather than its first act.

"We wanted it to be very cloudy and now we have this blue sky. It doesn't fit the concept," says the miserable Finn. "The first scene, when they meet, is supposed to be gloomy and the bright light spoiled the mood of the scene. It should possess a slight dreamy quality so the sunlight is wrong for it. We had the opposite problem in Los Angeles where the weather was quite bad. We shot in wintertime and they had the El Niño storm. Many times we were waiting for sun. Now it's the opposite. It's absurd."

title page: Undertakers David Tennant and Steve Huison and their client, stuntman Andy Bradford.

previous page: Filmmakers in Undercliffe Cemetery, Bradford.

above: Vinessa Shaw and David Tennant, who made his major feature film debut in L.A. Without a Map.

opposite: The crew sets up a dolly shot to follow a funeral as it wends its way through Undercliffe Cemetery.

As the crew sets up the new sequence 26-year-old newcomer Tennant looks down onto the cityscape of Bradford, laid out beneath hazy sunshine in the valley below. Thirty-five years earlier Tom Courtenay, as fellow undertaker Billy Fisher, observed a similar view while making *Billy Liar* in the same 19th century necropolis. History seems to be repeating itself. The difference is that Billy Fisher never escapes beyond his dreams; in *L.A. Without a Map*, the hero travels 6,000 miles in search of love and a new beginning.

"I play Richard, who starts off as an undertaker in Bradford and meets this girl from Los Angeles called Barbara who he falls for in the course of an afternoon," explains Tennant. "He decides, much to her surprise, that he's going to follow her home and make her his own. So that's what he sets

about trying to do. Basically he's the writer of the story, and it's his true-life escapade. I've not done a big movie before, just TV, theatre, some shorts and a day on *Jude*. So for me it was all about the experience. For a first film to get to play a lead role in Hollywood was quite a kick. And it's quite a cast: Johnny Depp, Julie Delpy, Amanda Plummer, James Le Gros and Vinessa Shaw, who's playing the lead girl. It's been very exciting from that point of view: meeting all these people you've seen in movies.

"On one of the scenes with Johnny I'd just arrived and said 'Hi, pleased to meet you.' I distinctly remember that we were actually shooting and there was one point where he turns round and puts his sunglasses down. You see his face and he says something to me. We were in the middle of the

above: Graveside conference: Steve Huison and David Tennant discuss the mechanics of a scene. Finnish director Mike Kaurismäki, who wanted a grey Yorkshire day, was unhappy with the bright winter sunshine.

opposite: Stuntman Andy Bradford, playing a lively corpse, peeps out of his coffin. "I've got no lines to learn," he joked.

shot and I said 'Bloody hell! Johnny Depp!' It completely freaked me out. Other than that you just try and keep calm and not think of it as being a big deal. As soon as you do that it starts to become intimidating. You start going 'Oh! Oh! Ooooh dear! That's Johnny Depp, this is Hollywood and I'm scared! You've got to try and treat it like just another day at work."

Away from the mechanics of the shoot, producer Sarah Daniel ruminates on the strange journey that has brought her to Bradford – birthplace of author Richard Rayner and his autobiographical tale. "It's quite funny how a Finnish director, a Finnish sound man, a French cameraman and a French focus puller have come into Bradford and are hoping that all the cultures will mix in an instant, which is what they have to do," she says. "So far it's gone great. I've been in Bradford for about three weeks and came up three times before on a recce with the director to choose our locations. Some of them are actually specified within the book and Undercliffe Cemetery is very much one of those. It's central to the writer's imagination and on the written page. It's a fantastic city. We've had nothing but enormous help from everybody."

The last word goes to stuntman Andy Bradford, a veteran of James Bond films, the *Indiana Jones* saga and a low-budget sci-fi movie called *Star Wars* and here playing the late Leonard Blenkinsop. "I've got no lines to learn," he quips. "I've been dead bodies before. I've had to die slowly, hang slowly, drown slowly. This is more tricky because what

the director would like is for the body to jacknife forward grotesquely for a second. There's foam in the bottom of the grave to absorb some of the shock because all the weight is going down to the base of the coffin. It means my legs don't come out of the end and I avoid being injured. It's a little bit of a shock, naturally. I shall have to concentrate because the actual jar as the lid comes off means I might just flick my eyes." Needless to say, the appropriately-named Mr. Bradford performs perfectly, receiving a round applause from mourners and pallbearers. And so the funeral games continue.

1999

Blow Dry

Love is in the hair

Director: Paddy Breathnach

Producers: Ruth Jackson, William Horberg, David Rubin

Writer: Based on the screenplay Never Better by Simon Beaufoy

Production Company: West Eleven Films/Mirage Enterprises

Year of Production: 1999 (Released March 30, 2001)

Where filmed: Dewsbury, Batley and Bradford, West Yorkshire during May and June, 1999.

Synopsis: Britain's most flamboyant hairdressers arrive in Keighley, West Yorkshire, to compete in the National Hairdressing Championships. At the heart of the competition is a dysfunctional family led by local barber Phil Allen who, despite his misgivings, locks tongs with his old adversary Ray Robertson.

Credited cast: Alan Rickman (Phil Allen), Natasha Richardson (Shelley Allen), Rachel Griffiths (Sandra), Rachael Leigh Cook (Christina Robertson), Josh Hartnett (Brian Allen), Bill Nighy (Ray Robertson), Rosemary Harris (Daisy), Warren Clarke (Tony, Mayor of Keighley), Hugh Bonneville (Louis), Heidi Klum (Jasmine), David Bradley (Noah Thwaite), Ben Crompton (Saul Thwaite), Ann Rye (Margaret Thwaite), Ray Emmett Brown (TJ), Mark Benton (George), Gordon Langford-Rowe (Stanley), Stephen Graham (Photographer), Peter Kay (Cyril the Barman), Elizabeth Woodcock (Sharon), Michael McElhatton (Robert), Peter McDonald (Vincent), Willie Ross (Pub Reject), Marshall Lancaster (Davo), Paul Copley (Ken), Lorraine Balinska (Ebony), Oliver Ford Davies (Doctor Hamilton), Janet Henfrey (Jean), Ken Kitson (Driver), Tony Barton (Workman 1), Philip Wright (Workman 2), Margaret Blakemore (Receptionist), Jukka Hiltunen (Rocker), Johnny Leeze (Journalist), Christopher Biggins (President).

Most people seem to have forgotten about *Blow Dry*, the film that brought Josh Hartnett to Yorkshire as a wannabe champion hair stylist who practises by cutting the hair of corpses in a funeral parlour. Looking back on the film it seems to offer a little bit of everything: pathos, drama, comedy, romance, social realism, clearly-defined characters and the largely unknown world of cut-throat clipping and coiffeuring: competition hairdressing.

It was conceived by *Full Monty* scriptwriter Simon Beaufoy as a quasi throwback to the 'kitchen sink' dramas of the 1960s but the film that eventually emerged was far from what he had in mind. American influences (and American finances) put paid to that. And so a thoroughly Yorkshire movie, written by a Yorkshireman, set in a

Yorkshire town and boasting a full cast of Yorkshire folk, became an entirely different project.

Beaufoy had set his film in Keighley, his home town. Yet into it ambled the amiable Hartnett, still some years from movies like *Pearl Harbor, Black Hawk Down* and *Sin City*. His love interest was Rachael Leigh-Cook, another Stateside import. Together they would lead a mis-matched cast that included Alan Rickman playing a West Yorkshire barber named Phil. No surprise, then, that Beaufoy left the project. A modicum of confusion and controversy surrounded the movie but diplomacy shielded the real reasons for the split between words and pictures. Beaufoy's name barely figured in publicity for the film and, at its world premiere during the Bradford Film Festival in 2001, he was nowhere to be

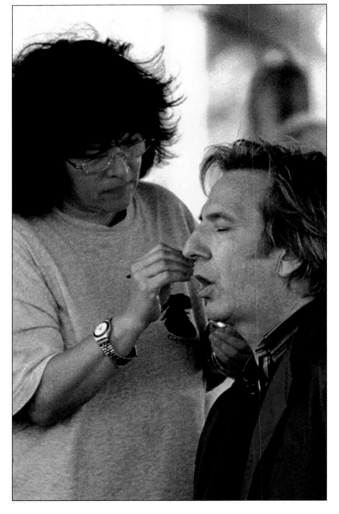

title page: Warren Clarke as the ambitious Mayor of Keighley.

previous: Scaffolding assists in capturing a shot.

above left: Natasha Richardson and Alan Rickman on location in Batley, standing in for Keighley where very little of the film was actually made.

above, right: Alan Rickman with real-life hair stylists Trevor Mitchell (left) who helped inspire the film.

right: Make-up artist Jenny Shircore who would win an Oscar for another film shot in Yorkshire, Elizabeth.

right: Writer Simon Beaufoy, Oscar nominated for The Full Monty, *who took his name off* Blow Dry.

seen. Explained director Paddy Breathnach: "Simon wrote a script called *Never Better*. It was pretty much the script we filmed but there were some changes to some characters that he wasn't convinced by. As it often is with movies the course of true love doesn't always run that smoothly. There was a modified credit because of that."

To add insult to injury the film, while set in Keighley – "a sleepy English town barely on the map" according to the publicity blurb handed out by Disney – *Blow Dry* was actually filmed in Batley, Bradford and Dewsbury. Keighley, it seemed, just didn't have what was required to play itself. At least the cast had fun. And what an ensemble it was. Alongside Rickman was Natasha Richardson as his estranged wife, Rachel Griffiths as her lesbian partner, Bill Nighy as Rickman's London rival and Warren Clarke as the ambitious Mayor of Keighley. Other familiar faces included Hugh Bonneville, Mark Benton, Peter Kay and supermodel Heidi Klum.

Bill Nighy enjoyed a brief but intense period of training with top stylists Glyn and Gary Taylor in Brighouse. The father-and-son team were a multi award-winning duo with a big, richly-deserved reputation. They were happy to help – and Nighy was delighted to get his hands on a pair of scissors. "I do all my own hair stunts," he laughed. "I was put into the back room with a dummy head for a week with a hair dryer and this variety of combs. They were very kind to me, very good to me and the girls were very patient. I could now probably blow dry your hair. There'd probably be tears in your eyes by the time I'd finished but I could just about pull it off."

Josh Hartnett threw himself into a crash course of hairdressing while learning the accent to play a Yorkshireman. "Brian loves hairdressing; it's his art," mused Hartnett. "It's what he wants to do with his life but his father doesn't want Brian to end up like him. So he's in a tough position. He lives in this small, quirky town with his depressed dad across the street from his estranged mom and her lesbian lover. He works in a mortuary and he's trying to find his own way. Clearly, things are a little bit askew."

Yorkshire, at least in the eyes of the Americans, became a place where life was tough – grey, hardscrabble, working class and harsh. Breathnach tried to avoid cliché and saw within the film an opportunity to explore a different side to the county. "We filmed in Dewsbury and Batley. I had a look at Keighley but it didn't have what I wanted. I decided to heighten it a little bit and make the place look a little more fictional than a reality. I wanted a place that was slightly cut-out – the film is like a series of islands visually. When you look at the hairdresser's it's like a graphic against the sky. The funeral parlour is like a cut-out piece in the middle. I wanted that sort of style. One of the things I was impressed with was the colour of the stone; it's beautiful. In a way it's very warm but in the way it's used it has a puritanical feel about the place. I liked the mixture of those two things. When I went to Batley and Dewsbury I just found that those two places were the locations I liked most and I so chose them."

2000

Harry Potter and the Philosopher's Stone

Let the Magic Begin

Director: Chris Columbus

Producer: David Heyman

Writer: Steve Kloves, from the novel by J.K. Rowling

Production Company: Warner Bros. Pictures

Year of Production: 2000
(Released November 4, 2001)

Where filmed: Goathland, Pickering and York, North Yorkshire during September, 2000.

Synopsis: Orphaned Harry Potter is thrust into a secret world of magic when he is plucked from his uncle's home and sent to the Hogwarts School of Witchcraft and Wizardry.

Credited cast: Richard Harris (Professor Albus Dumbledore), Maggie Smith (Professor Minerva McGonagall), Robbie Coltrane (Rubeus Hagrid), Daniel Radcliffe (Harry Potter), Emma Watson (Hermione Granger), Rupert Grint (Ron Weasley), Alan Rickman (Professor Severus Snape), Zoë Wanamaker (Madame Hooch), John Hurt (Mr. Ollivander), Ian Hart (Professor Quirinus Quirrell), Julie Walters (Molly Weasley), Richard Griffiths (Uncle Vernon), Fiona Shaw (Aunt Petunia), Leslie Phillips (Sorting Hat), John Cleese (Nearly Headless Nick).

It's the evening before the start of the new term at Hogwarts School of Witchcraft and Wizardry. Dozens of pupils throng the platform where the Hogwarts Express has just pulled into Hogsmeade Station. There to greet them is hulking giant Rubeus Hagrid. Among the newcomers is the legendary Harry Potter, an 11-year-old orphan who is about to take his first uncertain steps into a dark and dangerous world he never previously knew existed.

At Goathland Station, tucked away in the Esk Valley near Whitby, children wearing black robes throng the platform close to steam locomotive 5972, otherwise known as the majestic Olton Hall. Lost in the crowd is the star triumvirate of Emma Watson, Rupert Grint and Daniel Radcliffe, the unknown youngster who had beaten hundreds of other boys to land the coveted role of Harry Potter. Towering over them all is the heavily bearded yet still unmistakeable figure of Robbie Coltrane. The scene is set for one of the key sequences of *Harry Potter and the Philosopher's Stone*. Then, quite suddenly, the heavens open and everyone runs for cover. When the clouds clear, albeit temporarily, director Chris Columbus calls his young actors back to the set and the whole process begins anew.

It is hard to imagine anyone unconnected with the movie actually witnessing that scene due to the publicity clampdown surrounding the filming. When the first *Harry Potter* movie went before the cameras in the autumn of 2000 the entire production was shrouded beneath a blanket of secrecy. Warner Bros, all-too-aware of the rollercoaster

nature of the J.K. Rowling phenomenon, were anxious to keep the production under wraps. Thus observers were politely turned away. Locals with prying eyes were discouraged. And gawping fans were most definitely not welcome. So it was that resourceful photographers who did manage to sneak close to the set did so with all the guile and skill of a sniper.

As late as a fortnight before filming began, Warner Bros. were still being cagey about whether or not Yorkshire would play a part in the $125 million production. The sleepy rural location of Goathland, they said, had not yet been confirmed although it was revealed to be under serious consideration. "North Yorkshire is being considered currently but it may turn out that we can shoot the scenes that are needed down south," said a spokeswoman. A few days later the *Harry Potter* crew arrived en-masse. A nearby field was transformed into the production base replete with portable offices and personalised car parking spaces for senior personnel. The station's name signs were swiftly replaced. A small wall was made higher. The railway shop became the Prefects' Room. The ladies loo was transformed into the Wizards' Room and, hey-presto, Goathland became Hogsmeade.

The initial scenes at Hogsmeade take up little more than half a minute on screen. However following the climax of the story Harry and his pals return to their homes from the same station, thus giving Yorkshire two bites of the blockbuster cherry. Eagle-eyed fans claim that another smaller sequence, in which Hagrid hands Harry his ticket to Hogwarts, was shot on the pedestrian footbridge in York Station.

The isolated 18-mile stretch of line on which Goathland sits is owned and operated by the North Yorkshire Moors Railway (NYMR) and runs between Pickering and Grosmont. It has been featured in a number of films over the years including *All Creatures Great and Small* and *Possession*. During the 1990s the NYMR was perhaps best-known for providing some of the backdrop to Yorkshire Television's long-running series *Heartbeat*. However, the *Heartbeat* connection has been easily eclipsed by Rowling's septet of best-sellers and their resultant box office behemoths. As long as movies survive, this tiny moorland line will be associated with Harry, Hogsmeade and Hogwarts which, thanks to the magic of cinema, can be seen silhouetted on the far horizon as one looks from the station.

title page: Director Chris Columbus with his young cast – Rupert Grint, Emma Watson and Daniel Radcliffe.

previous page: Filming at Goathland in the Esk Valley. The tiny station doubles as Hogsmeade.

far left, top: Rubeus Hagrid, aka Robbie Coltrane, shelters from the rain.

far left, bottom: Hagrid greets new arrivals. The scene lasts less than a minute on screen.

bottom: JK Rowling.

2001

An Angel for May

She will be lost forever if he doesn't find her in time

Director: Harley Cokeliss

Producers: Michael Lionello Cowan, Harley Cokeliss, Jason Piette

Writer: Peter Milligan, from the novel by Melvin Burgess

Production Company: A Spice Factory/Barzo Production

Year of Production: 2001 (Released 2002)

Where filmed: Barnsley, Grimethorpe, High Bradfield, Penistone, Sheffield, South Yorkshire; Leeds, Marsden, Slaithwaite, West Yorkshire during 2001.

Synopsis: Schoolboy Tom, an asthmatic loner, finds he is able to travel back in time to World War II. There he meets May, a waif-like evacuee. Returning to the present, he learns that something terrible happened to May just days after he left her. Determined to save her, he resolves to alter time.

Credited cast: Tom Wilkinson (Sam Wheeler), Geraldine James (Susan Higgins), Hugo Speer (Bob Harris), Angeline Ball (Barbara Collins), Julie Cox (Alison), John Benfield (PC Clegg), Nina Wadia (Science Teacher), Matthew Beard (Tom), Charlotte Wakefield (May), Anna Massey (Rosie), Dora Bryan (Evelyn), Michael McNulty ('Sniffer'), Richard Fleeshman (School Team Captain), James Joyce (Big Kid), Daniel Mason (Short Hair), Jonathan Bradd ('Sir'), Andrew Foxcroft ('Number 2'), Ashley Rhodes (Small Boy), Bill Rodgers (Fat Man), Janine Birkett (WPC), Kate Anthony (Mrs. Cranshaw), Carol McGuigan (Nurse), Andy Devine (Drunken Man), Rob Riley (Desk Sergeant), Terence Maynard (Reverend Campbell), John Skevington (Jim) and Tess as herself.

As the director of two acclaimed 1970s featurettes for the late-lamented Children's Film Foundation, filmmaker Harley Cokeliss hadn't expected to be asked to make another movie 25 years later. Yet, in 2001, the London-based Californian was invited to choose a book that the renamed Children's Film and Television Foundation could develop into a screenplay. He chose *An Angel for May*, by Melvin Burgess, because of what he called "its emotional power and moral agenda".

Working with a modest £1.4 million budget he pulled together an impressive cast that included Geraldine James, Angeline Ball, Anna Massey, Dora Bryan and *Full Monty* stars Tom Wilkinson and Hugo Speer. Wilkinson, in huge demand after the runaway success of *The Full Monty*, turned

title page: Charlotte Wakefield as the waif-like May.

above: Bomb damage recreated in South Yorkshire.

above: Director Harley Cokeliss with Anna Massey, just one of the familiar faces scattered throughout An Angel for May.

opposite: The ruin, in the background, through which Tom travels through time. It was built on fields close to a farm in Penistone, South Yorkshire. The wind machines were used to conjure up stormy Yorkshire weather on fine days.

down big-money offers of significant American movies in favour of *An Angel for May*. The reason? He felt that Sam Wheeler, the Yorkshire farmer he played in the film, was uncannily like his own father, who had farmed land in Horsforth, Leeds.

Cokeliss shot his film entirely in South and West Yorkshire, creating an effective and believable patchwork of locations that represented two very different worlds: wartime Yorkshire in the 1940s and the same county 50 years later. He compared the necessity of moving his crew from one location to another to three-dimensional chess, but stressed it was entirely his own choice. "*An Angel for May* was written by somebody who's on the other side of the Pennines so it should be set in Lancashire, but everything described in the book was to be found in Yorkshire," he revealed. "The story had certain requirements. The boy needed to be able to go from one place to another. He needed to see the town change from present day to the past. There needed to be a farm, a ruin that we could use, housing that could become fields – all dictated by the story. By filming in South Yorkshire we were able to receive a modest stipend from what was then called the Yorkshire Media Production Agency. When you're operating on a budget as tight as we were, even that modest contribution was very significant."

A key element of the film was a ruin that acted as a wormhole, transporting juvenile hero Tom back to the 1940s. A set was built on fields close to a farm in Penistone which, for three weeks, hosted the principal production base. Using

cinema cunning Cokeliss used one nearby hill to represent '40s countryside and another for the present since it had windmills in the background. Time was constantly of the essence. In the village of Marsden, near Huddersfield, Cokeliss had just a few short hours to complete one vital scene. "The local council gave us one morning to film it. We'd taken down the road signs and had turned it back into circa 1941. Then they wanted us out of their hair."

Cokeliss was remarkably sanguine about the unpredictability of Yorkshire weather. He knew that making a movie on a landscape dotted with giant wind turbines mean one thing: it was likely to be beyond blustery. Occasionally he and his crew had to batten down the hatches while a momentary storm blasted the location and sets. Then, as soon as it had

arrived, the bad weather was gone leaving a window of beautiful late afternoon sunlight that Cokeliss, his crew and actors took full advantage of.

Full of praise for his cast, Cokeliss reserved his greatest admiration for Tom Wilkinson who, following an ad-hoc workshop with his young family, urged him to give the film a happy ending. During shooting the director and writer Peter Milligan had stuck to the novel's original bleak conclusion. Cokeliss was convinced by Wilkinson's argument. "Over lunch Tom said 'We'd really like to see the boy succeed. Why don't you guys see if you can come up with an ending where the audience can go out feeling positive?' We thought that was an intriguing idea. As it happens our funding got held up by three months, so Peter and I had the time to think about it. That was a very powerful message to send. When we showed the new script to Melvin Burgess he said 'I wish I'd thought of that ending.' It was very big of him and a great compliment to us."

far left, top: Oscar nominee Tom Wilkinson made **An Angel for May** because the role he played reminded him of his own father, a Yorkshireman who farmed in Horsforth, Leeds.

far left, bottom: Another rainy day. Cokeliss was remarkably sanguine about the unpredictability of Yorkshire weather.

far left, bottom: Like many actresses Charlotte demands a lift to work.

above: The real farm acting 'the farm'.

left: The clapperboard which marries sound and picture.

2002

Nicholas Nickleby

Every family needs a hero.

Director: Douglas McGrath

Producers: Simon Channing-Williams, John N. Hart, Jeffrey Sharp

Writer: Douglas McGrath, from the novel by Charles Dickens

Production Company: Hart Sharp Entertainment/Cloud Nine Films

Year of Production: 2002 (Released June 27, 2003)

Where filmed: Hardcastle Crags, Hebden Bridge, West Yorkshire, during April, 2002.

Synopsis: One of Charles Dickens' most successful novels follows the honest and decent young Nicholas through a darkly oppressive Victorian England, the story moves from a grim boarding school to colourful adventures in the theatre and beyond.

Credited cast: Charlie Hunnam (Nicholas Nickleby), Romola Garai (Kate Nickleby), Tom Courtenay (Newman Noggs), Christopher Plummer (Ralph Nickleby), Anne Hathaway (Madeline Bray), Jim Broadbent (Wackford Squeers), Jamie Bell (Smike), Juliet Stevenson (Mrs. Squeers), Heather Goldenhersh (Fanny Squeers), Kevin McKidd (John Browdie), Edward Fox (Sir Mulberry Hawk), Nicholas Rowe (Lord Verisopht), Nathan Lane (Vincent Crummles), Dame Edna Everage (Mrs. Crummles), Alan Cumming (Mr. Folair), Barry Humphries (Mr. Leadville), Phil Davis (Brooker), Sophie Thompson (Miss Lacreevy), Timothy Spall (Charles Cheeryble), David Bradley (Bray).

"Smike! Smiiiiiike!"

Wackford Squeers, his face twisted in rage, bellows through the bars of the gates that announce the name of his home: Dotheboys. His breath drifts like mist in the cold night air as he yells for his servant, Smike. He is impatient, angry, cruel. Moments later a crippled boy hobbles into view and Squeers, enraged by the boy's slowness, beats him to the ground. His companion Nicholas Nickleby looks on in mute horror.

Thus it was that the first scenes of *Nicholas Nickleby* were shot during April 2002 at Gibson Mill, built around 1800 and set deep within Hardcastle Crags on the outskirts of Hebden Bridge. Squeers, played by Jim Broadbent, is evil, sadistic and depraved. Smike, a lonely, malformed orphan, dreams

of someone to take him away from the monstrous Dotheboys Hall and its horrendous conditions of neglect and brutality.

Writer/director Douglas McGrath was deliberate in his choice of Hardcastle Crags and the early 19th century cotton mill. He wanted the Yorkshire scenes to contrast with later sequences in the film when Smike, accompanied by his friend and rescuer Nicholas Nickleby, escapes to London. Yorkshire, said McGrath, was all about leafless trees – "like someone set them on fire" – that added to the mood of dread that surrounded Dotheboys. The film makes the most of this moody Pennine milieu, introducing Dotheboys at night as Squeers and Nicholas arrive by carriage. The school emerges from the gloom like Dracula's castle – which was exactly the effect McGrath was seeking. "The location was really quite

extraordinary," he said, referring to the abandoned, derelict and partially unsafe mill. "Every angle of it brought some other dire bleakness into view."

Charles Dickens based Dotheboys on a real Yorkshire school run by a headmaster named William Shaw. Dickens based Squeers directly on Shaw – a man so devoid of humanity that two of the boys under his supervision went blind. A great social critic, Dickens wrote *Nicholas Nickleby* as a way of raising awareness of such institutions. Yorkshire had more than its fair share.

Production designer Eve Stewart transformed the authentic and well-preserved Gibson Mill into a viable film set. The first floor became a dormitory, with narrow, coffin-like boxes

packed with straw, and the second floor a schoolroom and kitchen. Around 60 local boys aged between eight and 12 were cast as extras for scenes involving Broadbent, Jamie Bell as Smike, Juliet Stevenson as Mrs. Squeers and 19-year-old Charlie Hunnam as Nicholas Nickleby. McGrath, already experienced with period drama as the director of *Emma*, was convinced that Nickleby should be played by someone as close to his age as possible. He hired Hunnam, a relatively untested actor but one with the requisite blend of courage, innocence and soul. "It was the youth in his face that struck me most," said McGrath.

As the villains of the piece, Broadbent and Stevenson opted for character over caricature. Broadbent's thinning hair was combed forward until it resembled black spikes hanging

over his forehead. A gnarled, sightless, dead eye completed the effect. As Mrs. Squeers, Stevenson emerged as a sinister, buttoned-down matron: starchy, clean and regal. McGrath wanted a look of Mrs. Danvers in Hitchcock's *Rebecca*, and he got it. If Squeers is aggressive and violent, his wife is controlled, cold and clinical. Pity the poor boys who fall under their spiteful spell.

Some of the interiors of Dotheboys were built on a sound stage but much of it was real. McGrath and his crew were careful not to push their luck: parts of Gibson Mill – unused since the Second World War – were dangerous and there was a real risk that the floor might collapse. When the boys ran around, little clouds of dust would erupt from the floor.

McGrath was anxious to complete the Yorkshire section of his film away from prying eyes; visitors, onlookers and autograph hunters were discouraged. "We need to avoid the disruption of hordes of people swarming all over the set because there is so much to accomplish in such a short time," said a brusque publicist. On film as it was in print, Dotheboys lived up to its reputation as a grim, unwelcoming place. And that's just how Dickens would have wanted it.

title page: Charlie Hunnan as Nicholas Nickleby in Dotheboys Hall with Jim Broadbent as Wackford Squeers.

left: Jamie Bell as Smike

above: Gibson's Mill doubling as Dootheboys Hall.

My whole goal my entire life has just to be in one film that was in a box and was there forever. I was so excited to be there for the first time. And that was in Yorkshire on a film called Whatever Happened to Harold Smith? *with Tom Courtenay. You get greedier and greedier as you grow older or you achieve one goal. But that was very exciting for me because it was my first film role.*

Nicholas Nickleby *was a bit of a tricky production for me because I wasn't in a position to turn that role down and yet I didn't particularly relate to it. I wasn't excited by the project. Douglas McGrath's philosophy and my philosophy towards the filming were definitely very, very different. You don't necessarily need to enjoy someone's personality to be able to achieve good results with them, but if your approach, philosophy or vision is completely the polar opposite of the director, then you find yourself with a big, big problem. So it was a tricky position I found myself in with that film. I don't want to bad-mouth the film itself but, career-wise, it was the one time that I felt I made a mis-step. I dislike my performance immensely.*

I loved Yorkshire. I grew up in the Lake District and I'd been living in America for three years so Nicholas Nickleby *presented a real opportunity to come and experience the wondrous English countryside, which was beautiful. I wasn't up there for very long – just two weeks – but it was incredible, breathing fresh air and eating good home-made food.*

I always found Tom Courtenay to be very keen and willing to take the mentor role. That was especially true on Nicholas Nickleby *where I was really suffering as an actor and looking for any help I could get and any kind of perspective outside of my own. It's very difficult in the thick of things to escape your own perspective of something. Tom's a wonderful man, and as smart as they come. I thoroughly enjoyed both experiences working with him and I hope he did, too. I hope he would count me as one of his friends.*

- Charlie Hunnam, August 2005

2005

Like Minds

Evil is of two minds

Director: Gregory J. Read

Producer: Piers Tempest

Writer: Gregory J. Read

Production Company: Bluewater Pictures

Year of Production: 2005 (Released May 11, 2007)

Where filmed: Bradford and Haworth, West Yorkshire; Giggleswick School, North Yorkshire; and Carlton Towers, South Yorkshire during February, 2005.

Synopsis: Two public schoolboys enter into a deadly psychological game that leaves one dead and the other suspected of his murder.

Credited cast: Toni Collette (Sally Rowe), Eddie Redmayne (Alex Forbes), Tom Sturridge (Nigel Colby), Patrick Malahide (Dr. Forbes), Richard Roxburgh (Inspector Martin McKenzie), Jon Overton (Josh), Amit Shah (Raj), David Threlfall (John Colbie), Cathryn Bradshaw (Helen Colbie), Kate Maberly (Susan Mueller), Hugo Sachs (Rev Donaldson), Liam McKenna (Fergus), Bryan Robson (Mr. Evans), Paul Sonkkila (Police Bureaucrat), Craig Crosbie (Coroner), Paul Blackwell (Geoff Burns), Jordan Prosser (Boy on Train).

There was something suitably chilly about the shooting of *Like Minds* in the grounds of Bradford Grammar School. It wasn't just the weather, though the actors certainly shivered in the icy blast of a wintry gale. It was also the atmosphere and mood of the place: austere, unforgiving, grim. The good people at the school are rightly proud of its record and reputation, but it was the impressive gothic majesty of the place that attracted the makers of *Like Minds*. The film, based on an original screenplay by writer/director Gregory J. Read, focuses on two 17-year-olds, both English public schoolboys and both deceptively normal. Yet each teenager is a psychopath, obsessive and controlling. Together they form a terrifying whole: a monster obsessed with medieval fables, morbid mythology and the legend of the Knights Templar. Their macabre pact will leave one of them dead, the other being investigated for murder.

title page: Evil incarnate: Tom Sturridge as Nigel Colby, with cinematographer Nigel Bluck.

above: A smiling Eddie Redmayne plays psychopath Alex Forbes.

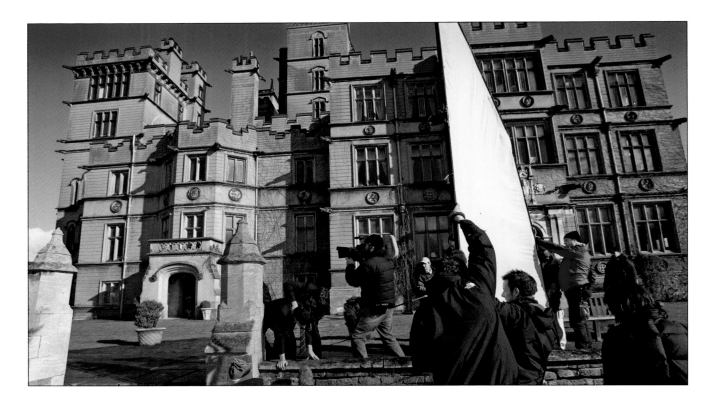

Half the £5 million film was shot in Yorkshire. The rest was made in Australia, where the cast and crew laboured in temperatures nudging 40 degrees centigrade to create the illusion of a bitter English winter. Said one: "It was a little tricky making Australia in 37°C look like Yorkshire in winter. They shipped in gallons of water to make it look like it was wet and wintry, but when you're standing there in an overcoat, nothing's really going to cool you down."

Leading lady Toni Collette, playing a forensic psychologist, was only available for the Australian end of the shoot, so the present-day aspect of the story was filmed on purpose-built sets in Adelaide. For the remainder – the back-story – the picture moved to Yorkshire. To cinematographer Nigel Bluck, the contrast presented some intriguing opportunities. "The Yorkshire scenery was great. The starkness of the leafless trees and the muted colours, the soft, low English light, the classical stone architecture and the atmosphere of the snow were perfect for the mood we were trying to create in the film."

Producer Piers Tempest lobbied hard to bring his film to his home county. Born in Skipton and educated at Ampleforth, his family owns 16th century Broughton Hall - scene of filming for *Wuthering Heights* in 1991. He was convinced Yorkshire provided everything needed to draw together a composite public school - the stalking ground for the two psychotic adolescents at the heart of the movie.

"Gregory Read, who wrote the script, had originally set the film in a non-specific place but, when I saw it, I immediately thought, 'It's just got to be Yorkshire'," said Tempest from the Bradford location. "It's very historically based, the school is very much an old boys' school, somewhere which can be daunting and impressive and the landscape we have on our doorstep just adds to the atmosphere of intrigue. Obviously there are disadvantages filming on location rather than in a studio where you have complete control of the environment. When we were out in Giggleswick there were training flights passing over from the RAF, but in terms of production values you can't beat being out on location. Yorkshire is often sold as a chocolate box location, but if we can do more films like this, then that's got to be good for attracting new business. It will change people's perceptions."

On set in Bradford were newcomers Tom Sturridge and Eddie Redmayne. With them was familiar British face Patrick Malahide, playing Redmayne's stern father who is

above: Patrick Malahide, in the role of Redmayne's stern father.

opposite: Filming at Carlton Towers, near Selby, for a confrontation between the principal villains: schoolboy killers Alex and Nigel.

left: The bleak landscape around Haworth lends chills to a graveyard scene.

below: Enter the headmaster: actor Patrick Malahide strides into the hall at Bradford Grammar School.

opposite, top: Cinematographer Nigel Bluck and producer Piers Tempest discuss an interior shot in Bradford Grammar School.

opposite, bottom: Game of death: Tom Sturridge and Eddie Redmayne.

also the humourless headmaster of the school where the various sinister occurrences take place. Malahide, an old hand at film acting with the likes of *Billy Elliot*, *The Killing Fields* and *Cutthroat Island* under his belt, was sanguine about the filming process and the length of time taken to achieve even the briefest shot. "You spend a lot of time catching up with people. I also write, so often I will go back to my hotel room," he revealed with a world-weary smile. "But this particular shoot has been very refreshing. Tom and Eddie have a sort of puppy dog enthusiasm, which reminds you why you're in this job in the first place and why you're so lucky to be an actor."

As well as filming at Bradford Grammar, *Like Minds* moved on to Carlton Towers, near Selby, and to Giggleswick School, North Yorkshire, and its glorious 19th century domed chapel. For Eddie Redmayne, the whole process gave cause for the most infectious excitement amidst the enforced boredom of hanging around while a scene was meticulously set up. Costumed in school uniform, his fresh-faced looks belied his actual age – 23 when the film was shot. "It's amazing, isn't it? There's a lot of breaks, a lot of standing around, a lot of doughnut eating, but to be honest I find it quite exciting. I play the son of the headmaster who is fantastically bright so, no, it's absolutely nothing like me. It's very weird being back in school. It was quite unnerving. The whole process is terrifying. You film everything out of sequence, so it's a completely different skill. In theatre, you follow a character's story from start to finish. On film, all of a sudden you have to turn on the tears, the anger or the happiness. There's no build up to anything.

A film built on a foundation of unease and ancient evil, *Like Minds* benefited enormously from the pervading atmosphere of arcane academia. Production designer Steven Jones Evans saw the violence within the story as a secondary character.

"Our approach to the story was to underplay the violence, never to represent it graphically. We wanted the film to have a sinister underbelly rather than being overt or playing it up. This is no slasher film. It's more psychological and we had to find a way to represent that intent. We contrasted the old world of the boarding school with the clean, modern fluoro-lit world of the police cell and the interview room. We wanted the film to have an almost crystalline beauty, a fragility to much of the imagery, to give a feeling that at any moment things could crack or shatter."

2006

Mrs. Ratcliffe's Revolution

Director: Bille Eltringham

Producer: Leslee Udwin

Writers: Bridget O'Connor, Peter Straughan

Production Company: Assassin Films

Year of Production: 2006 (Released September 28, 2007) UK Premiere September 23 in Leeds)

Where filmed: Halifax, West Yorkshire, during September, 2006.

Synopsis: Zealous Communist Frank Ratcliffe moves with his family from Yorkshire to the Germany Democratic Republic in search of an ideological Marxist utopia. But, on arrival, he finds a country under the iron heel of repression. His horrified wife, Dorothy, soon begins plotting their escape.

Credited cast: Catherine Tate (Dorothy Ratcliffe), Iain Glen (Frank Ratcliffe), Katharina Thalbach (Anna Kopleck), Nigel Betts (Uncle Phillip), Brittany Ashworth (Alex Ratcliffe), Jessica Barden (Mary Ratcliffe), Heike Makatsch (Fraulein Unger), Christian Brassington (Thomas), Alexander Scheer (Willi), Susan Tordoff (Mary's Teacher), John Kirk (Mr. Murray), Gábor Pintér (1st Border Guard), Ákos Horváth (2nd Border Guard), Ottília Borbáth (Frau Glock), Karl Kranzkowski (Rector), Robert Lowe (Otto), Imola Gáspár (Art Teacher), Fanni Futár (Uti), Piroska Móga (Ursula), Barna Illyés (Gym Teacher), Stephan Wolf-Schönburg (Herr Vort), Béla Fesztbaum (1st Stasi Officer), Ben O'Brien (2nd Stasi Officer), Arndt Schwering-Sohnrey (Jerzy), Uwe Lauer (Truck Driver).

Uncredited cast: Brian Norris (well-wisher).

A tiny car stacked high with luggage eases away from a small but vocal crowd of well-wishers holding banners proclaiming 'Bon Voyage'. Inside the cramped vehicle sit a husband, a wife, two daughters and a brother-in-law. All five are leaving West Yorkshire for East Germany. It is 1968, and Frank Ratcliffe – father of two, academic and ardent Marxist – is off to seek ideological bliss behind the Iron Curtain.

Strange, then, that this sequence is being played out in Elmfield Terrace, close to Savile Park, Halifax. It's the end of a long and difficult shoot but director Bille Eltringham and producer Leslee Udwin are actually filming the opening sequences of Mrs. Ratcliffe's Revolution, a £2 million comedy drama that begins in Bingley and

ends in the grey, oppressive and freezing town of Halle, deep in the German Democratic Republic.

As the title suggests, this is Mrs. Ratcliffe's story. Tate plays the dowdy provincial housewife who turns revolutionary heroine and in doing so combines comedy with drama. The film is based on the true story of a real-life family, led by passionate Communist Brian Norris from Bolton, who packed up and moved 1,038 miles to the German Democratic Republic during the height of the Cold War. Nine months later they were back, having fled the repression and brutality of a regime that routinely spied on its citizens, banned Elvis Presley records and revelled in petty restrictions. Naturally everyone grew weary, and Norris's wife quietly rebelled.

title page: Catherine Tate as Dorothy Ratcliffe, a resolutely cheerful 1960s Yorkshire mum

previous: En-route to a brave new world: Catherine Tate, Iain Glen, Brittany Ashworth and Jessica Barden set off from Halifax.

above: Catherine Tate takes direction from Bille Eltringham.

opposite: A Halifax backdrop for a political statement. Mary Ratcliffe (Jessica Barden) makes her point.

Norris was on set during the Halifax shoot along with his daughter, Maggie, whose book on their Eastern Bloc escapade had been adapted for the screen. "It seems a kind of dream to be here today. It's an unreal feeling but I am enormously pleased and grateful to Maggie for getting it made. We were supposed to be going to live there for some years and I was going to be lecturing in English at a university but it was a repressive place and there was a lack of freedom. In other words I came to my senses," he reveals.

In the movie, which swaps Bolton for Bingley, Dorothy is frumpy and something of a doormat for her husband's skewed idealism. Tate describes her, not inaccurately, as "resolutely cheerful". "I suppose she's the kind of woman who gets sidelined a bit, as I imagine quite a lot of women did in the '60s in Bingley. I think it was a fairly patriarchal society anyway – not just in Bingley, but generally in the '60s," says Tate, buying into the script's fantasy that Dorothy and her brood were from Yorkshire, not Lancashire.

In fact, the majority of the film was shot not in the former GDR but in Hungary. "I went out on a 10-day recce and basically scouted the whole of the former East Germany," says producer Leslee Udwin. "Within two days it became abundantly clear that it was no longer depressing enough and it had become so developed since that wall came down in 1989. Logistically it was a nightmare because the locations were so far flung, and there was so little left, that I thought 'This is not going to be

above: Fighting the fight: Frank Ratcliffe (Iain Glen) takes his message to the streets of Bingley. The scene was filmed outside Halifax Borough Market. The man in the black overcoat is Brian Norris, whose own real-life experiences inspired the film.

possible'. On the period side we were okay because little enclaves of Budapest looked as depressing as we needed them to be and there weren't that many TV satellites to change."

It was Udwin, also the producer of the hit Anglo-Asian comedy *East is East* (which was partly shot at Leeds's Hyde Park Picture House), who battled for, and won, Catherine Tate as her female lead. Having seen her in the hard-edged Neil LaBute play *Some Girl(s)* she became obsessed with Tate joining the cast to play Dorothy and fought off pressure to cast the likes of Julie Walters, Brenda Blethyn or an American star. "I withstood that with all my worth. How can you cast an invisible British housewife, which is the essence of Dorothy, with someone who carries baggage and is recognisable? The heart of this film is Dorothy and I wouldn't have wanted to make the film if Catherine hadn't been available but thank God she was. I just knew that she was the perfect Mrs. Ratcliffe," she reveals.

Tate and the rest of the British cast – co-stars Iain Glen and Nigel Betts, and newcomers Brittany Ashworth and Jessica Barden – were only fleetingly in Yorkshire, filming for two weeks in Halifax, which doubled as Bingley. "My mum came up and there was a billboard from Halifax and it said 'TV comic in our street'. My mum's still got that. Actually I hope that's the only time I'm on a billboard, given that usually it's not good news that they're telling," Tate laughs.

Tate was a popular figure during her brief sojourn in Halifax. Director Bille Eltringham, who previously co-directed another Yorkshire drama, *The Darkest Light*, with Keighley-born *Full Monty* writer Simon Beaufoy, was full of praise for her star. "Mostly we didn't get too bothered by onlookers but there were a couple of times when children would suddenly notice Catherine there. I thought they'd all start squealing but actually, because she was nice and always said hello to them, they were incredibly respectful."

On a sunny Halifax afternoon Catherine Tate is all smiles. She relishes the challenge of a genuine character part and, like all actors, points to the script as the source of her inspiration. "I am very lucky that I have been given the part. There was not that much deliberating. It's a great part, a great script and a great opportunity. What I loved about the script was that you had comedy and pathos in it. You never veer off into sentimentality and the comedy never becomes absurd. The comedy is really dry, bone-dry. It was so brilliant. That's the only thing that you can really do as an actor: look for the script and, if it's a great story, which it was, and fantastically written, which it is, it's irresistible. I think it's the only real criteria about work, really. And it is a Yorkshire accent that I'm doing. There are Yorkshire accents that are very, very thick, very specific and very broad, but if you put it on screen sometimes it sounds like a bit of a caricature. You just have to have an essence of where they're from rather than place it specifically in Bingley. You don't want to be accused of over-egging it."

"Mrs. Ratcliffe's Revolution *was written about a real man named Brian Norris. In the late '60s, at the time of the Vietnam War, a lot of people thought the ideology of Communism seemed really sound. People within the UK profoundly believed in the message of Communism, and that's where Frank finds himself in the film. He wasn't alone – there were a few people who moved to the GDR to live the dream. I'm not wise enough to know a great deal about it but, in my own way, I think the ideology of Communism was good. The practice of it was fucked but the ideology of it was good.*

"Frank was an interesting character and I enjoyed playing him. He was living a dream. He was very honest in his pursuit of that. He profoundly believed that when he went to live amongst the people who had 'chosen' that way of life that it would all be roses. And because his belief was so strong it took quite a long time for him to see the dream disintegrate.

"One thing that made me laugh was Catherine Tate. She's lovely to work with but very much kept herself to herself. We were very tight as a group, as actors and crew. I've got very fond memories of Budapest – we would all go out and have dinner together. Partly because she had a child there and partly because she's Catherine you always had to slightly persuade her to come out and do things with you. She was delightful company.

"We were in Yorkshire very, very briefly. When we were in Halifax, reasonably near the end of shooting, she came up and said "Will you come out with me? Apparently Shane Warne is at some club down the road and it would be great if we went there." It's my idea of a nightmare: going to some horrible, seething mass of people. But she was really, really excited about going to meet Shane Warne. And she was insistent.

So we ended up going to this club and she spent the entire evening with people coming up to her saying "Am I bovvered?" I just felt for her but she was loving it. She must have known that that would happen and she was handling it so well. I put up with it for about 40 minutes and left her with a sea of people asking "Am I bovvered?" and getting her autograph. But we never found Shane Warne."

- Iain Glen, 2007

2007

1920

Director: Vikram Bhatt

Producer: Vikram Bhatt

Writer: Dheeraj Rattan

Production Company: ASA Films Pvt. Ltd

Where filmed: Allerton Castle, Bolton Abbey, Bramham Park and Ripley Castle, North Yorkshire, during November and December, 2007

Synopsis: Supernatural thriller. An Indian boy and an English girl meet, fall in love and marry despite heavy opposition from all around them.

Credited cast: Rajneesh Duggal, Adah Sharmam, Anjori Alagh, Indraneel Sengupta, Ashish Pradhan, Rajendra Zutshi, Kuljinder Rayit

Steaming tea in plastic cups. Actors huddled beneath blankets. Hot breath floating in the cold air… it can only have been Yorkshire in winter. For the shivering Bollywood stars of *1920*, a horror thriller based in India, the freezing conditions came as something of a shock – especially when temperatures at home in Mumbai were nudging 40 degrees centigrade. The bright sun provided a hint of welcome warmth but producer/director Vikram Bhatt was not a happy man. He wanted murkiness, darkness and gloom. Wrapped up in woolly hats and thermals, he and his cast dodged the sun and set about shooting a scene in the only secluded spot they could find. "In a supernatural film you have blue-grey skies, so I wanted the grey," he revealed. "I suppose the rest of Yorkshire is happy that it's sunny today – it's glorious. But I'm not happy." He smiled a weary smile.

Bhatt and his performers – emerging stars Anjori Alagh, Adah Sharmam, Indraneel Sengupta and Rajneesh Duggal, aka Mr. India 2003, making his movie debut – were careful not to give too much away about the plot of *1920*. Alagh, playing a wealthy wife, owns a majestic Victorian home where she lives with a nanny and a little girl. Her husband, Arjun, wishes to demolish the isolated house and use the land for a hotel, but the house is cursed. Strange things happen to anyone who attempts to change things, and most wind up dead. Sengupta revealed that he played a pivotal role as a soldier from the 1857 Seboy Mutiny found wounded in the jungle that surrounds the old mansion where the film is set. "There's a lot of mystery to this character. He never smiles, he looks spooky," he said during a lull in filming. Like almost everyone else, he was wrapped in a heavy blanket to fight off the chill. "I like the weather," he ventured gamely. "It's pretty cold, but I like cold places."

To give the film the requisite atmosphere and influence of the British Raj, the makers of *1920* scoured the UK for the appropriate classical architecture of the Georgian, Victorian and Edwardian eras. They found what they wanted at Allerton Castle on the outskirts of Knaresborough, which doubled for a gothic pile in faraway India. "We fell in love with the place," said screenwriter Dheeraj Ratan. "It has been untouched by the changes that have gone on in the outside world." The magnificent 18th century estate previously hosted filming for 1992's *The Secret Garden*, starring Dame Maggie Smith. Other key locations on *1920* included Bolton Abbey, Bramham Park and Ripley Castle, the latter previously the scene of Disney's 1975 pit pony drama *Escape from the Dark* and Yorkshire Television's all-star version of *Frankenstein*, starring Robert Powell, Carrie Fisher, Sir John Gielgud and David Warner as the monster.

1920 offered huge opportunities to its cast of newcomers, and none more so than Kuljinder Rayit, a BBC cameraman who volunteered to work on the production as a camera assistant. Fluent in Punjabi and Hindi, he would quiz the director and other crew members on the complexities of operating and loading film cameras. Rayit was stunned when he was plucked from the background to play a cameo as a young priest in the film. "The second assistant director said 'You would be perfect for this part'. We both went to speak to the director and he just stared at me. Then he smiled and said 'We'll have to do something about his hair'.

They flattened it down and gave me a side parting. Although I could understand everything that was being said on the set, my main language is Punjabi, not Hindi. I knew I had lines to learn and I wanted them a couple of days in advance. Everything is so relaxed on an Indian set. So, 20 minutes before I had to do it, I got them on a piece of paper – written in pencil."

As Father Thomas, who has witnessed a miracle, Rayit had to sprint to a senior priest and breathlessly blurt out what he had seen. He got the lines right, but Bhatt felt his running lacked a certain urgency. "He said he couldn't feel the worry and panic in my running so, on the next take, I flailed my arms around. He was happy with that. Being in the film was a fun experience. It appeared from nowhere so it was an adrenaline rush to do something I'd never done before."

title page: Actress Anjori Alagh runs through a scene. On a frosty winter morning, it was perhaps the best way to keep warm.

previous page: Anjori Alagh and producer/director Vikram Bhatt view footage on a monitor.

below: Bollywood comes to Yorkshire as 1920 gets underway at Allerton Castle, near Knaresborough.

opposite: Beautiful Anjori Alagh smiles through the cold. The blanket, gloves and steaming tea tell their own story.

Filmmaking in Yorkshire

A Chronology 1920 - 2007

To attempt a complete and accurate chronology of all Yorkshire's films – particularly those produced during the embryonic years of motion pictures – would be a mighty and never-ending task. Consequently the list presented here concentrates solely on feature films with the exception of one featurette, Ken Annakin's *We of the West Riding*.

Films are listed by year of production – when they were actually made in Yorkshire – rather than year of release, which can often be considerably later. This chronology focuses exclusively on pictures that have received a cinema release.

Readers may be surprised by some entries, and puzzled by the non-appearance of others. Some movies were entirely filmed in the Broad Acres; others came and went in a matter of days. The Sylvester Stallone vehicle *F.I.S.T.* used steelworks in South Yorkshire to double for furnaces and coke ovens in 1930s America. The John Landis horror-comedy *An American Werewolf in London*, though set on the brooding, rain-drenched Yorkshire Moors, was filmed in Windsor Great Park and at Hay Bluff in Herefordshire. The memorably named pub The Slaughtered Lamb in East Proctor was (and remains) a private house in the South Wales village of Crickadarn, Powys. The interior, where Brian Glover warns two hapless American back-packers to "Beware the moon", was shot in The Black Swan in Effingham, Surrey, where rooms were partitioned off to give it a spooky, insular feel. Not a single frame of film was shot in Yorkshire.

Yorkshire's movie heritage is rich and vast: more than 130 films over 120 years. And, every year, the list grows longer.

1920

WUTHERING HEIGHTS
Director: A. V. Bramble
Where filmed: Kildwick, Haworth, West Yorkshire
Milton Rosmer, Colette Brettel, Warwick Ward, Annie Trevor

1921

THE PLAYTHINGS OF FATE
Director: Claude Verity
Where filmed: Harrogate, North Yorkshire
Cast unknown

1922

SHIRLEY
Director: A.V. Bramble
Where filmed: Oakwell Hall, Birstall, West Yorkshire
Carlotta Breese, Clive Brook, Harvey Braban, Joe Nightingale

1926

THE BALL OF FORTUNE
Director: Hugh Croise
Where filmed: Elland Road, Leeds, West Yorkshire
Billy Meredith, James Knight, Mabel Poulton,
Geoffrey B. Partridge

1935

TURN OF THE TIDE
See pages 20 - 31

HOPE OF HIS SIDE
Director: Jack Raymond
Where filmed: Featherstone, South Yorkshire
Sam Livesey, Sydney Howard, Wally Patch,
Mabel Constanduros

1941

THE MAN AT THE GATE
Director: Norman Walker
Where filmed: Robin Hood's Bay, North Yorkshire
William Freshman, Mary Jerrold, Wilfrid Lawson, Trefor Jones

1942

HARD STEEL
Director: Norman Walker
Where filmed: Sheffield, South Yorkshire
Wilfrid Lawson, Betty Stockfeld, John Stuart, George Carney

1943

THE LIFE AND DEATH OF COLONEL BLIMP
Directors: Michael Powell, Emeric Pressburger
Where filmed: Denton Hall, Denton, Wharfedale, North Yorkshire
Anton Walbrook, Roger Livesey, Deborah Kerr, Roland Culver

1945

THE WAY TO THE STARS
Director: Anthony Asquith
Where filmed: Catterick, North Yorkshire
Michael Redgrave, John Mills,
Rosamund John, Stanley Holloway

WE OF THE WEST RIDING
See pages 32 - 33

1946

MASTER OF BANKDAM
Director: Walter Forde
Where filmed: Hebden Bridge,
Huddersfield, West Yorkshire
Anne Crawford, Dennis Price, Tom Walls,
Stephen Murray

HOLIDAY CAMP
Director: Ken Annakin
Where filmed: Filey, East Yorkshire
Flora Robson, Dennis Price, Jack Warner,
Hazel Court

1948

A BOY, A GIRL AND A BIKE
See pages 34 - 39

1951

ANOTHER MAN'S POISON
See pages 40 - 47

1953

LEASE OF LIFE
Director: Charles Frend
Where filmed: Beverley, Lund,
East Yorkshire
Robert Donat, Kay Walsh, Denholm
Elliott, Adrienne Corri

1954

VALUE FOR MONEY
Director: Ken Annakin
Where filmed: Batley, West Yorkshire
John Gregson, Diana Dors, Susan Stephen,
Derek Farr

1958

ROOM AT THE TOP
See pages 48 - 55

1959

HELL IS A CITY
See pages 56 - 59

1960

NO LOVE FOR JOHNNIE
Director: Ralph Thomas
Where filmed: Halifax, West Yorkshire
Peter Finch, Stanley Holloway,
Mary Peach, Peter Barkworth

1962

THIS SPORTING LIFE
See pages 60 - 67

BILLY LIAR
See pages 68 - 75

1965

LIFE AT THE TOP
Director: Ted Kotcheff
Where filmed: Bradford, Ilkley,
West Yorkshire
Laurence Harvey, Jean Simmons,
Honor Blackman, Michael Craig

THE SPY WITH A COLD NOSE
Director: Daniel Petrie
Where filmed: Castle Howard,
near Malton, North Yorkshire
Laurence Harvey, Daliah Lavi,
Lionel Jeffries, Eric Sykes

LADY L
See pages 76 - 85

1968

THE GIRL WITH A PISTOL
Director: Mario Monicelli
Where filmed: Doncaster, South Yorkshire
Monica Vitti, Stanley Baker, Carlo Giuffre,
Corin Redgrave

WOMEN IN LOVE
Director: Ken Russell
Where filmed: Denaby, South Yorkshire
Alan Bates, Oliver Reed, Glenda Jackson,
Jennie Linden

KES
See pages 86 - 91

1970

THE RAILWAY CHILDREN
See pages 92 - 99

JANE EYRE
Director: Delbert Mann
Where filmed: Brimham Rocks,
Ripley Castle, North Yorkshire
George C. Scott, Susannah York,
Ian Bannen, Jack Hawkins,

WUTHERING HEIGHTS
Director: Robert Fuest
Where filmed: Ilkley, Otley, West
Yorkshire; Bolton Abbey, Blubberhouses,
North Yorkshire
Anna Calder-Marshall, Timothy Dalton,
Harry Andrews, Pamela Brown

1974

THE LIVING DEAD AT THE
MANCHESTER MORGUE
Director: Jorge Grau
Where filmed: Sheffield, South Yorkshire
Ray Lovelock, Cristina Galbo,
Arthur Kennedy

ALL CREATURES GREAT AND SMALL
See pages 100 - 105

1975

IT SHOULDN'T HAPPEN TO A VET
Director: Eric Till
Where filmed: Richmond, Reeth,
Arkengarthdale, North Yorkshire
John Alderton, Colin Blakely,
Lisa Harrow, Bill Maynard

BARRY LYNDON
Director: Stanley Kubrick
Where filmed: Castle Howard,
near Malton, North Yorkshire
Ryan O'Neal, Marisa Berenson,
Patrick Magee, Hardy Kruger

ESCAPE FROM THE DARK
Director: Charles Jarrott
Where filmed: Ripley Castle, Ripley,
North Yorkshire
Alastair Sim, Peter Barkworth,
Maurice Colbourne, Prunella Scales,

1976

THE LIKELY LADS
Director: Michael Tuchner
Where filmed: Helmsley, North Yorkshire
Rodney Bewes, James Bolam,
Brigit Forsyth, Mary Tamm

THE WATER BABIES
See pages 106 - 111

1977

AGATHA
See pages 116 - 125

F.I.S.T.
Director: Norman Jewison
Where filmed: Sheffield, South Yorkshire
Sylvester Stallone, Rod Steiger,
Peter Boyle, Melinda Dillon

1978

YANKS
See pages 126 - 135

BLACK JACK
Director: Ken Loach
Where filmed: Masham, Ripon,
North Yorkshire
Jean Franval, Stephen Hirst, Louise
Cooper and Brian Glover (narrator)

DRACULA
Director: John Badham
Where filmed: Whitby, North Yorkshire
Frank Langella, Laurence Olivier,
Donald Pleasence, Kate Nelligan

1980

CHARIOTS OF FIRE
Director: Hugh Hudson
Where filmed: Harrogate, York,
North Yorkshire
Ian Charleson, Ben Cross, Brad Davis,
Alice Krige

LOOKS AND SMILES
Director: Ken Loach
Where filmed: Sheffield, South Yorkshire
Graham Green, Carolyn Nicholson,
Tony Pitts, Roy Haywood

OMEN III – THE FINAL CONFLICT
Director: Graham Baker
Where filmed: Fountains Abbey, Ripon,
Kilnsey, North Yorkshire
Sam Neill, Rossano Brazzi, Lisa Harrow,
Don Gordon

1982

MONTY PYTHON'S THE MEANING
OF LIFE
Directors: Terry Jones, Terry Gilliam
Where filmed: Bradford, West Yorkshire;
Malham, North Yorkshire
Graham Chapman, John Cleese,
Terry Gilliam, Eric Idle, Terry Jones,
Michael Palin

1983

THE DRESSER
See pages 136 - 143

1984

A PRIVATE FUNCTION
See pages 144 - 149

WETHERBY
Director: David Hare
Where filmed: Harrogate, North Yorkshire
Vanessa Redgrave, Ian Holm, Judi Dench,
Stuart Wilson

1985

CLOCKWISE
Director: Christopher Morahan
Where filmed: Hull, East Yorkshire
John Cleese, Alison Steadman,
Stephen Moore, Sharon Maiden

1986

RITA, SUE AND BOB TOO!
See pages 150 - 155

1987

THE PRINCESS BRIDE
Director: Rob Reiner
Where filmed: Sheffield,
South Yorkshire
Cary Elwes, Mandy Patinkin,
Chris Sarandon, Robin Wright

TESTIMONY
Director: Tony Palmer
Where filmed: Alhambra Theatre,
Bradford, West Yorkshire
Ben Kingsley, Terence Rigby,
Brook Williams

1988

A CHORUS OF DISAPPROVAL
See pages 156 - 161

A HANDFUL OF DUST
Director: Charles Sturridge
Where filmed: Selby, North Yorkshire
James Wilby, Kristen Scott-Thomas,
Rupert Graves, Anjelica Huston

THE FRUIT MACHINE
Director: Philip Saville
Where filmed: Flamingo Land, Kirby
Misperton, North Yorkshire
Emile Charles, Tony Forsyth,
Robert Stephens, Clare Higgins

BERT RIGBY, YOU'RE A FOOL
Director: Carl Reiner
Where filmed: Barnsley, South Yorkshire
Robert Lindsay, Robbie Coltrane,
Anne Bancroft, Bruno Kirby

DIAMOND SKULLS
Director: Nick Broomfield
Where filmed: Duncombe Park,
Thirsk, North Yorkshire
Gabriel Byrne, Amanda Donohoe,
Struan Rodger, Douglas Hodge

1989

SLIPSTREAM
Director: Steven Lisberger
Where filmed: Malham, North Yorkshire,
Bob Peck, Mark Hamill, Kitty Aldridge,
Bill Paxton

1990

KING RALPH
Director: David S. Ward
Where filmed: Harewood House,
West Yorkshire
John Goodman, Peter O'Toole, John Hurt,
Camille Coduri

ROBIN HOOD: PRINCE OF THIEVES
See pages 162 - 165

1991

BELTENEBROS
Director: Pilar Miró
Where filmed: Scarborough,
North Yorkshire
Terence Stamp, Patsy Kensit,
José Luis Gómez, Geraldine James

**EMILY BRONTË'S
WUTHERING HEIGHTS**
See pages 166 - 175

1992

LEON THE PIG FARMER
Directors: Vadim Jean, Gary Sinyor
Where filmed: Clapham, North Yorkshire
Mark Frankel, Janet Suzman, Brian Glover,
Connie Booth

THE SECRET GARDEN
Director: Agnieszka Holland
Where filmed: Allerton Park, near
Knaresborough, North Yorkshire
Kate Maberly, Maggie Smith, John Lynch,
Andrew Knott

1993

JAMES HERRIOT'S YORKSHIRE
Director: Joy Perino
Where filmed: Harrogate, Robin Hood's
Bay, Scarborough, Swaledale, Thirsk,
Wensleydale, Whitby, North Yorkshire
Alf Wight (aka James Herriot),
Christopher Timothy

1994

SWEET SURRENDER
See pages 212 - 217

CARRINGTON
Director: Christopher Hampton
Where filmed: Goathland,
North Yorkshire
Jonathan Pryce, Emma Thompson,
Steven Waddington, Samuel West

WHEN SATURDAY COMES
Director: Maria Giese
Where filmed: Sheffield, Rotherham,
South Yorkshire
Sean Bean, Emily Lloyd,
Pete Postlethwaite, Craig Kelly

I.D.
Director: Philip Davis
Where filmed: Bradford, West Yorkshire;
Rotherham, Sheffield, South Yorkshire
Reece Dinsdale, Warren Clarke,
Claire Skinner, Sean Pertwee

JANE EYRE
Director: Franco Zeffirelli
Where filmed: Brimham Rocks, near
Harrogate, North Yorkshire
William Hurt, Charlotte Gainsbourg,
Joan Plowright, Billie Whitelaw

1995

BRASSED OFF
See pages 176 - 181

JUDE
Director: Michael Winterbottom
Where filmed: Richmond, North Yorkshire
Christopher Ecclestone, Kate Winslet,
Liam Cunningham, Rachel Griffiths

1996

THE FULL MONTY
Dir. Peter Cattaneo
Where filmed: Sheffield, South Yorkshire
Robert Carlyle, Mark Addy, Tom
Wilkinson, Steve Huison

BROTHERS IN TROUBLE
Director: Udayan Prasad
Where filmed: Bradford, West Yorkshire
Om Puri, Pavan Malhotra, Angeline Ball,
Ahsen Bhatti

FAIRYTALE: A TRUE STORY
See pages 182 - 187

MONK DAWSON
See pages 188 - 191

1997

MY SON THE FANATIC
Director: Udayan Prasad
Where filmed: Bradford, Halifax,
West Yorkshire
Om Puri, Rachel Griffiths,
Akbar Kurtha, Stellan Skarsgård

ELIZABETH
See pages 192 - 195

AMONG GIANTS
See pages 196 - 201

SOLO SHUTTLE
See pages 202 - 205

LITTLE VOICE
See pages 206 - 211

AMY FOSTER
Director: Beeban Kidron
Where filmed: Keighley, West Yorkshire
Rachel Weisz, Vincent Perez,
Ian McKellen, Kathy Bates

1998

PROMETHEUS
Director: Tony Harrison
Where filmed: South Yorkshire
Michael Feast, Walter Sparrow,
Jonathan Waistnidge, Fern Smith

FANNY AND ELVIS
See pages 212 - 217

L.A. WITHOUT A MAP
See pages 218 - 223

CAPTAIN JACK
Director: Robert Young
Where filmed: Whitby, North Yorkshire
Bob Hoskins, Sadie Frost, Gemma Jones,
Anna Massey

1999

EAST IS EAST
Director: Damien O'Donnell
Where filmed: Leeds, West Yorkshire
Om Puri, Linda Bassett, Jordan Routledge,
Archie Panjabi

THE DARKEST LIGHT
Directors: Simon Beaufoy, Bille Eltringham
Where filmed: Ingleton, North Yorkshire
Stephen Dillane, Kerry Fox, Keri Arnold,
Kavita Sungha

**WHATEVER HAPPENED TO
HAROLD SMITH?**
Director: Pete Hewitt
Where filmed: Sheffield, South Yorkshire
Tom Courtenay, Michael Legge,
Laura Fraser, Stephen Fry

BLOOD
Director: Charly Cantor
Where filmed: Sheffield, South Yorkshire
Adrian Rawlins, Lee Blakemore,
Phil Cornwell, Nicholas Harvey

2000
BETWEEN TWO WOMEN
Director: Steven Woodcock
Where filmed: Bradford, Keighley,
Huddersfield, West Yorkshire
Barbara Marten, Andrina Carroll,
Andrew Dunn, Paul Shane

SECRET SOCIETY
Director: Imogen Kimmel
Where filmed: Doncaster, South Yorkshire
Charlotte Brittain, Lee Ross,
Annette Badland, James Wootton

THIS FILTHY EARTH
Director: Andrew Kotting
Where filmed: North Yorkshire
Rebecca R. Palmer, Shane Attwooll,
Demelza Randall, Xavier Tchili

GABRIEL & ME
Director: Udayan Prasad
Where filmed: Sheffield, South Yorkshire
Iain Glen, David Bradley, Sean Landless,
Billy Connolly

BLOW DRY
See pages 224 - 227

HARRY POTTER AND THE
PHILOSOPHER'S STONE
See pages 228 - 231

2001
POSSESSION
Director: Neil LaBute
Where filmed: Pickering, Ravenscar,
Runswick Bay, Whitby, North Yorkshire
Gwyneth Paltrow, Aaron Eckhart,
Jeremy Northam, Jennifer Ehle

MIRANDA
Director: Marc Munden
Where filmed: Scarborough,
East Yorkshire
Christina Ricci, John Simm,
Kyle MacLachlan, John Hurt

2002
HARRY POTTER AND THE
CHAMBER OF SECRETS
Director: Chris Columbus
Where filmed: Goathland,
North Yorkshire
Daniel Radcliffe, Emma Watson,
Rupert Grint, Robbie Coltrane

AN ANGEL FOR MAY
See pages 232 - 237

NICHOLAS NICKLEBY
See pages 238 - 241

NINE TENTHS
Director: Jon Gritton
Where filmed: North Yorkshire
Sarah Cartwright, Phil Craven, Luke Goss,
Elizabeth Heaney

CALENDAR GIRLS
Director: Nigel Cole
Where filmed: Kettlewell, North Yorkshire
Helen Mirren, Julie Walters,
John Alderton, Ciarán Hinds

THE PRINCIPLES OF LUST
Director: Penny Woolcock
Where filmed: Sheffield, South Yorkshire
Alec Newman, Marc Warren,
Sienna Guillory, Lara Clifton

2003
MY SUMMER OF LOVE
Director: Pawel Pawlikowski
Where filmed: Brighouse, Cornholme,
Todmorden, West Yorkshire
Nathalie Press, Emily Blunt,
Paddy Considine, Dean Andrews

JELLY DOLLY
Director: Susannah Gent
Where filmed: Sheffield, South Yorkshire
Rachael Walton, Ashley Barnes,
Stuart Laing, Litza Bixler

2004
ASYLUM
Director: David Mackenzie
Where filmed: Menston, West Yorkshire;
Sheffield, South Yorkshire
Natasha Richardson, Ian McKellen,
Marton Csokas, Hugh Bonneville

THE JEALOUS GOD
Director: Steven Woodcock
Where filmed: Bradford, Huddersfield,
Halifax, West Yorkshire
Jason Merrells, Denise Welch,
Mairead Carty, Pamela Cundell

CHARLIE AND THE
CHOCOLATE FACTORY
Director: Tim Burton
Where filmed: York, North Yorkshire
Johnny Depp, Freddie Highmore,
David Kelly, Helena Bonham Carter

KEEPING MUM
Director: Niall Johnson
Where filmed: North York Moors,
North Yorkshire
Rowan Atkinson, Kristin Scott Thomas,
Maggie Smith, Patrick Swayze

THE LEAGUE OF
GENTLEMEN'S APOCALYPSE
Director: Steve Bendelack
Where filmed: Marsden, West Yorkshire
Mark Gatiss, Steve Pemberton,
Reece Shearsmith, Michael Sheen

A COCK AND BULL STORY
Director: Michael Winterbottom
Where filmed: York, North Yorkshire
Steve Coogan, Rob Brydon,
Keeley Hawes, Shirley Henderson

2005
GARFIELD: A TALE OF TWO KITTIES
Director: Tim Hill
Where filmed: Castle Howard,
near Malton, North Yorkshire
Breckin Meyer, Jennifer Love Hewitt,
Billy Connolly and the voice of
Bill Murray

FLYBOYS
Director: Tony Bill
Where filmed: East and North Yorkshire
Jean Reno, James Franco, Tyler Labine,
Abdul Salis

DRIVING LESSONS
Director: Jeremy Brock
Where filmed: North Yorkshire
Julie Walters, Rupert Grint, Laura Linney,
Tamsin Egerton

THE HISTORY BOYS
Director: Nicholas Hytner
Where filmed: Halifax, West Yorkshire;
Ripon, North Yorkshire
Richard Griffiths, Stephen Campbell
Moore, Dominic Cooper,
Samuel Barnett

MISCHIEF NIGHT
Director: Penny Woolcock
Where filmed: Beeston, Leeds,
West Yorkshire
Kelli Hollis, Ramon Tikaram,
Christopher Simpson, Gwyn Hollis

THE PENALTY KING
Director: Chris Cook
Where filmed: Elland Road, Leeds,
West Yorkshire
Nick Bartlett, Claire Grogan,
Samantha Beckinsale, Frank Jarvis

LIKE MINDS
See pages 242 - 247

THE LISTENING
Director: Giacomo Martelli
Where filmed: Menwith Hill,
North Yorkshire
Michael Parks, Maya Sansa,
Andrea Tidona, James Parks

2006
NATASHA
Director: Jag Mundhra
Where filmed: North Yorkshire
Algina Lipskis, Sheyla Shehovich,
Richard Lintern, Serena Gordon

BAD BLOOD
Directors: Lightning Bear,
Kenny Richards
Where filmed: Hull, Scarborough,
East Yorkshire
Kenny Richards, David John,
Jennifer Lynn, Amanda Elizabeth

HEAVEN AND EARTH
Director: Marleen Gorris
Where filmed: North Yorkshire
Sean Pertwee, Miranda Raison,
Janet Suzman

MRS. RATCLIFFE'S REVOLUTION
See pages 248 - 253

STARDUST
Director: Matthew Vaughn
Where filmed: Menwith Hill,
North Yorkshire
Michelle Pfeiffer, Robert De Niro,
Claire Danes, Charlie Cox

2007
HUSH
Director: Mark Tonderai
Where filmed: Sheffield, South Yorkshire
Robbie Gee, Andreas Wisniewski,
Clare Keelan, Stuart McQuarrie

THE COTTAGE
Director: Paul Andrew Williams
Where filmed: Harewood House,
West Yorkshire
Andy Serkis, Jennifer Ellison,
Reece Shearsmith, Doug Bradley

TIED IN BLOOD
Director: Matthew Lawrence
Where filmed: Haworth, Hebden Bridge,
Wakefield, West Yorkshire
Paul McEwan, Kenneth G. Hodgson,
Laura O'Donoughue, Chris Leach

WILD CHILD
Director: Nick Moore
Where filmed: Haworth, West Yorkshire;
Harrogate, Robin Hood's Bay,
North Yorkshire
Emma Roberts, Natasha Richardson,
Aidan Quinn, Alex Pettyfer

BRIDESHEAD REVISITED
Director: Julian Jarrold
Where filmed: Oakworth, West Yorkshire;
Castle Howard, near Malton,
North Yorkshire
Emma Thompson, Michael Gambon,
Ben Whishaw, Matthew Goode

SUMMER
Director: Kenny Glenaan
Where filmed: Sheffield, South Yorkshire
Robert Carlyle, Sean Kelly

1920
See pages 254 - 257

Also dedicated to Stephen, Richard and Louise.

AUTHOR'S ACKNOWLEDGEMENTS

Made in Yorkshire has been in my mind for almost 20 years. For some of that time Jim Moran and I have spent many hours on film locations all across the county. However it would not have been possible to chronicle the history of this wonderful region's cinematic heritage without the assistance, generosity and enthusiasm of a great number of people. Some, sadly, have died since I first began researching this project. Others continue to work in movies and to provide inspiration. I am indebted to the following actors, directors, writers, producers, publicists, extras, stand-ins, stunt performers, cinematographers, costumiers, editors, make-up artistes, industry colleagues and fellow writers:

Jenny Agutter, John Alderton, the late Roy Alon, Ken Annakin, Martin Armstrong, Annette Badland, Simon Beaufoy, Lynne Benjamin, Scott Beswick, Andy Bettridge, Mark Bickerdike Cate Blanchett, Brenda Blethyn, Toni Booth, Simon Bosanquet, Reg Brace, Andy Bradford, Paddy Breathnach, Jim Broadbent, Sir Michael Caine, Steven Carter, Ann Catterall, Jane Chippindale, Julie Christie, David Cohen, Harley Cokeliss, Sarah Collis, Michael Coulter, Daphne Couplan, Eleanor Course, Sir Tom Courtenay, Terry Cryer, Sarah Daniel, Brian Daniels, Peter Djordevic, Marie Donaldson, Michael Durnford, Ben Eagle, Elizabeth Earl, Jane Ellis, Bille Eltringham, Ralph Fiennes, Mike Fisher, Tara Fitzgerald, the late Freddie Francis, Helen Fraser, Morgan Freeman, Shuna Frood, John Furbisher, Tony Garnett, Stephen Garrett, Kulvinder Ghir, Iain Glen, the late Brian Glover, Simon W. Golding, Paul Goodman, Jim Greenhalf, Bruce Greer, Rachel Griffiths, the late Willis Hall, Duncan Hamilton, Keith Hampshire, Maggie Hanley, David Hanson, Michael Harvey, Ronald Harwood, Anthony Hayward, Mark Herbert, Mark Herman, John Herron, Mike Hine, Barry Hines, John Hirst, Florence Hoath, Keith Holliday, Brian Hopps, the Hon. Simon Howard, Steve Huison, Simon Hulme, Mel Hulme, Charlie Hunnam, Philip Jackson, Paul Jennings, Tony Johnson, Robert Kandt, Elizabeth Karlsen, Elliott Kastner, Mika Kaurismäki, Dr. Arnold Kellett, Diane Kelly, Ian Kerrison, Ruth Kitchin, Bill Lawrence, Pete Lazenby, John Ledger, Margaret Le Lohé, Brian Liddy, Sandy Lieberson, Ken Loach, Nick Lockett, Tony Lytle, Jean MacQuarrie, Dave McCall, Paul McGann, Ewan McGregor, Karl Magee, Jayne Marsden, Mavis Marshall, Undine Marshfield, Norman Masters, Keith Meatheringham, Kay Mellor, Bill Mitchell, Richard Moran, Derren Nesbitt, Phoebe Nicholls, Bill Nighy, Mike North, Martin Oates, the late Bob Peck, Phil Penfold, Bryan Percy, Chris Phipps, Jill Pitts, Robin Platt, Colin Pons, Pete Postlethwaite, Kuljinder Rayit, David Rayner, Peter Rayner, Kevin Reilly, Darren Rhodes, Michael Rhodes, Natasha Richardson, Malcolm Robertshaw, Andrew Robinson, Charles Round, Tim Rowbotham, the late Shirley Russell, Addy Rutter, Liz Rymer, Sir James Savile the late John Schlesinger, Paul Seeley, the late Mary Selway, Peter Sharpe, Dinah Sheridan, Jean Simmons, Deb Singleton, Frances Smith, Patricia Smith, Sean Stowell, Charles Sturridge, Bob Sykes, Catherine Tate, Joyce Taylor, John Teasdale, Piers Tempest, David Tennant, Paul Thompson, Stephen Tompkinson, Jean Trotter, Leslee Udwin, Dominic Walker, Tom Waller, Colin Welland, James Westwood, Peter Yates, and Andrew Youdell.

For the use of images we are grateful for the support of the following newspapers and the generosity of their editors and picture desks:

Ackrill Newspapers Ltd (Harrogate), *Bradford Telegraph & Argus, Halifax Courier* Ltd, *Hebden Bridge Times, Huddersfield Examiner, The Press* (York), and the *Yorkshire Post*, which gave us unlimited access to its amazing archive of photographs and previously published reports.

We extend particular thanks to James Westwood, one of more than 800 extras on *Yanks*, who covered the shooting of the film with an impressive array of photographs, which he placed at our disposal.

From the publishers:
Special thanks to Su Swan, Jane & Russell Burden @ Nebulo Strata, Tracey Broderick & Helena Corydon @ CC Offset Printing UK and Stephen Atkinson & Glen Marks @ Rex Features for their hard work, efficiency, care and great eye for detail.

Thank you –
Leeds City Council, Emma Hayley @ MetroMedia Books , Brian Percy, Steve Abbott, PA, Lady L photographs reproduced from the Castle Howard collection with kind permission of the Hon. Simon Howard, A Chorus Of Disapproval photographs reproduced with kind permission of Elliott Kastner, Amanda Booth @ Kirklees Images, Dobson's, Canal + Images UK, Bronte Parsonage, Maggie Ellis and Helena McKenzie @ Film London , Dave McCall@ BFI, Tony Lytle @ 111 Productions, Jim Wight, Robin Woods, Emlyn Price, LS (Tony) Lewis, Christopher Timothy, Michael Ryan and Alexei Slater @ Handmade Films PLC and Jo Nolan Chief Executive, Screen South.

PICTURE CREDITS